The Undergroundtrader.com™ Guide to Electronic Trading

*Day Trading Techniques
of a Master
Guerrilla Trader*

The Undergroundtrader.com™
Guide to Electronic Trading

Jea Yu

McGraw-Hill

New York   San Francisco   Washington, D.C.   Auckland   Bogotá
Caracas   Lisbon   London   Madrid   Mexico City   Milan
Montreal   New Delhi   San Juan   Singapore
Sydney   Tokyo   Toronto

Library of Congress Cataloging-in-Publication Data
Yu, Jea.
    The undergroundtrader.com™ guide to electronic trading / by Jea Yu.
    p. cm.
    ISBN 0-07-136016-6
    1. Electronic trading of securities.   I. Title.
    HG4515.95 .Y93 2000
    332.64'0285—dc21   00-025088

McGraw-Hill

A Division of The **McGraw·Hill** *Companies*

1 2 3 4 5 6 7 8 9 0 DOC/DOC 0 9 8 7 6 5 4 3 2 1 0

ISBN 0-07-136016-6

This book was set in Plantin by Inkwell Publishing Services.

Printed and bound by R.R. Donnelley & Sons Company.

This publication is designed to provide accurate and authoritative information in
regard to the subject matter covered. It is sold with the understanding that neither the
author nor the publisher is engaged in rendering legal, accounting, futures/securities
trading, or other professional service. If legal advice or other expert assistance is
required, the services of a competent professional person should be sought.
                    —*From a Declaration of Principles jointly adopted by a Committee*
                        of the American Bar Association and a Committee of Publishers.

Contents

Part 2 Implementing the Tools

Appendix B

Index   *243*

Introduction

A skilled fighter puts himself into a position where defeat is
impossible, yet never misses the opportunity to defeat the
enemy.

Sun Tzu

Day trading has been around in one form or another ever since the
beginning of the financial markets. However, the advent of the
Internet has allowed the public to access the markets more cheap-
ly, quickly, and efficiently through electronic day trading. It can be
quite a rewarding, gratifying, and exciting profession or hobby.
The income potential is unlimited. On the flip side, it can be the
most frustrating, costly, and expensive endeavor one might ever
experience. You can feel like a hero one minute and the world's
biggest loser the next. The pure adrenaline rush and excitement of
a successful and profitable trade will keep most coming back for
more.

The purpose of this book is to make you aware of the true
activities of the markets and provide you with real techniques on
how to capitalize on and profit from the volatility and fluctuations
in the markets. This book is not about hype or theory, but about
the realities of electronic day trading. One untold reality is that 9
out of 10 day traders fail. In fact, most people who play the markets end up losing money.

Why is there such a high failure rate for day traders? Simple.
The markets are a zero-sum game—one big pot of money where
everyone contributes to buy stock. When one person walks away
with a $1000 profit, it had to come from another person who lost
that very same $1000, or 10 people who lost $100 each. When one

wins, someone else loses. In essence, the markets are nothing more than musical chairs, and there are only a limited number of chairs. Therefore, you can pretty much guess that it is everyone for himself. Within these markets are the cast of characters, a food chain of sorts.

You are pitted against other day traders, the proverbial SOES bandits, momentum players, market makers, speculators. The markets are a cruel battlefield, and every single investor, trader, market maker, speculator, money manager, and institution is an opponent.

Welcome to the most expensive speculator sport in the world. You will be pitted against some of the sharpest minds and deepest pockets in a head-to-head zero-sum match where winner takes all. As a day trader, you are up against other traders, market makers, money managers, institutions, speculators, and investors. Within the traders, you have several subspecies, such as the SOES bandits, the electronic day traders, momentum players, bottom fishers, and bargain hunters.

You will come under attack through bear raids, get head-faked and wiggled out by the market makers, get pinned to the wall by other day traders, and have the rug pulled out from underneath you by the SOES bandits. It will leave your head spinning. This is the day in the life of an electronic day trader.

The goal of day trading is to preserve your capital. In other words, you want to enter into the safest possible trades with the greatest and surest profit potential so that you do not take on any unnecessary risk. You must condition yourself to trade like a sniper—to carefully observe and wait for the right window of opportunity to arise and then to take your shot with split-second timing and accuracy.

Forget all that you have heard about Wall Street. Forget about fundamentals, and most importantly forget about the "buy and hold" philosophy. As a day trader, you must shift paradigms and recondition yourself. You must understand that you will have an even number of trades a day. In other words, you hold no overnight positions. That would make you an investor. It is my feeling that being an "investor" is much riskier than being a trader. An investor will *buy and hold* onto a stock day in and day out *long term*. In theory, the longer you hold a stock, the less risk of loss, but in reality that's far from the truth. Thousands of examples prove otherwise. In reality, an investor is often completely blinded to trend and intraday price movement—and in essence is nothing more than a sitting duck in the path of a Mack truck, blinded by the inability to either take profits or cut losses quickly. Is investing terrible? No, not if that is your intention. However, the subject of this book is electronic day trading, and in day trading, yes, investing is terrible because it is not the game plan. (We will, however, discuss one of the very few reasons to hold a position overnight and that is for the morning gap plays or stochastics.)

THE PURPOSE OF THIS BOOK

This book is about trading Nasdaq stocks intraday utilizing a Level 2 screen, charts, and momentum indicators. It is not about investing, and we offer no guidance in evaluating p/e ratios, stock fundamentals, or long-term investment decisions. There is a galaxy of investment publications and books to that effect. In this book, we only target trading intraday and profiting from volatility and price fluctuations in stock prices. The average investor who reads *The Wall Street Journal* every morning with his or her coffee and doughnuts will likely not understand or care about what goes on with a stock price throughout the day. The average investor will remain unaware of the constant jockeying for position by market makers; of the wiggles, jiggles, head fakes, panic selling, and panic buying; of the drama, the tension, the politics, and the action—all of which are elements of this wonderful speculator sport we call day trading.

As noted earlier, the markets are a game of musical chairs. When a trend emerges, traders pile into a position, drive up the price, and then pull out, they hope, with profits, leaving the last ones in hanging with a short-term loss. Knowing this, traders are always trying to outguess each other about when a trend will begin and when to take profits. And the traders aren't the only players. The Nasdaq market makers are also trying to fake out the traders and other market makers constantly jockeying for positions. It is war.

We have a trading system that consistently performs. The main tools that we use are the Nasdaq Level 2 screen, time of sales report, 3-minute moving averages chart, futures, and 1-minute stochastics chart (attached to a 1-minute price chart). We believe the way to win is to hit as many singles, doubles, and triples as possible to accumulate larger profits taking advantage of the volatility of the markets. We don't go for home runs because the world-class nature of the professional market makers on the opposite sides of our trades guarantees that we will strike out the majority of the time. Thus, our attitude that every little scalp counts is the foundation of our actions. In that vein, we act like snipers who wait in the bushes for the right opportunity to come along, assuring that the scales are tipped in our favor on every trade before we pull the trigger. All this is done in a matter of seconds.

Our goal is to educate and provide a foothold for understanding and profiting from the intraday swings in the markets. The information in this manual is very specific to the reality of real-time trading. This information is valuable. If you have ever attempted to day-trade only to end up with a series of losses, depressed and confused at the end of the day, then this manual is specifically tailored for you. We left out the fluff and only include straightforward, useful, hard-core, and rare information.

Confidence comes from knowledge. On the other hand, gaps in knowledge lead to self-doubt and frustration. We want to help fill those gaps and train you to be a more confident and profitable day trader. Day trading has a very expensive learning curve, and most people will lose either the majority of their capital or their sanity in the learning process. We want to help the beginner, the average, and even the experienced day trader survive the learning curve and start on the way to a more profitable future in the markets.

Understand that everything stated in this book is based on our experiences—what we learned through trial and error (going through our own expensive learning curve)—and is only our opinion. We, of all people, know what it feels like to be shaken out of a position and lose money, and therefore we speak as day traders based on our experiences and offer our techniques and opinions in the hope that we can provide you guidance in your education as a day trader.

The key point that you must understand is that all the information presented in this book is based on personal experience and personal frame of reference. There is no sure system that works every time. There are always exceptions to the rules. Trading is a subjective endeavor that only proves your actions right or wrong after the trigger is pulled. The environment is always changing, and the playing field is always moving. Therefore, it is best to ingest everything covered in this book to complement your own experience in an effort to further build your own frame of reference. The step-by-step setups we describe apply to most movements, but there is no sure guarantee when playing the markets. So long as we can present to you our own proven methods to better your own judgment calls on potential plays, we feel our work is complete and worthwhile. Always take the time to think through your actions and anticipate all potential results before taking a position.

We believe in our hearts that experience is the greatest teacher, and mistakes make up a substantial portion of that experience. A very successful hedge fund manager once said that "All I bring to the table is 17 years of mistakes." This lends credence to our belief that every time you make a mistake and learn from it, you will be less likely to make that mistake again, consciously or subconsciously. This is the inevitable learning curve that every trader needs to overcome. We wish to help you through that learning curve so that you can develop into a successful equities trader. With that in mind, let's get to work!

Let's be blunt right from the get-go. Electronic day trading is not investing. Company fundamentals and news have a knee-jerk effect on a stock's price—and that's it. As a day trader, you concern yourself with the price fluctuations in a respective stock.

The markets are a zero-sum game, and the playing field is far from even. While the average investor has no clue about market maker tactics and capabilities such as head faking, price fading, loading bid and ask sizes, controlling spreads with multiple ECN access and order flow information, the astute day trader must be aware of all the advantages of the market makers. In a perfect world, there would be only one system of execution, with *real* sizes showing true supply and demand and with universal access to this one limit book. This doesn't and can't exist. It is in this gray area away from the public that you find the true core of the markets.

As the cliché goes, "Give a man fish and he eats for a day. Teach a man to fish and he eats for a lifetime." This is the underlying theme and the approach we will take in the book. The first part of the book presents a full explanation of all the tools, indicators, and theories—in essence you will become familiarized with the markets as you sit down to your meal.

The second part of this book gives you the tools and the strategies—in essence laying out your utensils methodically before you—your soup spoon, salad fork, dinner fork, knife, etc.

Then we teach you how to implement all the tools—how to use your utensils to get the most out of your meal. This is where we feel most books on day trading fail. They fail to present the real methods as they would apply in a real market. Our methods are used in the trenches every market trading day. We avoid the fluff that the majority of the books on day trading seem to overwhelm readers with. We tell it like it is, with plenty of examples to hammer the points across.

Lastly, we apply the tools in two simulated trading sessions as we place you inside the mind of an underground day trader, giving you an insight into the thinking process. We will methodically detail the proper use of all the tools and concepts in the book to give you a full understanding of what sniper trading is all about. This chapter (Chapter 13) is aptly titled "Putting It All Together," and well ... the name says it all.

As an extra bonus, Dr. Russell Arthur Lockhart contributes a very special section (Appendix A) on Fibonacci targets, the Japanese three-price break, pivot points, and natural trading units. This section is quite complicated and encompasses a whole different methodology of day trading.

Our goal here is to provide you with the best tools and techniques to build your foundation of knowledge. Eventually, we hope that you will be able to combine the techniques that work for you to create your own personal best style of trading for consistent profits. We know these methods work since they are practiced and demonstrated successfully every trading day. Good luck, and let's get going!

Jea Yu

PART ONE

LEARNING THE TOOLS

CHAPTER 1

What Makes the Markets Tick?

THE STOCK MARKET—THE GREAT OCEAN

The average investor has no clue why a stock moves intraday. News can have a short-term effect on a stock, but what is the cause of the movement behind price fluctuations? When most people read the morning paper and see MSFT at $93^1/_4$ on Monday and then see MSFT at $93^1/_2$ on Tuesday, they assume MSFT only moved $^1/_4$ of a point and think nothing more of it. In reality, MSFT may have had an intraday high of 95 and low of $92^1/_2$ and closed at $93^1/_2$. How does one explain the fluctuation in price intraday? Contrary to popular beliefs, a stock does not need news to move. In fact, news is a very temporary catalyst for stock movement. To find out why it moves, we need to take a look at the whole market from a different perspective. Consider a giant totem pole where momentum flows from the top down. The stronger the momentum is, the farther down the totem pole it flows. Here's a quick breakdown:

Futures (S&P 500 and Nasdaq 100)

Tier 1 generals

Tier 2

Tier 3

Tier 4, etc.

(More details on the tiers in the "Tier Synergy" portion.)

When you hear the saying "A rising tide lifts all boats" in relation to the stock market, it is implying that a strong market lifts all stocks. This is true in a sense. To be specific, a strong market moves stocks in the above-mentioned order, and the stronger the market is, the more stocks it lifts (and the lower down the tiers the strength flows). The market moves in this manner. The futures are the lead indicator that pull the Tier 1 generals, which pull the Tier 2 stocks, which pull the Tier 3 stocks, and so forth. This applies in a strong as well as a weak market. We can break this down in further detail.

THE FUTURES: INSTITUTIONAL PROGRAM TRADING

The futures become a lead indicator because they directly influence institutional program trading from the arbitrage situations they provide when there is a divergence in value with the respective stock index (also referred to as *cash*). It is commonly believed that the markets are random and that stocks pop and diverge on their own fundamentals based on news. Nothing can be further from the truth. The markets are very orderly and flow like a gigantic ocean. Huge undercurrents dictate what is seen above the waters as waves crash and churn.

Let's understand the premise of top down. Market momentum moves from the top on down like a wave. Imagine the markets as being a giant ocean and stocks move with the tide. This is how the markets move intraday:

Cash and futures spreads enter into buy or sell program territory, triggering program trading. For example's sake, let's assume buy programs are triggered. Buy programs, as their name states, are designed to buy a bulk amount of stocks on a market index with the press of a button. This causes a flurry of buying in the Tier 1 index stocks. Market makers start stepping off asks and increasing their bids while they watch the other Tier 1 stocks move, and when they begin to move, then the buying focuses on Tier 2 stocks. If the momentum is strong enough, Tier 3 stocks may also be affected by this wave of buying, and so forth on down.

PROGRAM TRADING

Program trading is like the strong undercurrents in the ocean that oscillate the momentum into waves that can be viewed on the surface. To understand what makes the market fluctuate, we have to gain a grasp of institutional program trading. These buy and sell programs hit the market like a tidal wave with the press of a button from the major brokerage houses. Although the New York Stock Exchange (NYSE) defines program trading as the simultaneous buying and selling of 15 different stocks totaling a market value of $1 million or more, it is understood that a minimum autoload buy program starts at $15 million and moves up from there. These buy-sell programs can cause immediate ripples in the stock market.

To understand why brokerage houses or institutional traders would hit a buy program or sell program that appears to be nothing more than a mad buying or selling spree in the designated index stocks, we need to understand the opportunities that lie with cash versus futures arbitrage. This is where the big money is.

The Standard & Poor's (S&P) 500 index stocks are often referred to as cash since they have a liquid intrinsic value based on a formula that takes into account the prices of all the stocks and converts them into a cash value. The cash has an inverse relationship with the S&P 500 futures, also known as *futures and spoos* for short. As the name implies, the spoos are a lead indicator on the S&P 500 index. Imagine money getting transferred from cash (S&P 500 index) to futures (spoos) back and forth all day long. The question is why.

The answer has to do with fair value and arbitrage. There is a formula know as fair value. Fair value is the equation that measures the benefit of owning cash versus owning futures. The premium (also known as the spread) is the *difference* in value between the cash and the spoos. Theoretically, the premium should equal the fair value. When the premium equals the fair value, there is no difference between owning the cash and owning the futures. However, when the premium diverges from fair value, an arbitrage situation arises.

Every brokerage has its own version of buy and sell premiums. CNBC will often show buy and sell premiums in the morning, which can be roughly about 70 percent accurate to most quote vendors' own interpretations. Let's try an oversimplified example here:

S&P 500 index (also known as cash)	=	1025
S&P 500 futures (also known as spoos)	=	1030

The premium (or spread) is 5.

Depending on fair value, brokers will have their program trading parameters set. For example's sake, let's say:

Fair value	=	5
Buy premium	=	6
Sell premium	=	3

The cash versus spoos is at fair value and priced accordingly.

Now it's later in the morning, and we get the following values:

S&P 500 index	=	1023
S&P 500 futures	=	1029

Now the premium is 6.

This is the point at which the buy programs would kick in. They would buy the S&P 500 index and sell the S&P 500 futures, also known as *buy the cash and sell the spoos,* to bring the premium back to fair value. This is index arbitrage.

The buy and sell premiums are just estimations, based on information from the quote vendors, of the point at which most brokers would trigger program trading. There is no exact figure that would trigger program trading, as that would make things far too predictable.

The spoos are a lead indicator to the cash. The inverse is what happens to the spoos when the premium hits buy. It will often result in a sell in the spoos, and the spoos will go down until the spread hits fair value.

SPOTTING PROGRAM TRADING

As we just pointed out above, the buy and sell premiums are just estimations that vary by quote vendors. Only the actual institutions that implement the program trading know when they will really trigger. Spotting program trading can be fairly easy. Usually, the time when the premium is within the buy-sell ranges is the time when you should be looking at the 3-minute futures chart (overlaid with a line chart). When a buy program is triggered, you will see an immediate jump in the spoos chart and the spoos. It literally shows up on a line chart as a gap, as the Tier 1 stocks will usually start getting taken out on the ask. The 3-minute stochastics chart (Figure 1.1) will confirm the buy program by continuing to show an extended uptrend on the %d and %dslow. Finally, the tick improves, and most evidently the indices will pop.

Indices are the laggard indicator. Unless the institutions are leapfrogging each other, by the time the indices reflect buy programs, they are usually nearing the end of the cycle. However, this does not necessarily mean that buying in the market will dry up immediately. The program trading oftentimes acts as a catalyst that will bring either more buyers or more sellers into the markets. If the markets have strength, buy programs can act as a catalyst to bring in more buyers off the fence, and vice versa for sellers in a weak market.

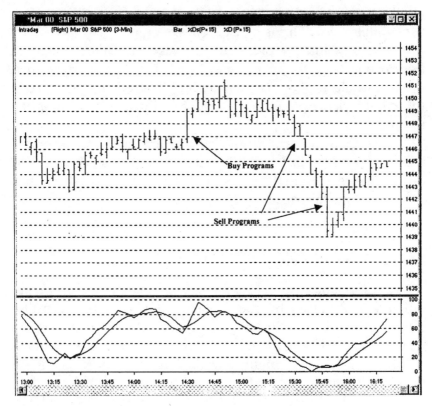

Figure 1.1 Program trading on a 3-minute stochastics chart. (SOURCE: RealTick™ ©
1986–2000 Townsend Analytics, LLC. Used with permission.)

HOW TO USE THE FUTURES AS
YOUR MARKET BAROMETER

The main thing to remember from all this is that the futures are the
undercurrents of the stock market. If the futures are in an uptrend
and rising, that is good for the market in general, starting with the
Tier 1 generals, and vice versa if the spoos are downtrending.

You will have to consult your individual quote vendor for
exact symbols on the S&P 500 futures and Nasdaq 100 futures.
On Cybertrader and Mbtrader, we use the /sp and /nd prefix for
the futures (e.g., /spz9 and /ndz9 = Dec 1999 futures). In addition
to the futures, it's a good idea to have the other following indica-

tors on a market minder window (a chart is prime if you have the space): $spx.x (premium), $tyx.x (long bond yield).

We like to put the S&P 500 futures on 3-minute stochastics charts. We don't use the 1-minute stochastics since it invites too many wiggles (short-term pullbacks), resulting in a very choppy chart. The 3-minute stochastics gives us a smooth and very real visual on the trend of the futures (Figure 1.1, top). When the two oscillator lines (%d, %dslow), shown in the bottom portion of Figure 1.1, fall under the 20 band, the futures are in oversold territory and one anticipates a reversal up. When the two oscillator lines run above the 80 band, the futures are in overbought territory and one anticipates a reversal down.

TIER SYNERGY

The stock market can be divided into sectors by industry. Within these sectors, there are the bellwether stocks, also known as the Tier 1 generals. These stocks are usually the most liquid and widely held stocks in the market. For example, INTC would be a Tier 1 general of the semiconductor chip sector, and YHOO would be a Tier 1 general for the Internet sector. Remember that Tier 1 stocks are the bellwether for their respective sector. If a Tier 1 general is tied to a market index (Dow, S&P 500, or Nasdaq 100), its position as a Tier 1 is even more solidified due to the program trading linked directly to the index stocks. Tier 1 stocks hibernate, but rarely die unless something drastic happens fundamentally (e.g., getting replaced on the indexes).

To give you an example of tier synergy in action, you can usually overlay a Tier 1 and a Tier 2 stock on a bar chart and notice the similarities in the pattern and trend. Usually the Tier 2 stock mimics the Tier 1 stock in a mirrorlike fashion, but a few minutes behind.

This is not simply coincidence. The markets have already deemed which stocks are which tiers in their category. The Tier 1 stocks are linked directly with the indexes and various program trading modules, thus also linking them to the S&P 500 and Nasdaq futures. This is a key point.

Whenever taking a position in a stock, a trader needs to know how the lead indicator is performing. For Tier 1 stocks, that would be the futures and/or another Tier 1 stock in the sector to confirm the momentum. For example, when watching YHOO, a trader should also be watching AOL and EBAY to confirm the uptrend in YHOO, since the whole sector of Tier 1 generals should be moving in unison. However, YHOO is an even better lead indicator to a Tier 2 stock like ATHM. When trading ATHM, one should observe how YHOO is trading, as ATHM tends to lag a few minutes behind YHOO. This makes for a nice tool since YHOO will usually pull back minutes before ATHM, thereby giving you a heads-up on what to expect for ATHM's movement in general.

Tier 1 stocks, also known as generals, rarely die, but rather hibernate. However, they can get downgraded to a lower tier. As far as the lower-tier stocks go, they can fluctuate daily, so you have to understand that the key word here is *generally*. Tier 3 stocks *generally* lag the Tier 2 stocks, which *generally* lag the Tier 1 stocks. Table 1.1 shows Tiers 1, 2, and 3 stocks as of the printing of this book. You can get a current updated list on the Internet. Just keep in mind that momentum flows from top down in the stock market, starting with the Tier 1 generals.

Although the prices may be different, you can usually see the similarity of the chart pattern. This is visual proof that a tier system exists in the market within the sectors. This makes using the tier synergy an excellent confirmation tool as far as a respective stock's trend is concerned.

The list in Table 1.1 is by no means absolute or complete, but it should give you a general idea. However, remember that this list can and will change as time moves on. The Tier 1 generals do have great staying power and usually stay in their position from months to years. The Tier 2 and lower stocks tend to change with more frequency. The table shows the basic long-standing Tier 1s and Tier 2s and a few Tier 3s.

Note that when a Tier 1 stock splits, it will sometimes step down to a Tier 2 status until the price appreciates to allow for more upward movement on lesser volume.

Table 1.1

Sector	Tier 1	Tier 2	Tier 3
Internet	YHOO, EBAY, AOL	AMZN, RNWK, DCLK	ATHM
Networkers	CSCO, LU	COMS	PAIR
Telco equip	JDSU, TLAB	CIEN	AFCI
Box makers	IBM, SUNW, GTW	DELL, AAPL, HWP	MUEI, CPQ
Chips	INTC	AMD	
Semi equip makers	NVLS, AMAT, KLAC	RMBS, HIFN	KLIC, CYMI

TIER DIVERGENCE

Tier synergy is a phenomenon but not a perfect science. There will be days where the respective sector tier stocks may diverge for one reason or another. One or a handful of the tier stocks may move up while the rest of the sector moves down. Usually, this is attributed to some fundamental reason—be it earnings, news releases, rumors, insider selling, or broker downgrades and upgrades.

Any of the aforementioned fundamental catalysts may cause a top-tier stock (Tier 1, 2, or 3) to initially diverge from the sector. This initial divergence can be a short-term (minutes) or extended (hours) knee-jerk reaction, as the stock trend usually returns to move with the same pattern as the Tier 1 general, albeit at higher or lower prices in its own range.

In rare instances, a lower-tier stock may get strong news that will cause it to become a temporary Tier 1 stock for the day and actually help drive the sector higher. A great example of this was AMZN when the company announced the opening of its online Zshops. The Internet sector for the most part was down; however, AMZN surged from 65 to 82 on tremendous volume, causing upward momentum to the Tier 1 stocks such as EBAY and AOL. This is a case of the tail wagging the dog, and it does not happen very often. This is temporary, as evidenced by the sector the very next day when the Tier 1s continued to sag lower, taking AMZN along with them.

CHAPTER 2

The Nasdaq Market

The U.S. equities markets are separated into two systems: the specialist and the market maker. The New York Stock Exchange and the American Stock Exchange are known as specialist systems and auction markets. Every stock on these exchanges is assigned to a specialist whose job is to maintain a fair and orderly market by matching up buyers and sellers in an auctionlike style. Supply and demand cause price movements. The specialists do not establish price. What they will do is adjust their bid and offer prices in order to stabilize the market.

The Nasdaq and over-the-counter (OTC) markets are known as market maker systems. These markets have no geographical locations and boundaries. They exist through an electronic network linking market makers, registered representatives, and regulators. This electronic network makes it possible for brokers to attain quotes and for market makers to post quotes on terminals. A market maker is a person who represents an institution that "makes a market" in a Nasdaq stock. There are three levels of service on the Nasdaq:

- Level 1 is used by registered representatives (brokers) and provides real-time quotes that reflect only the best bid and best ask prices and their accompanying sizes. This is usually the only screen the public is aware of—it's mostly used by retail stockbrokers.

- Level 2 is used by retail traders. It allows them to see the depth of the price on the bid and ask sides. This snapshot allows an experienced trader to judge the trend, support, and resistance of a stock's price at any given time. These provide very little indication or insight about price movement. Thanks to the advent of the Internet, the public now has access to these informative screens.

- Level 3 is used by market makers. The Level 3 screen has all the features of a Level 2 but also allows users to enter, delete, and update their quotes for the securities they are making a market in. Level 3 screens are restricted and are only available for authorized market makers who meet NASD qualifications.

THE LEVEL 2 SCREEN

One important difference between the Level 2 screen and the Level 1 is this: The Level 2 screen shows all the market makers that participate in a stock, whereas the Level 1 screen (as noted before) shows only the best bid and best ask quotes along with their respective sizes.

The Level 2 screen is split into two sides. The left side shows the market makers on the bid (buyers) and the market makers on the ask (sellers). The bid size represents the number of shares a market maker will buy at the current price. The ask size represents the number of shares a market maker will sell at the current price. The display shows the abbreviation for the market maker, the market maker's bid or ask (what the market maker is willing to pay for shares or sell shares for), the size (whatever the number × 100), and the time of the quote.

The market makers are stacked from best to worst quote on each side. Markets makers are positioned by price, size, and time of quote.

On the bid side (left), the market maker offering the highest price to buy stock is listed first and foremost and is considered the best bid. If multiple market makers are offering the same best bid price, then size is considered the next indicative positioning factor. If multiple market makers are offering the same best bid price and same size, then time of quote is the final indicative factor. The latest quote will be positioned in front. For example, a stockbroker will pull a quote on CYMI (on Level 1) and see that it is bid $15^{1}/_2$ and ask $15^{9}/_{16}$ with 15 × 5 respective bid-ask sizes. This means that you can sell up to 1500 shares at $15^{1}/_2$ or buy 500 shares at $15^{9}/_{16}$. On Level 2, we see two market makers on the best bid price at $15^{1}/_2$. Although GSCO, MSCO, and PWJC all show the same best bid price, GSCO has a higher size and therefore takes the lead ahead of MSCO as the best bid. Although MSCO and PWJC have the same bid price and size, MSCO has a later post time—14:50 versus PWJC's 14:39—and thus takes the lead over PWJC. This pecking order continues on down, and likewise on the ask side.

CYMI	B: 15-1/2 A: 15-3/4		N: +1/2	VOL: 324,500			
MMID	BID	SIZE	TIME	MMID	BID	SIZE	TIME
GSCO	15-1/2	15	14:59	INCA	15-9/16	5	14:30
MSCO	15-1/2	10	14:50	ISLD	15-5/8	2	14:29
PWJC	15-1/2	10	14:39	GSCO	15-3/4	10	14:15
ISLD	15-7/16	15	15:02	SALB	15-3/4	5	14:18
BEST	15-7/16	10	14:45	FBCO	15-13/16	10	14:15
MONT	15-3/8	10	14:38	MSCO	15-7/8	10	14:14
HMQT	15-3/8	10	14:35	PWJC	15-7/8	5	15:01
NAWE	15-3/8	10	14:29	MONT	15-7/8	2	15:15
FBCO	15-5/16	10	15:01	BEST	15-15/16	15	13:25
MASH	15-1/4	10	15:25	MASH	16	10	15:10
LEHM	15-1/4	5	14:20	HMQT	16	10	15:05
NITE	15-3/16	10	14:45	NAWE	16	10	14:56
DEAN	15-1/8	10	13:25	LEHM	16	5	15:10

Although we don't indicate it in this book, all Level 2 screens are color-coded by price levels. Usually the best price is yellow, second best is green, third best is light blue, fourth best is red, and fifth best and beyond is dark blue. This is a blessing on the eyes when market makers are scrambling around, jockeying for position. In addition, most Level 2 screens will also make a click noise whenever a market maker adjusts her price or size or position.

The Level 2 screen for CYMI shows buying pressure and short term stability at 15^1/$_2$ bid. However, it appears that CYMI is looking to uptick (move to a higher price), judging by the size and depth (number of market makers supporting a price level) on the ask side. Let's imagine that an investor puts in a market order to buy 500 shares of CYMI and gets it at 15^9/$_{16}$. What happens next is that INCA (the market maker at best ask) is taken out, and if there are no more market makers at 15^9/$_{16}$, the second best ask price moves to best ask, the price upticks, and ISLD becomes the best ask at 15^5/$_8$.

Since there are more market makers and shares at the 15^1/$_2$ bid than at the 15^9/$_{16}$ ask, we can safely say that the 15^1/$_2$ has more depth and even buying pressure than the 15^9/$_{16}$ ask, which only has one market maker with only a 5 size. Therefore, the stock will most likely uptick rather than downtick (move to a lower price). This is just a very basic illustration of what happens on a Level 2 screen.

CYMI	B: 15-1/2 A: 15-3/4		N: +1/2	VOL: 324,500			
MMID	BID	SIZE	TIME	MMID	BID	SIZE	TIME
GSCO	15-1/2	10	14:59	INCA	15-3/4	10	14:30
MSCO	15-1/2	10	14:50	ISLD	15-3/4	10	14:29
PWJC	15-1/2	5	15:01	GSCO	15-13/16	10	14:15
ISLD	15-7/16	15	15:02	SALB	15-13/16	5	14:18
BEST	15-7/16	10	14:45	FBCO	15-7/8	10	14:15
MONT	15-3/8	10	14:38	MSCO	15-7/8	10	14:14
HMQT	15-3/8	10	14:35	PWJC	15-7/8	5	15:01
NAWE	15-3/8	10	14:29	MONT	15-7/8	2	15:15
FBCO	15-5/16	10	15:01	BEST	15-15/16	15	13:25
MASH	15-1/4	10	15:25	MASH	16	10	15:10
LEHM	15-1/4	5	14:20	HMQT	16	10	15:05
NITE	15-3/16	10	14:45	NAWE	16	10	14:56
DEAN	15-1/8	10	13:25	LEHM	16	5	15:10

Judging from the size, it appears that there is pressure on the buy side—and that is all one can assume. The Level 1 screen has its limitations in that it does not give any indication of exactly how many market makers are sitting at the 10 bid price or the 10^1/$_8$ ask price. If there were 10 market makers sitting on the bid at 10 and only 2 market makers sitting on the ask at 10^1/$_8$, one can come to the conclusion that there are more interested buyers than sellers and therefore an uptick would be in the cards, especially if a trend develops and market makers end up chasing a stock.

By viewing the patterns of the prices a trader can get a bird's-eye view of the momentum of a stock.

READING THE TIME OF SALES REPORT

The time of sales screen is a dynamically updating report that shows every trade made for a stock throughout the day. This screen is just as essential as a Level 2 screen, and we highly advocate the use of both. The screen will display the time of the trade, the price of the trade, and the size. The screen also quotes the current inside (best) bid and ask and their respective prices and sizes. Every time a trade is made, the time of sales screen will update. The most current trade appears at the top, and the respective bid and ask are constantly updated.

From this report, we can maintain an actual visual picture of order flow and perceive the kind of strength a trend has by the size of the trades. The Level 2 screen is a theoretical view of what the market makers perceive the direction of the trend will be. The time of sales is the actual real-life, real-time implementation of the trend.

PAIR		19-1/4 +1/4	
9:42 -	19-1/4	1000	
9:42 -	19-1/4	500	
9:42 -	19-1/4	3000	
9:42 -	19-1/4	2000	
9:42 -	19-1/4	1000	
9:41 -	19-1/4	500	
9:41 -	19-3/16	1000	
9:41 -	19-1/4	500	
9:41 -	19-3/16	800	
9:41 -	19-3/16	500	

Another valuable option with the time of sales report is the trade summary report. This report takes a cumulative account of all trades that happen throughout the day at the bid, mid (in between bid and ask), and ask. When we take a look at the total trades at the bid and at the ask, we should be able to tell how a stock has traded for the day, logically speaking. If the trades at the bid greatly outnumber the trades at the ask, this means there were more sellers than buyers (also known as *negative money flow*) and generally the stock should be down. If the trades at the ask far outnumber the trades at the bid, this means there were more buyers than sellers (also known as *positive money flow*) and generally the stock should be up.

When there is a discrepancy between the stock price and the trade report, one can often assume some market maker manipulation is occurring. This phenomenon usually happens during midafternoon, during lunch hour, and in smaller-volume stocks.

For example, COMS's stock price might be down $1\frac{1}{4}$ points for the day, but the trade summary report shows that there were 50 trades at the bid and 180 trades at the ask, indicating a positive money flow and a major discrepancy in the price. Whenever you spot this phenomenon, it should immediately signal a buy flag. Usually, the market makers will take the price back up by the close of the day to fall in line with the trading summary report to cover their tracks. Oftentimes, this will also signal a bottom and intraday low. When the trade summary report is used in conjunction with the time of sales and Level 2, the odds of catching the bounce from the intraday low are dramatically in your favor.

BLOCK TRADES ON THE TIME OF SALES: NASDAQ VERSUS NYSE

There is a misconception among traders and investors alike regarding block trades (trades in excess of 10,000 shares or more). On the Nasdaq, these prints are irrelevant at best, as we will show you.

As mentioned earlier, Nasdaq market makers spend a great deal of time filling orders for their clients. Who are these clients? Big mutual funds and institutions. For example, a multibillion dollar hedge fund might want 100,000 shares of WSTL and place its order with MSCO (Morgan Stanley). WSTL opens the day at 15 × 15$^1/_{16}$. MSCO will then start accumulating shares throughout the day, always trying to get the best price. MSCO will use all its resources to get cheap shares via electronic communication networks (ECNs), head fakes, and wiggles and perhaps even fading the trend (these techniques will be explained later). MSCO might skillfully try to shake the trees and cause a mini panic by sitting on the inside bid with a 10 size and using INCA to display a 150 size on the inside ask, shorting anyone that hits the ask and collecting cheap shares on the inside bid. He might continue to try to pound the price lower, using INCA to jump lower and lower and intimidating the other market makers. If MSCO is effective, he will have attained his 100,000 shares of WSTL without showing his cards. Needless to say, if other market makers and traders realize that MSCO has a motivated block buyer, they will run the price in anticipation. Let's say by 3 p.m., MSCO has attained the 100,000 shares at an average price of 15$^3/_8$. All his trades have appeared on the time of sales report. WSTL is currently trading at 15$^5/_8$ × 15$^3/_4$. MSCO will then turn around and fill his client order at a markup— perhaps 15$^3/_4$, the current ask. At 3:01 p.m., you might see a 100,000-share trade at 15$^3/_4$. Yet the price doesn't uptick, obviously, because the 100,000 shares have already been purchased throughout the day and "the price" is printed when the shares change hands from MSCO to his client. Many times this block trade print will often cause an intraday reversal, and other market makers will take this opportunity to short the stock all the way back down. There will initially be a small pop and then a pullback.

On block sales, the market maker will actually sell/short the shares in his own account and then cover by purchasing the block from the client, which is then printed on the time of sales report. This applies to an infamous technique market makers use called *fading the trend* (which will be explained in more detail later), in which the market maker will sit at the inside ask and not budge. Obviously he has a ton of shares that he is shorting, and when traders realize this they panic and sell back the shares at a lower price, at which time the market maker will cover. It takes deep pockets and/or a ton of shares to be able to strong-arm a stock into submission and reverse the trend. Therefore, usually this lead market maker, known as the ax (a term that also will be explained in detail later), should be in your crosshairs at all times, and in cases where he is fading the trend, it's best to follow his coattails and short at his level or $1/16$ below.

If you are a hedge fund that needs shares, you will go to the ax market maker because of his skill in getting you the best price (often by, as it is said, shaking the trees and causing panic). His in-depth experience, capital resources, and inventory shares will be utilized to get you good fills. It is no wonder the axes in a stock remain the axes. Being a lead market maker is almost a self-fulfilling prophecy. The difference between the men and the boys among market makers is the ability to collect a huge amount of shares with relatively little net change to the stock price, if not the opposite effect, in essence a risky game of liars poker.

So you see, the ax market makers rarely lose. They have the inside track on the demand for a stock through requested block orders from their clients. Knowing this, market makers on the Nasdaq are fully within their rights to front-run the orders, with the argument being that the market maker himself takes the brunt of the risk with his account should the trend reverse and pin him to the wall. In reality, the market maker can't lose, especially when he has the leverage to cripple a stock's momentum. It's a license to kill.

On the NYSE and AMEX markets (also known as specialist systems), block trades are more accurate. Since these exchanges only have one middleman, the specialist, these block trades are usually instant and accurate and very indicative of trend and buying. Therefore, it always pays to watch the block trades on the NYSE and AMEX. Front-running on the specialist exchanges is illegal.

CHAPTER 3

Watching the Market Makers

Market makers are allowed to adjust their prices at any time as many times as they want, because they take the risk on both sides of the trade on their bid and ask. Market makers also need to be able to gauge the conditions of the market and will often adjust their prices and keep narrow spreads to get a feel for the trend.

As a rule of thumb, you should always be familiar with the Level 2 action on any stock before you start trading it. Always keep your Level 2 screens and time of sales screens on several stocks and observe the movements of the market makers. It is usually helpful to watch some of the more heavily traded stocks to witness the constant motion and movements, especially during the first and last half hours of the trading day. Set the highlight feature to target a specific market maker (usually an ax, e.g., GSCO) and follow him along to see how he reacts to sellers and buyers. Watch how he sets his bid and ask based on the trend and trades on time of sales. Observe what he does during a string of straight sellers or buying panic. See which market makers follow suit with his price posts. Develop a comfort level with this particular market maker and get comfortable in his trading patterns. Eventually, you want to be able to anticipate how he will react to trades and what he does with the trend. It may take hours and even days of viewing these screens before you will learn to get into the rhythm of the dance of the Level 2 and most importantly develop the ability to anticipate what the market makers are doing.

Start off by watching your market maker around 9 a.m. EST every morning and see where he positions himself before the open. Watch if he takes the bid higher to gap the stock up or lower to gap it down. Note if he is usually the first market maker to set a price (bid or ask) or the last. Most importantly, always watch his spread (the difference between his bid and ask price). See if your market maker loosens his spread—e.g., GSCO $21^1/_2$ bid × $21^3/_4$ to $21^1/_2$ bid × 22—or tightens his spread—e.g., GSCO $21^1/_2$ × $21^3/_4$ to $21^1/_2$ × $21^9/_{16}$. At the 9:30 a.m. bell watch to see if he is sitting on the best bid and takes it higher for the first 2 minutes, only to step onto the best ask side and drive it lower. Keep note of the intraday low and high for the stock and view where the market maker is in relation to them.

THE MARKET MAKERS

There are key market makers who will consistently perform as the ax on the majority of stocks they make a market in. Once again, the difference between the men and the boys of the market-making game is the ability of the men to get as many shares as needed without severely affecting the stock price and tipping their cards. They offer their clients the best prices and greatest liquidity in the stocks they make a market in and therefore attain repeat business as their reputation continues to grow. These market makers are like world-class pitchers, and the biggest mistakes most inexperienced traders make is trying to hit home runs on every pitch (striking out the majority of the time). The key in trading is to go for as many singles, doubles, and triples as possible. Take small consistent scalps throughout the day and you will end up ahead.

Experienced traders will tell you that GSCO (Goldman Sachs) and MSCO (Morgan Stanley) swing the biggest sticks in any stock they make a market in. Even among the men, traders unanimously agree that GSCO is the baddest market maker on the block. What makes GSCO so dangerous besides his deep pockets is the skill of the market maker. GSCO is a magician that can pull the strings of fear and greed to move a stock in any direction he wants. When trading a stock in which GSCO is the ax, you are up against the very best in the world.

Let's get a good grip on exactly what market makers do and how they make money. The job of a market maker can be broken down into two categories. First and foremost, market makers are there to fill orders for the clients of the brokerage, including retail and institutional. Second, market makers also trade inventory and make profits playing the spread in a group of stocks.

When a brokerage doesn't make a market in a particular stock, it will often outsource the order to retail market makers like HRZG, NITE, and SLKC.

Traders often think a market maker can be making several points in a stock that may run 5 to 6 points on the day. The reality is that market makers play the spreads, and they play in volume to make their money. In other words, even if a stock runs 6 points on the day, a good market maker may have only averaged about $1/4$-point profit on the stock. That doesn't sound like a lot until you realize that the market maker made that $1/4$ point on 300,000 shares plus a commission oftentimes of $0.0025 a share. This results in a profit of $75,000 on the spreads and $750 on commissions, for a total of $75,750 profit on that particular stock. This is only a very general example, as many factors, such as float and volume, play a big role in how a market maker would adjust his spreads.

SO HOW DO MARKET MAKERS MAKE MONEY ON SPREADS?

As a rule of thumb, market makers buy on the bid and sell on the ask. They have complete access to Instinet and various ECN books, as well as to Level 3 data, which tend oftentimes to reveal the real size not chosen to be reflected on Nasdaq Level 2. Market makers also have a special program that is their respective brokerages' proprietary market maker software that calculates spreads for them. To make a long story short, market makers usually straddle a stock to build up inventory. If a market maker feels bullish on the stock, he will build a larger long inventory, and vice versa for short inventory on a bearish stock. The goal of the game is to zero out the majority of inventory by the close with a profit, which is usually the average spread. Therefore, in essence, when a stop is strong, a market maker may buy more shares on the bid, but will also continue to short and fade the run in order to continue to build a bull straddle, and vice versa on weak stocks. Do market makers always make money? No, not always. If a market maker guesses wrong on the trend, he will be overloaded and put into a very tight situation where he will look to eat losses. However, don't feel too bad for the market makers, as they also enjoy the benefit of 9 to 1 margins with firm capital and the ability to short the downtick.

THE AX

Aside from entry and exit, the other reason for using Nasdaq Level 2 is to find the ax. The ax market maker is the market maker you want to lean on. In other words, you want to use the ax as your stabilizer and foothold support. For example, if MSCO is the ax in ARBA and he is on the inside bid eating shares, then you should make sure that when you enter a long position, MSCO is on the bid side holding a price level as your support. Vice versa if MSCO is holding the ask price level down firm. Then you want to make sure you can lean on MSCO on a short position. Should the ax step off his level, that should be your first clue to take a minimal stop loss before the stock reverses.

Before going any further, let's take a good look at the key market makers.

GSCO (Goldman Sachs) Characteristics

- *Notorious for head fakes.* Might sit on the best bid and instantly jump on the best ask as buyers slow down or even in the middle of a buying spree.
- *Rarely tips his hand.* Tough to tell if GSCO is accumulating or dumping. However, during the opening bell, if there is a mad rush on a stock, GSCO will usually be real and usually be easy

to trade. When the action slows down, GSCO starts playing his games.

- *Often uses INCA to take the opposite side of a trade to panic shares his way.* It appears that the GSCO market maker is fully aware of his birthright as the king of the Street (even though he has recently been dethroned by MSCO), and anticipates having his actions carefully watched and followed by legions of traders. This allows him to use INCA (Instinet) to take the other side of his trades. In this way, GSCO is actually his own decoy and picks up shares on INCA. So, for example, if GSCO wants to buy PAIR at 18, he might sit on the best bid at 18×10 size and use INCA to jump on the best ask at $18^1/_{16} \times 100$ size. This will usually panic traders into dumping their shares fast.

As just noted, the GSCO market maker knows how much clout he carries and realizes that his every move is being watched and interpreted by hundreds of traders every second of the trading day, and he will use his notoriety to fool traders all day long. The ability to interpret GSCO's actions is the proverbial "key to the bank." A trader must invest full days observing GSCO on the Level 2 screen. From 9 a.m. to 4 p.m. (EST), a trader needs to pick a stock that GSCO makes a market in and just watch what GSCO does at premarket, the open, mid-morning, lunch hour, mid-afternoon, and the close. See what GSCO does in relation to market indicators (Dow, Nasdaq, and S&P futures) throughout the day. Most importantly, watch what happens to a stock's price when GSCO jumps on inside ask (selling) and inside bid (buying). You will often notice a pause on time of sales after GSCO jumps on the ask and then an onslaught of sellers. This is the nail on the coffin that shows how much of a self-fulfilling prophecy GSCO's actions are. Every trader needs to find a foothold indicator in the potential direction of a stock, and that usually is the ax. GSCO is usually the ax in any stock he makes a market in.

Watch GSCO's rhythm and spread. Our goal as traders is to seek the truth behind GSCO's actions. Does he have a large buyer or seller? Is he accumulating or selling or shorting? Is his position real or fake?

When observing GSCO, watch how long he will sit on the inside bid and ask as trades come in and he gets hit. Does he sit there and absorb all the sellers on the inside bid as all the other market makers jump to a lower price? If so, he could be accumulating shares to fill a block order, or he could be covering using INCA on the inside ask with larger size to panic traders. Does he sit there on the inside ask with a firm 10 size while a flurry of buys come in as all the other market makers jump to a higher price? If so, he could be fading the trading and selling or shorting for his own account to choke out the buyer who will inevitably end up selling back the shares at a lower price moments later.

Or does GSCO step higher when he gets hit with a few 1000-share trades on the ask? Or does GSCO step lower when he gets hit with a few 1000 sells? If so, then he is probably just catching orders and feeling out the market.

When GSCO widens his spread, this is usually a good indicator of where GSCO thinks a stock is going. This usually happens on the open, when news hits throughout the day or when a big buyer or seller comes into the market. We have seen GSCO widen his spread to $3/4$ to 1 point from his usual $1/4$ spread as he sits on the inside ask. Initially, this would tell us that GSCO is going out on a limb, predicting a decline in the price of the stock. Or he is setting up a head fake. Thus it is very important to see if INCA is the other side of the trade. If not, then he is probably for real.

MONT (Montgomery Securities), HMQT (Hambricht & Quist), RSSF (Robertson Stephens)

These market makers travel around in packs. They are the premiere "boutique" brokerages that specialize in technology and biotech stocks. They are usually the underwriters in these smaller stocks, and with the absence of GSCO, BEST, and MSCO, any one of these market makers can be the ax.

Unlike GSCO, these market makers often tip their hand and are less prone to playing games than a major market maker. Generally, when they are on the bid, they are usually buying, and when they are on the ask, they are usually selling. This is not to say they never head fake or try to jiggle traders out of their positions, but they are generally true to their positions. The main reason could be that they are axes in securities that have a smaller daily trading volume and fewer outstanding shares than the more widely held popular stocks. MONT (Montgomery Securities) usually shows his true position and maintains a strong control over the stocks in which he is the ax. Usually, after observing Level 2, we will feel him out, get to know his stance, and follow his lead. Often when a stock makes its run and MONT sits on the ask, we will go short, especially if he has taken a ton of hits and hasn't budged.

MSCO (Morgan Stanley Dean Witter) Characteristics

MSCO is growing as the power broker on the Street, knocking GSCO off the pedestal. MSCO is the king. MSCO has the strongest IPOs in the aftermarket, and unlike other underwriters, he tends to support most of his IPOs in the aftermarket. MSCO will tip his hand as an ax especially when he is filling institutional orders. You can often see MSCO hold a bid or ask for an extended period of time. In fact, MSCO is so bold as to be obnoxiously strong when he plays, which is just a sheer testament to the fact he wants everyone to know he is the ax of the moment. Eventually, traders and market makers alike mimic MSCO as his bids and asks become a self-fulfilling support or resistance, respectively. This strategy started with IPOs like CMTN, BRCD, and ARBA, where MSCO would sit on the bid in the wake of selling (literally 1 market maker on the bid versus 10 on the ask), eating so many shares that the sellers would pull their asks and buyers would quickly take MSCO's cause on the bid. The bidders would trip over each other trying to bid above MSCO. This became a routine. Every time MSCO upticked his bid, the stock would be 1 point ahead of him. When the sellers and profit takers came in to take out the bidders, downticking the stock, MSCO would hold firm and once again more followers would step in ahead of him. Folks, this is sheer muscle backed by massive institutional order flow and firm capital and damn good market making.

One particularly interesting incident occurred on December 7, 1999. YHOO was to be added to the S&P 500 index after the market close. YHOO had already gapped 18 points, retraced from 300 on the open to 286, and bounced steadily back. When YHOO retested (returned back to) 300 and reversed, MSCO held the support at 298^1/$_2$. I mean he *held* the bid. There was sheer panic selling, and MSCO sat at 298^1/$_2$ against up to 20 market makers and massive ISLD and INCA sell size. He sat there and ate and ate and ate shares on the bid until the shorts realized that YHOO was not going down. As YHOO upticked, so did MSCO. The members of our company (the Trading Pit) were alerted to this and a buy alert was issued at 300^1/$_2$ as MSCO upticked to 300 and held the bid firm. When MSCO upticked to 300^1/$_2$, the buyers stepped in front of him, sellers stepped off, and the stock stayed a full 1 point above his bid. Eventually, the bidders were taken out and panic set in, dropping the spread again from 301 on the bid to a quick fall to 300^1/$_2$. MSCO would be the only market maker at the bid versus literally "the world." In fact, we even commented like sportscasters that day: "It's MSCO versus the world, folks. Who will win? MSCO holding a 300^1/$_2$ bid versus 15 market makers on the ask." Needless to say, MSCO prevailed and squeezed the shorts in the process to just over 304^1/$_2$ on YHOO before he stepped off to let it breathe. When MSCO stepped off, the stock snapped back, and short sellers rushed the asks only to have MSCO jump back on the bid and squeeze the stock higher. We would say that MSCO literally squeezed YHOO through the 300 resistance that day to near 310 before the true momentum kicked in, taking YHOO to 330 and then a strong wiggle back to 317, where MSCO again showed firm support. The rest is history as YHOO entered the last half hour of the market and fund-buying momentum drove YHOO to 351 into the close!

Like we said, MSCO is the new king. When MSCO is an ax in a stock, you will know it along with everyone else. The best way to play is to follow his lead and play the momentum as he upticks. However, never sit in through the whole run, because when MSCO steps off the bid, the price will collapse short term. Therefore, take your profits early and use the momentum ticks to exit. The best time to exit is when he holds a bid and new bidders come in to mimic him. Usually the ISLD players will step in at MSCO's bid with size that causes all the market makers on the ask to quickly step off. Then market makers come in to bid higher, and so on, until you get ISLD buyers above the ask. In a stock where MSCO is the ax, you will often see $1/2$-point to 1-point pops when he upticks. Use these opportunities to pare out (break the order into manageable parts). You can ride the winners, but always lock in your profit and always realize that MSCO will eventually step off the bid, so keep these plays as sheer momentum based on MSCO's self-fulfilling prophecy. Take them for what they are worth—a nice scalp opportunity—and always sell into buyers; don't sell in a panic with the other sellers.

THE NEW POWERHOUSE TRADING MARKET MAKERS

As we discussed earlier, the classic market maker usually spends most of his time filling orders. Market makers like GSCO and MSCO are the white-collar royalty-type brokers that manhandle their respective high-volume Tier 1 general stocks. Rarely will you see them in many of the smaller Internet stocks that carry huge one-day momentum. There is a new movement on Wall Street to grow proprietary in-house hedge trading units. These in-house hedge traders trade firm capital margined 9 to 1 and play massive volume on spreads. The new breed of market maker caters to day traders, and it is these market makers who are becoming the new axes to watch. Market makers like NITE, MASH, HRZG, and SLKC were known to be weak retail market makers that only filled orders for firms that did not make a market in certain stocks. They are now becoming the new powerhouses in the industry. Not only are they generating more volume due to increased online trading activity, but they are growing into powerhouse hedge traders that have a hand in every momentum stock that hits the radar. These are the blue-collar monster market makers that play heavy and hard head-to-head with the day traders. They don't have analysts or keep much inventory stock. Instead, they trade big volume for spreads. Any day trading momentum stock of the moment will have one of these three market makers as the ax. NITE is notori-ous for running the momentum on the smaller madness movers, only to clamp down and short the life out of an overblown runner, literally choking the life out of the buying pressure. These hedge traders are young, hungry, and aggressive. They are the future.

When playing a momentum stock, always look for these market makers as the ax. Many times, they are responsible for the run or the squeeze. SLKC often works with NITE and HRZG, and so it is wise to keep an eye on all three. The difficulty is that it's hard to tell client orders from hedge trading, and so it takes time to recognize. Use volume pops to see how they lean. Here is a brief sketch of the three:

- *MASH (Meyers & Schwartz)*. This market maker controls all the orders for Charles Schwab and other discounter firms. He represents small investors and rarely controls the action in a stock. MASH has a very fast-growing hedge trader arm.

- *HRZG (Herzog)*. This market maker is usually used by retail shops like Smith Barney or other brokerages that don't make a market in a stock that an investor wants to purchase. He also fills order flow for the online brokers like E*trade and Ameritrade. HRZG is growing fast, and it is quickly becoming a blue-collar powerhouse on momentum stocks.

- *NITE (Knight Trimark)*. These guys are hard-core aggressive. They fill orders for retail brokers much in the same way HRZG does. However, their hedge traders are the most furious, gutsy, and aggressive traders we have ever seen. These traders are tough, hungry, and mean—and damn good. They don't have the luxury of billion dollar hedge fund clients like GSCO or MSCO. They are real traders that use firm capital (peanuts compared with GSCO or MSCO) to run or crush momentum. Folks, these guys trade hard core. Our hats off to NITE.

The market makers discussed in this section by no means account for even a fraction of the market makers on the Nasdaq. There are hundreds of market makers, and they all have their own characteristics. However, the companies we just discussed tend to have a presence in all the stock we tend to trade.

MARKET MAKER TACTICS

Market maker tactics are a hot topic with every day trader. There are also the easiest excuse and scapegoat for poor trading results. We can't tell you the numerous times that traders complained to us about the "blatant manipulation" by the market makers which caused their losses when, in reality, their losses were a direct result of poor trading and money management.

Interpreting the true intentions of a market maker is a game of speculation at best. Remember, market makers do not need even a single trade to change their bid or ask price higher or lower. They are taking on the risk of making a market on both sides of the trade and will naturally seek to move their prices to where they feel there is the greatest security and profitability. Unlike the specialist system on the New York Stock Exchange and American Stock Exchange, market makers on the Nasdaq can change their quotes at will. However, by only offering investors stock at the best bid and ask prices, we assume that is enough incentive for market makers to be competitive with their pricing and allow investors access to fairest possible price.

What happens when the market makers for a particular stock all of a sudden decide to step off their current bids? *Panic!* For example, suppose XYZ is trading at $18^{1}/_{4} \times 18^{15}/_{16}$ and suddenly the inside market drops to $17^{3}/_{4} \times 17^{7}/_{8}$ on very low volume. At this point, sellers show up and immediately start dumping their shares in a panic, thinking that there is a fundamental reason for the fall. "Perhaps it was a bad press release, a downgrade, or someone knows something I don't? Who knows, just dump it! Cut my losses!" This is the attitude displayed by the panic sellers, causing the stock to tumble even lower. Eventually, the market makers will accumulate cheap shares on the way down and at the bottom and then sell some for a profit on the way up. Does this sound familiar?

The above mentioned example is termed by traders as a *head fake*. Head fakes are actions by market makers to create an illusion of a short-term trend to induce panic (buying or selling) and usually result in a trend reversal, faking out the poor panic sellers or buyers of their shares. Many traders tend to think head faking only occurs in the smaller-volume stocks, but in our opinion, head faking happens across the board with all Nasdaq stocks.

The ax in the larger-cap stocks is also notorious for head fakes, especially with the help of INCA (Instinet). Instinet is an ECN often used by institutions, traders, and market makers. Usually, all the market makers in a stock have their sights set on the movements of the ax. This can be a blessing and a curse at the same time.

In one sense, the ax's movements are often mimicked, and a self-fulfilling prophecy occurs. For example, if GSCO is buying heavy, then the other market makers will rush in to outbid him, taking the stock price higher. And if GSCO is selling, the other market makers will take his lead and sell, taking the stock price lower. This can make things tough when GSCO really wants to buy shares at a reasonable price. Therefore, he will often use INCA to take the opposite side of a trade (often with a larger size) to intimidate traders into selling or buying.

In the above example, you'll see GSCO increase his bid price and then sit on the inside bid. Meanwhile, you'll see INCA on the inside ask with a large intimidating size comparable to GSCO, indicating selling pressure. We can hypothesize that if GSCO really wanted some shares, he would disguise himself as INCA with a large enough size to intimidate some traders into dumping their shares to GSCO at the inside bid.

THE AX: HOW TO SPOT HIM AND PLAY HIM

In every particular stock, there will always be an ax. As mentioned earlier, the ax is usually the market maker that will determine the trend. The myth behind the Nasdaq system is the belief that the competition among the various market makers jockeying for business in a stock will result in the best possible price for investors. The reality is that very few market makers every compete. Instead, most market makers usually follow a lead market maker, the ax.

This is because the ax will actually take firm positions with firm capital and has the deep pockets to do it, not to mention that the ax probably controls a major interest of the float (firm capital and clients) due to being an underwriter (if not the head underwriter). It is very interesting in that most of the other market makers and traders will follow the movements of the ax, thereby making the ax's movements a self-fulfilling prophecy. The ax usually has enough capital to spark a trend or stifle it dead in its tracks.

Therefore, whether the ax knows it or not (and he does), he can move a stock based on how traders interpret the ax's positions. Knowing this, the ax will at many times try not to reveal his true hand and will often try to fade the trend or wiggle traders out. *Fading the trend* refers to the ax sitting on the best ask during a buying spree or sitting on the best bid during a selling spree. In other words, the ax will try to shake you by going the other way. Due to these movements, it can be very hard to interpret the true intentions of the ax unless you are familiar with the stock and the behavior of the ax. If the ax jumps on the best bid with a heavy size, most of the other market makers may even jump off their current bid to a lower bid in anticipation of the sellers. If the ax jumps heavy on the bid size, many market makers will jump on the bid in anticipation of the buyers. Many times, the ax may not want to reveal his hand at any price and will use INCA (Instinet) to jump on the opposite side to add pressure to the opposite position. For example, suppose GSCO wants to accumulate shares of XYZ stock. He might jump on best bid at 23 with a 10 size and use INCA to jump on the best ask with a 200 size at $23^1/_{16}$. This will scare traders into rushing to sell. As the sellers come in, GSCO will eat up the shares or even jump to a lower bid price, taking the other market makers with him until he accumulates as many shares as he wants. He'll then pull INCA off the ask, jump on the bid as GSCO with a heavy size near bottom, and see the traders come right back in and sell the shares at a higher price.

Once again, do not mistake market makers on the Nasdaq with specialists on the NYSE. The Nasdaq is *not* an auction market, and market makers do not exist to maintain a "fair and orderly" market for the stock that they make a market in. The Nasdaq is a dealer market. Market makers profit from buying at the bid and selling at the ask (long) or selling at the ask and buying at the bid (short). Throughout the day, market makers are constantly jockeying for position on the Level 2. However, not all market makers are created equal. One must be able to distinguish between the significant market makers and the market makers that just go along with the trend. The reality is that the majority of the market makers are not committed to making a market, taking risks with firm capital, or keeping an inventory. The majority of the market makers take on very little risk, because they are usually in a stock in an effort to catch an order they can trade against (turn around and fill an order already in hand) without the liability of taking a position. In these cases, they will receive orders from different customers for both the buy and sell sides of a transaction, making it a riskless transaction. These market makers are considered the "herd," or followers. So who are the leaders? They are the ax in the stock.

Identifying the ax in any stock should be a priority even before considering taking a position. There are two ways to identify the ax. First, you can do some research on the company (www.nasdaqtrader.com) and find out which firm trades the most monthly volume on the underlying stock. Usually, the ax will far outshadow even the closest market maker in volume. The second way is to utilize the Level 2 screen. In heavily traded stocks (usually on the Nasdaq's most active list), the ax will usually be GSCO (Goldman Sachs), MSCO (Morgan Stanley), BEST (Bear Stearns), MLCO (Merrill Lynch), LEHM (Lehman Brothers), and or SBSH (Smith Barney Shearson). In lesser held stocks (smaller tech stocks, biotechs, etc.), the ax will usually be smaller boutique brokerage firms like HMQT (Hambricht & Quist), MONT (Montgomery Securities), PIPR (Piper Jaffray), OPCO (Oppenheimer), FBCO (First Boston), and UBSS (UBS Securities). These firms are by no means an end-all comprehensive list. However, in our experience they are the likely axes in most Nasdaq stocks and usually in the order presented. For example, if GSCO is a market maker in a stock (in addition to BEST, HMQT, and FBCO), it can be assumed that GSCO is the ax. However, it is a good idea to keep an eye on where MSCO and BEST line up in regard to GSCO. Chances are very high they will follow GSCO's lead.

To find the ax in a stock using Level 2:

1. Pull up the stock's Level 2 market maker screen.

2. See which market makers are sitting at the best bid and ask.

3. Apply the above list to the market makers.

4. Watch the movement of the market makers as they jump on and off their prices.

5. Look for the last market maker at the best bid (after all other market makers jump to a lower bid price) during a rash of selling (absorbing all the buys) or the last market maker on the ask (while all other market makers jump to a higher ask price) during a rash of buying (thereby keeping a lid on the price). This market maker is probably the ax.

PAIR	B:17-1/2 A: 17-5/8 N: +1/2		VOL: 432,500			
MMID	BID	SIZE	TIME	MMID	BID	SIZE	TIME
GSCO	17-1/2	10	14:59	INCA	17-5/8	10	14:30
MSCO	17-7/16	10	14:50	ISLD	17-5/8	10	14:29
PWJC	17-7/16	5	15:01	HMQT	17-3/4	10	14:15
ISLD	17-7/16	15	15:02	SALB	17-13/16	5	14:18
BEST	17-7/16	10	14:45	FBCO	17-7/8	10	14:15
MONT	17-3/8	10	14:38	MSCO	17-7/8	10	14:14
HMQT	17-3/8	10	14:35	PWJC	17-7/8	5	15:01
NAWE	17-3/8	10	14:29	MONT	17-7/8	2	15:15
FBCO	17-5/16	10	15:01	BEST	17-15/16	15	13:25
MASH	17-1/4	10	15:25	MASH	18	10	15:10
LEHM	17-1/8	5	14:20	GSCO	18	10	15:05 GSCO is the ax
NITE	17	10	14:45	NAWE	18	10	14:56
DEAN	17	10	13:25	LEHM	18-1/4	5	15:10

The ax's position gives you your basic foothold in determining where a stock price is headed. However, you need to be able to determine if an ax's position is firm and real or if he is just scalping. This is the most difficult aspect of trading. For the newcomer, the ax can make you do whatever he wishes by bringing out that most common emotion in trading—panic.

To avoid acting out of panic, look closely. If you see an ax sit on the best bid and see many trades on time of sales at the bid as he absorbs a ton of shares, then you can assume the ax is taking a firm position. Likewise on the short side. If you see an ax sit on the best ask as a ton of trades come in at the ask, you can assume the ax is unloading shares or even shorting them, and so the stock may very well be heading back down.

Since the ax usually is the real market maker, he will take risks and commit firm capital to take a position. The irony is that the other market makers (as well as experienced traders) know and respect the actions of the ax and will usually follow his lead. For example, GSCO happens to be the ax on ABC stock as it free-falls $3/4$ off the intraday high to $18^{1}/_{2}$. It is common to see GSCO jump on the best bid at $18^{1}/_{2}$ and eat up all the shares at bid. A few moments later, more market makers will jump on $18^{1}/_{2}$ in front of GSCO once they realize the coast is clear. Several moments later, the traders realize that GSCO is serious about taking a firm position at $18^{1}/_{2}$. At this moment of realization, the bottom has been reached as the traders promptly jump in at the ask, causing several upticks as the market makers jump over each other, taking the price higher to accommodate the demand. This is how an ax will move the markets. The ax has the deep pockets and the notoriety to instill fear and panic in the hearts of the other market makers and the traders alike.

What does it take to be an ax? It takes plenty of firm capital and big-money clients, namely multibillion dollar mutual funds and institutions that command hundreds of millions of dollars in funds. Perhaps the most useful tool in a market maker's arsenal is his leverage. A market maker has a 9 to 1 margin, whereas most traders only have a 2 to 1, or 50 percent, margin requirement. In essence, while a day trader needs to put up $45,000 to leverage himself to own 10,000 shares of a $9 stock (a 2 to 1 margin), a market maker only needs to put up $10,000 to buy the same 10,000 shares (a 9 to 1 margin)!

These market makers make money two ways. First they have clients that happen to be institutions and mutual funds with billions in funds. A mutual fund client might go to GSCO and say, "I'd like to buy 200,000 shares of XYZ stock between 24 and $24^{1}/_{2}$." Then the market maker goes to work. Rarely does a market maker ever buy all 200,000 shares at once. Instead, the market maker will "work" the price of the stock. In cases like these, the goal of the market maker is to accumulate 200,000 shares between 24 and $24^1/_2$. GSCO might sit on the bid and start buying up as many shares as possible at $24^1/_8$. However, this might be too obvious. Experienced traders realize that when GSCO is looking to buy shares at the bid, it will usually mean a run-up in price. Other traders and market makers will also try to buy shares at the bid and even try to outbid GSCO. The very sight of GSCO sitting on best bid will oftentimes cause buyers to show up, causing a rally in the price. In essence, GSCO's own reputation would cause GSCO to pay a higher price for shares. Therefore, when either the sellers run out or other traders are watching GSCO's every move GSCO will try to panic the traders into selling him more shares.

For example, if XYZ stock is sitting at $24^1/_8 \times 24^3/_{16}$, GSCO might sit on the best bid at $24^1/_8$ and then use INCA to jump on $24^3/_{16}$ with an intimidating size like 100. You will see GSCO 10 size at $24^1/_8$ and INCA 100 size at $24^3/_{16}$. This will usually scare traders into panicking and selling their shares in anticipation of a run down in price. And sure enough, as the sellers come in, GSCO will sit there and buy up the shares, and might even drop the bid and take INCA lower on the ask with the same size to $24^1/_{16} \times 24^1/_8$. GSCO will eat up all the shares all the way down to perhaps $23^3/_4 \times 23^7/_8$. What happens if someone buys shares at the ask from INCA (which is actually GSCO at the ask)? INCA will simply short at the ask and buy back as GSCO on the bid—it's beautiful. In essence, GSCO will strong-arm a stock lower. If GSCO has accumulated all the shares he needs, and wants to trade some or sell some for a profit, GSCO will jump on the bid and have INCA jump on the bid with a 100 size. A trader will see INCA's massive size and GSCO on the best bid and will buy in a panic frenzy, taking the price higher. GSCO doesn't have to be on the ask to sell shares. GSCO can stay on the best bid and chase the stock higher and sell his shares on SelectNet directly to the market makers on the inside bid. When the ax has attained all the shares for his client, then he will average the cost and sell them to his client at a premium. This is how the institutions attain shares and how the market makers make money.

Once you have identified the ax in a stock, you need to keep note of his spread. As discussed earlier, the spread is the difference between ax's bid and ask price. The ax's spread will usually indicate where the ax feels the short-term range of the stock price will be. It is critical to immediately notice when the ax has decided to take the stock price back up and either set the trend or initiate a trend reversal.

How do you determine a trend initiated by the ax? Look for these moves:

1. The ax jumps to best bid and loosens his spread from $1/4$ point to $1/2$ point.
2. Time of sales shows all buyers coming in on the ask.
3. More market makers jump on the best bid with the ax.
4. Market makers jump off the current best ask to a higher ask price.
5. The ax continues to jump to a higher bid price as the other market makers join him, causing the stock price to go higher.
6. Soon other market makers jump in front of the ax in a panic, taking the price even higher.

It is very important to note that at this point the ax could be ready for a head fake or a wiggle. The above steps can usually take anywhere from 30 seconds to several minutes and then the head fake.

How do you determine an ax head fake? Look for these actions:

1. Once the stock price has increased $1/4$ point, the ax immediately jumps to the best ask and drops off the best bid.
2. Time of sales will show straight sells.
3. Other market makers jump on the best ask and jump off the best bid.
4. At this time, INCA might step on the best ask with a heavy size (for example, INCA 100).
5. INCA will pound the ask lower as market makers get hit on the bid or step off to lower bids.

17-5/16	+5/16	
15:00	17-5/16	1000
15:00	17-3/8	3000

PAIR   B:17-1/2 A: 17-5/8 N: +1/2   VOL: 432,500

MMID	BID	SIZE	TIME	MMID	BID	SIZE	TIME
GSCO	17-1/2	10	14:59	INCA	17-9/16	10	14:59
MSCO	17-7/16	20	14:50	ISLD	17-5/8	10	14:45
PWJC	17-7/16	20	15:01	HMQT	17-5/8	10	14:15
ISLD	17-7/16	15	15:02	SALB	17-3/4	5	14:18
BEST	17-7/16	10	14:45	FBCO	17-13/16	10	14:15
MONT	17-3/8	10	14:38	MSCO	17-7/8	10	14:14
HMQT	17-3/8	10	14:35	PWJC	17-7/8	5	15:01
NAWE	17-3/8	10	14:29	MONT	17-7/8	2	15:15
FBCO	17-5/16	10	15:01	BEST	17-15/16	15	13:25
BTRD	17-1/4	10	14:35	GSCO	18	10	15:10
LEHM	17-1/8	5	14:20	BTRD	18	10	15:05
NITE	17	10	14:45	NAWE	18	10	14:56
DEAN	17	10	13:25	LEHM	18-1/4	5	15:10

15:00	17-3/8	1000
15:00	17-3/8	1000
15:00	17-7/16	1000
15:00	17-7/16	1000
15:00	17-7/16	1000
15:00	17-7/16	1000
15:00	17-1/2	a 100
15:00	17-7/16	b 10
15:00	17-9/16	1000
15:00	17-9/16	1000
15:00	17-9/16	1000
14:59	17-9/16	1000
14:59	17-9/16	1000
14:59	17-9/16	5000
14:59	17-9/16	2000
14:59	17-9/16	500
14:59	17-9/16	1500
14:59	17-9/16	1000
14:59	17-1/2	2000
14:58	17-1/2	1000

PAIR   B:17-7/16 A: 17-1/2   N: +3/8   VOL: 455,500

MMID	BID	SIZE	TIME	MMID	BID	SIZE	TIME
INCA	17-7/16	10	15:00	INCA	17-1/2	100	15:00
MSCO	17-3/8	10	15:00	GSCO	17-1/2	10	15:00
PWJC	17-3/8	5	15:01	HMQT	17-3/4	10	15:00
ISLD	17-5/16	15	15:02	SALB	17-13/16	5	15:01
BEST	17-5/16	10	15:00	FBCO	17-7/8	10	15:00
MONT	17-1/4	10	15:01	MSCO	17-7/8	10	15:00
HMQT	17-1/4	10	14:59	PWJC	17-7/8	5	15:01
NAWE	17-3/16	10	14:59	MONT	17-7/8	2	15:15
FBCO	17-3/16	10	15:01	BEST	17-15/16	15	13:25
MASH	17-1/8	10	15:25	MASH	18	10	15:10
LEHM	17-1/16	5	14:20	TNTO	18	10	15:05
GSCO	17	10	14:45	NAWE	18	10	14:56
DEAN	17	10	13:25	LEHM	18-1/4	5	15:10

Note that the purpose of a head fake is usually to wiggle traders out of their positions. As you can see, when the ax initiated what appeared to be a trend, the traders immediately jumped in with 1000-share buys (time of sales). As the traders bought in looking for an uptrend and perhaps a quick scalp profit, the ax allowed the price to rise about a $1/4$ point before he jumped on the best ask. If traders don't get shaken out at this point, the ax might employ INCA with an intimidating size (which is quite effective), causing traders to take an immediate profit. Unfortunately, not everyone can take a profit. As the traders end up selling their shares right back, most of them will sell them back in a panic and end up with a loss. Market makers usually perform head fakes during lunchtime and when there is a slowdown of trades. This is quite an interesting way to kill some time (and traders), we must admit.

How do you determine when an ax is fading the trend, shorting with the ax? The term *fading the trend* (as noted previously) describes a technique used by the ax where he takes the opposite side of an apparent trend and wears it out until the trend reverses. The ax would sell into the uptrend and buy into the downtrend, literally strong-arming it into changing directions. Needless to say, this takes a tremendous amount of capital. Without having a Level 2 screen and time of sales screen, one would never be able to interpret this action.

CREAF	B:17-7/16	A: 17-1/2 N: +3/8		VOL: 325,500			
MMID	BID	SIZE	TIME	MMID	BID	SIZE	TIME
INCA	17-7/16	10	15:00	GSCO	17-1/2	10	15:00
MSCO	17-7/16	10	15:00	INCA	17-9/16	10	15:00
PWJC	17-7/16	10	15:00	HMQT	17-3/4	10	15:00
ISLD	17-7/16	15	14:59	SALB	17-13/16	5	15:01
BEST	17-3/8	10	15:00	FBCO	17-7/8	10	15:00
MONT	17-5/16	10	15:01	MSCO	17-7/8	10	15:00
HMQT	17-1/4	10	14:59	PWJC	17-7/8	5	15:01
NAWE	17-3/16	10	14:59	MONT	17-7/8	2	15:15
FBCO	17-3/16	10	15:01	BEST	17-15/16	15	13:25
MASH	17-1/8	10	15:25	MASH	18	10	15:10
LEHM	17-1/16	5	14:20	TNTO	18	10	15:05
GSCO	17	10	14:45	NAWE	18	10	14:56
DEAN	17	10	13:25	LEHM	18-1/4	5	15:10

The market maker screen above shows an example of GSCO fading the trend. You will notice a ton of buys at the ask on the time of sales report screen, and yet GSCO will be the only market maker sitting on the ask with the same 10 size. If the trend is extremely strong, GSCO might uptick $1/16$ at a time until the buying slows down. Eventually, the buying will subside as GSCO sits on the inside ask firm. The traders who originally entered the position at $17^1/2$, anticipating a short-term uptrend, will immediately begin selling upon realizing that GSCO is not moving higher. As the trades start coming in at the ask, the other market makers will jump to a lower bid price, causing more panic selling. GSCO will continue to drive the ask down (as more market makers join him on the ask), and often you will see INCA on the inside bid, which very likely could be GSCO covering his shorts. His shorts? Yes, the trades that went off at the inside ask were shorted by GSCO.

When the ax is actively fading the trend, usually near the end of the day or at or near the intraday high, we can usually assume that the ax is shorting. When the buyers disappear and the sellers show up, the ax (GSCO in the above example) will cover on the way down, often disguised as INCA on the best bid (leaving his bid several ticks underneath to portray the illusion that he is not covering yet). The ax relies on the inevitability of the profit takers coming into the market and taking their cue from the Level 2 screen, selling into the downtick.

CHAPTER 4

Charts: The Most Powerful Tools

One of the key mistakes most day traders make is they wear their emotions on their sleeve, being influenced mostly by Nasdaq Level 2 screens. The reality is that Nasdaq Level 2 is generally an illusion based on anticipation. In a perfect market, the sizes displayed on Level 2 would be real sizes with real orders. But this is not the case, as market makers will often use ECNs to head fake, fade the trend, and not refresh quotes to give the illusion of less or more size than they really have. This brings emotions out in traders, who often get wiggled out in a knee-jerk reaction by the mesmerizing dance of the Level 2 screen. A successful day trader needs more than just Nasdaq Level 2. Consider everything on Level 2 as theory. The trades on time of sales are *fact*. These are real trades that have been executed and accounted for.

Traders need objectivity and reality. This makes charts an indispensable tool. Charts are based on real trades that have been executed. Therefore, charts are fact and reality. Charts give you the real story, an objective view of price action and trend based on real trades. Charts give you a very real visual history on a stock. Although there is no substitute for watching a stock's movements on Nasdaq Level 2 for several hours to learn the range and the rhythm, charts allow you to cut through much of that information gathering and point out the immediate and historical intraday trends. A perfect analogy would be like having *Cliff Notes* to get the quick picture rather than reading through the whole novel. *Cliff Notes* are fast and get the job done. However, many of the smaller details are left out, the same as with straight charts. When you combine reading the novel with the *Cliff Notes,* you get an even more thoroughly comprehensive understanding of the story. In the same sense, we highly suggest you use charts to complement your Nasdaq Level 2 reading. Naturally, there will be times when you will be playing momentum on the fly or finding a new stock to play and need to make immediate moves for a scalp. The chart can be your quickest way to get briefed on trend coupled with Nasdaq Level 2 for ax spotting and entry and exit of your scalp.

When it comes to technical analysis and charting, there is a universe of simple to complicated methods to select from. Beware, however, of information overload. The bottom line is that the good technical tools will usually confirm each other—thus having a whole arsenal of oscillators and different charts can be a waste of time.

We use only two types of charts. Of all the tools we have seen, these very simple, easy-to-use charts pretty much say it all. We are only concerned with short-term momentum and intraday trend. The two charts that cover these areas are the 1-minute stochastics chart and the 3-minute moving averages chart. We will delve into detail in both of these indispensable charts

1-MINUTE STOCHASTICS CHART

We have discovered a powerful tool that helps to clarify and fill in the gaps with Level 2 and time of sales. This tool visually depicts a stock price's momentum and gives clear entry and exit points throughout the day. This powerful tool will allow you oftentimes to avoid head fakes and take advantage of stock spikes. This tool will allow you to position yourself perfectly before the big runs and big drops. When you couple this tool with Level 2 and time of sales, your chances of trading success increase dramatically. It is an essential component of your arsenal to ensure that the scales are tipped in your favor on every trade.

This powerful tool is a charting technique called *stochastics.* Imagine a stock's price like a stretched rubber band. When the stock is sitting, the rubber band is still. Now, suppose that you grab the middle of the rubber band and pull it down as far as you can until it reaches its elastic threshold. What happens when you let go? It snaps back up and eventually relaxes again. The same thing would happen if you grabbed the middle, pulled it up, and then let go. The theory behind using stochastics is that every stock is like a rubber band. When momentum enters into a stock, it is stretched either too far up or too far down and the stock will retrace. Understanding this helps you understand that the best way to make a good scalp is to enter a stock as it's being pulled down like a rubber band, right at the point where it will be let go to bounce back up—and vice versa when shorting. The stochastics oscillator tells you when a stock has reached that short-term point where it should bounce back like a rubber band. The stochastic oscillator compares a current price relative to its price range over a given time period. It is a complex formula, and we highly advise getting software that will provide an intraday stochastics chart attachable to or overlaid on a 1-minute tick chart (be sure you have a real-time feed!). Make sure that you can enter three variables for %d and two variables for %dslow. The stochastics graph will show two lines that usually move with each other up and down throughout the day on any particular stock. One of the lines is the stochastics oscillator, and the other line is the moving average of the stochastics oscillator.

Let's get the setup correct. Your package should have the %d and %dslow. And you should enter the following values:

For %dslow:

%K interval:	15
%d interval:	5
%dslow-interval:	2

For %d:

%K interval:	15
%d interval:	5

Make sure you overlay the chart at the bottom and set your setting to intraday 1-minute intervals. This should produce a chart like the one shown in Figure 4.1.

The %d is the stochastics oscillator and the lead indicator. The %dslow is the moving average of the %d. Together they make up the meat of the 1-minute stochastics chart. The %d will lead and make the initial move. Then the %dslow will usually cross over and follow. When they both move in the same direction, this tells you the immediate trend.

As a stock's price fluctuates throughout the day, the stochastics oscillator will also fluctuate. When the lines fall, it means the price momentum is dropping, and vice versa when the lines rise.

The nice thing about stochastics is that the historical data (whether using the 1-minute tick looking at price action a few hours back or daily) when cross-referenced with a price chart

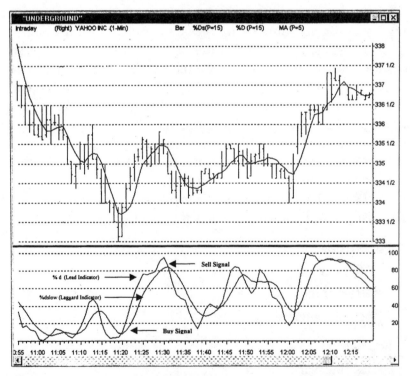

Figure 4.1 1-minute stochastics (bottom chart). (SOURCE: RealTick™ © 1986–2000 Townsend Analytics, LLC. Used with permission.)

prove that it works and, as well, the data support its validity and accuracy. All you really have to do is look at the stochastics and the attached price chart to see where the stochastics bounces resulted in bounces in the stock's price and likewise for reversals.

There are many ways to use stochastics, but we are only going to go over what works for us. Stochastics should be used in every stock play to give you an idea of where the momentum is and how long the trend has lasted. Stochastics is ideal for intraday-trading your basket of stocks. Together, knowledge of ax market maker behavior on Level 2, access to time of sales, and stochastics-based entry points will make your positions even safer, giving you an edge on your trade and a competitive advantage over other day traders.

The beauty of stochastics is that it takes the human element of emotions out of the analysis. It is very mechanical and frightening-ly accurate. In most cases, we would pick the stochastics over the Level 2 indicators when there is a divergence because of the decep-tive nature of the ax market makers and their ability to cause unforced errors resulting from traders' emotions, namely panic and fear. There have been several times when Level 2 would suggest an immediate uptrend (e.g., INCA with 100 size on the inside bid and GSCO right underneath him), only to have stochastics indicate a sell/short opportunity (indicators reversing from the 95 band). And amazingly, it would turn out that GSCO was head faking and would switch to inside ask along with INCA, driving the stock lower.

In the *Underground Level 2 Daytraders Handbook*, I explained that we use the 80/20 bands as our alerts. However, to better the odds in our favor *or* in weak markets, we look for reversal through the 90 and 10 bands.

Buy Signals

Buy signals occur when the %d falls below the 20 or 10 band and *reverses* to above the 20 or 10 band. The points at which the %d and the %dslow lines cross on the reversal are the *buy points*. The depth of this convergence (crossing) is very important. The *wider* the *gap* and *higher* the *angle* of the lines when they cross, the more dynamic the bounce should be.

The most common parameters that traders use are 20 and 80 (the scale on the right of the chart, from 0 to 100). Usually, when the stochastics oscillator goes through the 20 line on the way down and then bottoms and hits it again on the way up, it is considered a buy signal. When the stochastic oscillator goes through the 80 line on the way up and hits it again on the way down, it is considered a sell/short indicator. A stochastics oscillator will often move (on active stocks) without a tremendous amount of price movement, which makes it an excellent tool for scalping a basket of stock all day long. The big killing comes when it foreshadows a big move in the stock intraday.

We usually tend to use the 20 and 80 parameters on most trades. However, we will also jump the gun using the 15 and 85 parameters, provided that the ax on Level 2 appears to be buying and shows plenty of support. This is why you will get fake signals as the lines converge, only to peter out and fall back below the 20 or 10 band again.

The best buy signals are the *zero band* bounces. This is where the %d oscillator reverses off the zero band and then crosses the %dslow wide and at a steep angle. These are excellent signals on the initial bottom bounces on a down day. The reason we like the zero band so much is that the oscillators simply cannot fall below the zero band, and therefore we have reached the extreme limit short term to the price fall. In reality, the stock price could continue to fall while the stochastics remains on the zero band. This is fine, because we are reacting to the *reversal* as the %d reverses and heads higher to cross the %dslow.

The price difference in entry points between 15 and 20 can usually mean 1/8 to 1/4 points and is quite a compelling reason to jump in early. Keep in mind that jumping in prior to the 20 band also incurs greater risk but makes for a greater reward.

When we are playing a very fast mover, we love to play the 0 and 100 bands (if and when they get hit). There is always the risk that if a stock is falling hard and it hits that 0, it moves lower (and off the scale figuratively), or if it rises meteorically, it hits the 100 band and keeps going higher. Therefore, it is always important to wait for a slight reversal before pulling the trigger. For example, suppose SEEK runs to the intraday high 42, up 5 points for the day, and the stochastics oscillators are on that 100 band. We will wait until it reverses slightly, perhaps to the 98 band, before pulling our trigger to short. In fast movers, the %dslow might be ideal and smooth while the Level 2 might be buzzing like crazy.

Sell/Short Signals

Taking what we have learned about 1-minute tick stochastics on buy signals and reversing that, we can derive the same principles when it comes to shorting signals. We look for the %d and %dslow to pop above the 90 band and preferably reverse off the 100 band and cross down. This is a sell/short signal. The short position would be taken on the reversal.

Typically, a sell signal on the stochastics chart is when the %d and %dslow cross again to the downside. However, exits are subjective to the risk tolerance of each individual trader. We can easily say that 80 percent of the time the zero band bounces can produce a minimum of $1/8$ to $3/8$ gains on the initial pop (on thin-float Internet stocks, the initial zero band bounces can produce several points on the initial pop). How long you stay in is really at the discretion of your risk tolerance. The longer you stay in a position, the more risk you take. However, you can opt to ride the bounce based on stochastics and hold off on selling your position when the %d and the %dslow lines cross again, this time to the downside.

Therefore, if you are simply looking to reach your profit target of, say, $500 a day, you should aim to take two $1/4$-point scalps, which can easily be made on these zero band bounces on 1000 shares.

The biggest complaint about stochastics is that it is hard to determine the difference between a wiggle and a trend reversal on that 1-minute tick. Stochastics will fluctuate regardless of whether the selling is a wiggle or a trend reversal. A wiggle is a pullback on a stock that is in an uptrend. The pullback is usually caused by profit takers. A trend reversal occurs when the buying momentum completely dries up in a stock and the sellers continue to bleed the stock lower—lower highs and lower lows. A wiggle often accompanies a quick burst of buyers that take the price to a peak followed by a sell-off by profit takers. When the bottom is reached, the buying resumes. The stock's price chart shows higher highs and higher lows. On uptrending stocks, you can opt to play the wiggles (this takes skill) by buying into the panic selling on the bid and selling into the panic buying at or above the ask. Always remember that a stock can be toppy without being topped out; and it can look bottomed without being bottomed out. What is the confirmation that a stock is topped or bottomed? The reversal is the key. Always remember that you are looking for the reversals. A stock can fall and fall and fall and ride the stochastics zero band, but until the stochastics reverses, it has not bottomed. The same applies for stocks that ride the 100 band and keep rising higher. Until that stochastics reverses off the 100 band, the stock is toppy but not topped out. Do not predict any moves. Do react.

Now you have an idea of the best short-term momentum tool to use. Be aware, however, that there will always be instances when you will use stochastics and then realize that you got out too soon. Oftentimes, you will take a $1/2$-point scalp on a stock that runs 6 points. A profit is a profit, true. However, you should always look to maximize your profit when you get the opportunity. To capture the larger gains, you need to be able to watch the overall trend of a stock. If you can think of a 1-minute stochastics as looking at a rock from 3 feet away, then consider the 3-minute moving averages chart as looking at the rock from a block away. The little details are not obvious, and yet the trend is very apparent. You need this chart to capitalize on the overall trend.

3-MINUTE MOVING AVERAGES CHART

This chart will be the most powerful tool in your chart arsenal. This chart measures a stock's trend in 3-minute intervals by using 5- and 15-period simple moving averages. The advantage of this chart versus the 1-minute-tick stochastics is that it doesn't register wiggles, which makes the lines much smoother to read. Since it uses 3-minute intervals, this chart allows the trader to step back and measure the whole trend on a macro basis rather than a micro basis, allowing the trader to ride the winners out much longer than a 1-minute stochastics chart would. This chart shows us the trend of a stock and its respective trading range. The trading range is also referred to as a trading channel, which consists of an upper envelope and a lower envelope. These are the respective resistance and support prices for the stock. When a resistance is broken (to the upside), that is referred to as a *breakout*. When a support is broken (to the downside), that is referred to as a *breakdown*. Breakouts are usually prime entry points and bring in a whole new ball game of sorts to the price action. Breakdowns are usually prime exit points and/or short-sell points and the beginning of a retracement in the stock's price.

This chart should be initially used for risk assessment on a trade. Entry price is a big factor in risk control. Obviously, getting in early on an uptrend is safer than getting in later. We prefer to take positions in a stock as close to the convergence as possible, as opposed to taking a position later on in the uptrend as the gapping and rising slow down. Therefore, we always use this chart before we take a position, be it a scalp or swing trade, just to confirm that we are on the right side of a trend and to evaluate our risk into the trend.

Figure 4.2 shows a bar chart set to 3-minute intervals. The 5-period moving average line in the bar chart is used as a lead indicator and the resistance point. The 15-period moving average line is used for the support. The space between the 5- and 15-period lines is the trading range or channel.

When the 5- and 15-period moving average lines run horizontal, they are consolidating or in *consolidation*. This means that the buyers and sellers are even, and therefore a consistent trading range has developed. Consolidation means a steady and slow trading range. Volume is usually minimal. We like to consider this the calm before the potential storm. One of two things can happen after consolidation. They are breakouts or breakdowns. This is not to discount the possibility that a consolidation can go on for hours.

Buy Signals

When the 5-period moving average line starts to move higher and the 15-period line follows, this is a sign of a *breakout and is a buy*

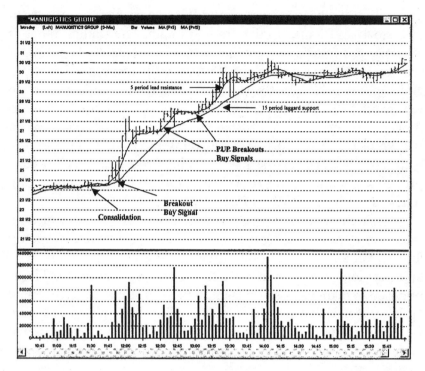

Figure 4.2 3-minute moving averages (top chart). (SOURCE: RealTick™ © 1986–2000
Townsend Analytics, LLC. Used with permission.)

signal, meaning that the upper envelope of the trading range is
being pushed higher by buyers. Usually, buying brings in more
buyers off the fence and the stock starts an uptrend here. The earlier you enter on a breakout, the less risky your entry price. And
vice versa—the farther along in the breakout you enter a trade (at
a higher price), the higher your risk. The entry price is key, and
therefore always assume that you want to enter a stock long as
close to the breakout as possible.

Some breakouts are stronger than other breakouts. The angle
of the breakout is also a means of measuring the momentum. An
angle higher than 40 degrees is a very strong momentum breakout that can result in very high volatility as well as a strong retracement since the 15 period is usually very lagged behind. Breakouts
that extend at a 20 degree angle or less are slower and safer with

less retracement. Always keep in mind that the 15-period moving average line is your support area, and the further you are from that support area, the higher your risk if you are in a long position.

Sell/Short Signals

When the 15-period moving average line starts to move lower and the 5-period line either follows or crosses over lower, this is a sign of a *breakdown and is a sell signal,* meaning that the lower envelope of the trading range is being pushed lower by sellers. Usually, selling brings in more sellers off the fence and a stock will start a downtrend here. The earlier you sell your position or enter a short position, the less risky your entry price or exit price if you are exiting a position.

The angle of the breakdown is also very important. A steeper angle means more selling pressure and a continued followthrough on the breakdown. If you are shorting a stock on the breakdown, make sure you understand that the 15-period moving average line is the stock's support and retracement point and therefore should be your trailing stop loss.

Cup and Handle Pattern and Filling the Gap

The *cup and handle* chart formation is an extension of the term traders often use called *filling the gap.* When a stock gaps (bids higher than the previous closing price) prior to the open, hits the daily high on the open, and sells off, we are looking for the stock to find a support and then try to head back to the highs of the open. This means the stock is in essence trying to fill the gap. This may take minutes to happen, or it may take hours.

When a stock fills the gap, it basically means that the stock gapped on the open as profit takers sold the gap, causing the stock price to tumble until it finds a bottom. Once that bottom is established, we can assume that the profit takers have sold out of the stock. As the stock rises, we can assume new buyers are coming in. When the stock finally fills the gap and reestablishes the highs on the open, two things happen. First, the cup formation has formed. Second, this often triggers a flurry of new buyers, causing the handle to form on the charts. In essence, a breakout occurs.

What makes this pattern so powerful is that the initial high resistance is tested and fails. When it comes back to retest, it is on the shoulders of the new buyers. When the old resistance is usually tested, it brings back many of the old buyers that were stopped out initially on the first attempt. This is a very strong psychological breakout.

Consolidation Pattern

A consolidation pattern shows up on the 3-minute moving averages chart when the 5- and 15-period lines are parallel for an extended period of time. The 5-period line is the upper end and resistance of the trading channel, and the 15-period line is the lower end and support of the trading channel. A consolidation simply means that the buyers and sellers are at a stalemate, causing the stock to move sideways. When there is consolidation, the stock is stable. This is great for traders because it buys them plenty of time to assess the situation and get a less risky entry position on either the breakout or the breakdown. Once a consolidation has begun, you have to assume there are either buyers or sellers waiting on the fence to see which way the consolidation breaks. For this reason in particular (traders on the fence), consolidation usually results in rather dynamic moves upon breaking.

Consolidation is a very important formation. When it comes to safety in trading, consolidation should be viewed like a pit stop for stock. The stock is taking a breather (sometimes all day long). From the consolidation, you will get a break either up or down. The safest way to play any stock is to enter from the consolidation. The consolidation solidifies the trading channel. Most importantly, it allows traders to slow down, take a deep breath, watch, and wait. This means everyone watching the stock gets a chance to rest and wait to react. Buyers line up "on the fence" during consolidation. If a stock breaks the upper trading envelope (the 5-period moving average), that signifies a breakout. The buyers that come in off the fence are more confident because they realize that a support has been tested and hammered out (the 15-period moving average line). This is cause for stronger breakouts from firmer and more anxious buyers. This also applies, vice versa, to breakdowns. When the 15-period support is broken, this causes nervous sellers to take stop losses as well as attracts short sellers that lean on a proven resistance in the form of the 5-period moving average line.

PUP Breakout

At our company, we have coined a special type of breakout called a PUP (Power Uptik Productions) breakout. This particular breakout usually occurs on strong stocks that run to a high, pause to let the support catch up, and then break out to a new high, also referred to as the "next" leg in the breakout. To spot this particular breakout, we pull up the 3-minute moving averages chart, usually on a strong-volume momentum stock, and look for a 5-period line that tends to peak and then go sideways. Meanwhile the 15-period line is usually rising at a 45 degree angle, looking to run right into the 5-period line. We do not like to predict the breakout, but rather react to it by entering as close to the new leg of the breakout as possible.

PUP breakouts mean that momentum is brewing as the buyers are starting to get itchy and impatient. When the buyers realize that a breakout is ready to occur, they rush the seller and break out the stock, bringing more anxious buyers off the fence. The fact that the 15 period catches up gradually as the 5 period stays firm means that the buyers are building and bidding on top of each other. This is extra-added safety when entering just before, at, or near the break point.

The makeup of a PUP breakout can be explained as a steady flow of buyers into a stock, with an even heavier amount of sellers at the upper envelope (resistance). However, rather than retrace and pull back, there is also a steady supply of motivated buyers bidding up the lower envelope of the price range until these motivated buyers can no longer wait for sellers. At this point, the buyers attack at the upper-envelope price ranges in volume, causing the sellers to either retreat or run out of shares—in essence starting another leg in the breakout formation and creating a new trading range in the process at higher levels.

13-MINUTE MOVING AVERAGES CHART

This chart is the same chart as the 3-minute chart except that the time interval is 13 minutes instead of 3. The number 13 is significant in that it is a pivot point based on the Fibonacci series and is often used by technicians.

This chart basically performs the same functions as the 3-minute chart; but it is much smoother, ignores the minor trend reversals in the 3-minute chart, and gives the overall intraday trend, which is very useful. The only drawback is that by the time a true sell signal is given, the stock has pulled back significantly from its peak. Therefore, the 13-minute chart is rarely used for buy or sell indicators, but instead is used strictly to determine a stock's price trend on a longer time interval.

We like to use a combination of the three charts. The 1-minute stochastics can be used for short-term entry and exits at the extremes of the price range. The 3-minute chart is used to judge short-term trends. Finally, the 13-minute chart is used to gauge the price trend on a longer time frame. However, if you do not have enough monitor space or bandwidth, you can opt to leave out the 13-minute chart, which is used more for swing plays (defined later).

Of course, you can sometimes step into a stock even when the stochastics is "topped out," meaning the stochastics oscillators are in the 90–100 range. This is because you will see the beginning of an uptrend on the 3-minute chart. Would it be smarter to wait for the stochastics to pull back below the 20 band before entry? Yes and no. Remember that the stochastics gauges momentum based on the last trades. The stochastics will always be moving, and therefore the stochastics could fall like a rock, only to have the stock pull back fractionally before it resumes a dynamic uptrend. This occurs because there may be market makers who are anxious to buy shares and will gladly support the inside bid to get them. By the time the stochastics shows a buy signal, the stock could have already taken off, and therefore we would get in early to ensure that we got in on the next run. Stochastics measures short-term momentum on the 1-minute chart, while moving averages measure the actual trend. A stock can be toppy and not yet topped out.

The bottom line is that you should experiment with these charts and use them in your trading. The beauty of these charts is that their effectiveness and accuracy can be seen in the historical price data intraday, current day, or at any historical period prior. CIEN on Friday, January 22, 1999, is an excellent case study in using stochastics for the nice bounces and entries and in using the 3- and 13-minute charts to stay in on the swing trade for several point gains. Please take a look at the price action on CIEN for January 22, 1999, and see what we mean.

MOMENTUM STOCKS

Momentum stocks usually pop strong on immediate bursts of volume and tend to stay one or more points above the 15-period support, oftentimes trading through the 5-period band. Usually, the stock has volume and a thin float. This always causes overreaction in buying or selling, but eventually the stock stabilizes. You will also notice extended momentum pops above the 80 band on the 1-minute stochastics. This will definitely convince you that this is a momentum stock since such stocks often tend to make nice but fast extended runs above the 80 band.

A nice example of this is ENTU. On November 12, 1999, a momentum trade alert was issued in our company at 38^1/$_2$ at 2:14 p.m. EST. We were alerted to play the momentum and not chase the stock for any kind of swing purposes, but rather wait for a stochastics retracement. At that time the stochastics was crossing above the 80 band, indicating overbought conditions on a normal stock. However, ENTU was a momentum stock, up four times average trading volume with a thin 7 million share float. The 15-period 3-minute chart support was 37^1/$_2$. The stock was 1 full point ahead of support. ENTU popped through 38^1/$_2$, 39, 39^1/$_2$, hitting the momentum ticks very strong. We were then alerted to lock in profits at the 40-round-number momentum tick, as the 10 round numbers are also very tough resistance points. (Round numbers will be explained in detail later.) On momentum stocks, however, they usually pop through the 10 round number initially for an extra point or two before retracing back under. In the case of ENTU, that is exactly what happened—the 40 momentum tick generated nice buying as we were exiting for profits. ENTU eventually popped to the 41 momentum tick as stochastics topped just above the 98 band on the 1-minute stochastics and proceeded to tank to the zero band, taking ENTU back down to 38 on a panic wiggle. It tested a new support on the 3-minute chart at $38^{1}/_{4}$, where it proceeded to return when the panic was over. When playing momentum, traders have to sell when there are buyers and that means selling on the ask into the buying. When traders get too greedy on momentum runs, they miss getting filled early and get stuck in a panic wiggle. Therefore, it is better to get a guaranteed fill on an exit into buyers and take profits too early, instead of waiting too long to get out and let a profit turn into a loss. Experienced traders know this from experience. New traders will eventually learn.

The moral of the above real-life example is that momentum stocks usually wiggle above and below the 5-period resistance and 15-period supports and then proceed to resume the trend. There are only two ways to play them: (1) Play the momentum in and out on the momentum tick *prior* to a reversal above the 80 (overbought) band on the 1-minute stochastics chart, or (2) play the breakout from extended consolidation for safety (on ENTU the breakout was at 37, with tight 15-period support at $36^{3}/_{4}$—this entry is safe).

CHAPTER 5

Order Routing
and ECNs

One of the key skills good day traders have down cold is order routing for Nasdaq-traded stocks. Order routing only applies to traders who are using a professional day trading broker like CyBerTrader (www.cybercorp.com) or RealTick™ (www.mbtrading.com). These kinds of brokers allow you to choose your order routing, opposed to most Internet browser–based brokers, which usually execute through a market maker. The day trading brokers also provide you with a complete trading platform that includes real-time Nasdaq Level 2 screens, quotes, charts, market minders, and flawless point-and-click order execution and routing. Having these tools is imperative if you are serious about attaining any measure of success in day trading. We often hear new traders talk about starting off with a cheap online broker and "working up" to a day trading broker, and that completely baffles us. It is like learning to ride a motorcycle and telling the instructor that you will "work up" to getting pads and a helmet as you get better. In the game of day trading, you don't want any unforced errors, much less start the game with a major strike against you, by not having proper real-time information, tools, and order-routing capabilities.

Order routing allows traders the ability to choose how and where to place their orders. We can break the routing systems down into order-routing systems and ECNs (electronic communication networks). Order-routing systems are in essence the messengers, and ECNs and market makers are the receivers.

On the Nasdaq, there are primarily three order routing systems, SOES (Small Order Execution System), SelectNet, and ARCA (to alleviate any confusion, we will go into greater detail on ARCA at the end of this section, as it acts as an order-routing system and an ECN). Order-routing systems allow the individual investor to deal directly with the market makers in a timely fashion (SOES), and SelectNet also allows access to ECNs. SOES and SelectNet must not be confused with the ECNs. Understand that ECNs are primarily electronic limit books that automatically match up bid and ask orders as they come in. ECNs are wonderful in that they are cut and dried—what you see is what you get. The day trading brokers offer direct access to various ECNs, which makes them all the more efficient and, most importantly, fast.

"MONSTER KEY"

Before we go any further, let us explain a term often used by traders: *monster,* and its variations *monster fill* and *monster key.* In short, a monster or monster key order is simply a front-of-the-line pass when it comes to trying to get a fill on your order before everyone else. The name stems from the late eighties, shortly after the 1987 crash, when SOES bandits were the early pioneers of day trading. These bandits would rush the market makers on the Nasdaq SOES, flooding them with buy orders that allowed the bandits to attain fast fills as the market makers assumed there was a big demand and overzealously upticked their bids, only to get sold the same shares back at a higher price. (Yes! They weren't too bright back then.) Even among the bandits, there was much competition since SOES is a first-come first-served–based system. A group of hacker traders had discovered and exploited a glitch in the Nasdaq SOES allowing them to step in front of all the existing SOES orders to get filled first. This glitch was called the "monster key," and from that point on the term referred to the ability to step in front of existing orders to get priority on fills.

ORDER-ROUTING SYSTEMS (THE MESSENGERS)

SOES

The Nasdaq Small Order Execution System was created for the nonprofessional investor shortly after the market crash of October 1987. This system was designed to allow the individual investor to get fast fills for up to 1000 shares. Many modifications have been made to the original design and rules. Basically, SOES allows an individual investor to hit a market maker for up to 1000 shares or his displayed size. The market maker is required to fill the order within 17 seconds or change or update his quote. This makes for fast fills. SOES only allows you to hit the inside (best bid or best ask) market maker. SOES does not allow you to route to ECNs. Professionals are not allowed to use SOES; this includes market makers and the professional-margin day trading brokerages (usually a 10 to 1 margin).

Size on fills is limited to 1000 shares, but every stock has a SOES tier minimum amount, starting with 100 shares. The tier size limit is there to protect the market makers, especially in a thinly traded stock. You will find that on many Nasdaq Internet stocks with thin floats, market makers often only display 100 or 200 shares on the bid and ask even though you may see 1000-share trades on time of sales. Since the stock may be thinly traded, market makers like to protect themselves from the fast SOES orders by only displaying the minimum tier requirement. However, they may take more shares on SelectNet, where they have more time and leeway with price.

SOES is a first-come, first-served system. If trader A and trader B both want shares of COMS at $29^{1}/_{4}$, the trader who executes the SOES button first is the first to get filled. If more shares are available, then the next trader gets shares, and so on. In high-volume stocks, SOES can turn into a major traffic nightmare, as everyone is trying to SOES at the inside price level and gets stuck in a traffic jam waiting for shares.

SOES orders can be broken down into *limit* and *market*. SOES limit orders go directly to the inside market makers and continue to hit the inside market makers up to your requested size (limit 1000) and price limit, assuming you are first in line. SOES market orders are sent directly to the inside market makers with no price limit. In theory, this means you have a monster preference on fills, with the downside being that it is a market order and therefore you still have no control over the price. SOES market orders are faster than limit orders because the only goal is to get filled at the inside price, whatever that price may be (as market makers can continue to update their quotes rather than fill the order within 17 seconds). If a stock ticks above a SOES limit order price, then it is automatically canceled and the trader must decide whether she wants to reenter her order at a higher limit price. This can take time, whereas a market order is probably filling at higher prices. If you place yourself in the shoes of a market maker, you can understand that when faced with a limit order and a market order, you would prefer to fill your shares at a higher price; and if you are fast enough, you may choose to uptick your quote rather than fill the limit order and thus fill the market order instead at a higher price. This is possible provided there are no other market makers on the inside at your same price level.

The 5-minute rule was also implemented by the Nasdaq as another measure of protection for market makers. In the days of the SOES bandits, market makers would get flooded by the same bandits continuously on the same stock with no breathing room. The 5-minute rule applies to the individual trader, stipulating that he cannot use SOES on the same stock for more than one round-trip (a buy and a sell) within 5 minutes. Many traders misunderstand this rule and assume they can only use SOES every 5 minutes, as it applies to the Nasdaq market in general. This is wrong. The rule applies only to one Nasdaq stock at a time. Therefore, a trader could do a round-trip SOES order (buy and sell or short and cover) on COMS, and then do a round-trip order on YHOO, and so on with different Nasdaq stocks. The trader could not execute another round-trip SOES order on COMS until 5 minutes after her last roundtrip on COMS.

In summary, here are the pros and cons of using SOES on the Nasdaq.

Speed of fill. Very fast fills executed in 17 seconds or less.

Market makers cannot use the system for their own orders. Professional usage is prohibited.

CONS

Traffic jams. If you are one of many traders trying to SOES an order, it's first-come, first served, so unless you are fast, you will wait and risk the stock moving away from your limit price.

Tier size restraints. Since market makers only have to post minimum tier size limits, you may not be able to get close to the size of the fill you desire.

Strange fills. Sometimes you will get stuck with odd lots (e.g., you SOES for 500 shares and get 393).

No ECN access. SOES only deals directly with market makers on the inside price.

Accessible only during market hours. No premarket or postmarket accessibility.

SelectNet

Nasdaq's SelectNet system is used widely by market makers and individual traders. SelectNet is another order-routing system that allows you to send orders directly to the market makers and ECNs. There are no size limits on SelectNet orders. Professionals as well as nonprofessional traders have access to SelectNet. SelectNet orders can be filled at the discretion of the market maker within 27 seconds. Markets makers can opt not to fill the order also, depending on how many market makers are on the price level and whether the order has been broadcast or preferenced. This is where SelectNet gets sticky.

SelectNet orders are broken down into broadcast and preference. A SelectNet broadcast order takes your limit order and announces it to all the market makers at your requested inside price level. If a market maker wants to fill your order, then he will accept it; if not, he will sit it out, allowing any other market maker at that level to fill your order. A SelectNet preference order requires you to pick a specific market maker on the Nasdaq Level 2 screen and will send your order directly to that market maker. That market maker has 27 seconds to fill your order or update his quote. Understand that in this case 27 seconds is an eternity and gives the market maker more time to measure the momentum and make a decision.

SelectNet also allows traders to route to all ECNs on the Nasdaq exchange. This is a nice feature. However, never choose a SelectNet to ECN when you have the option (depending on your broker) for direct ECN access (usually with a button on your order page). There is a time difference involved. First, you have to SelectNet and preference the respective ECN and then place the order, which can take an extra 10 to 15 seconds longer than just clicking the button for direct ECN routing. However, the best ECN routing from SelectNet in our opinion is SelectNet preference to INCA, unless you happen to be lucky enough to have an Instinet terminal.

SelectNet to ECN routing is especially beneficial premarket (before 9:30 a.m. EST) and postmarket (after 4 p.m. EST). However, understand that market makers are not obligated to fill any orders premarket or postmarket, even if they are bidding up a stock multiple points.

In summary:

PROS

Full access to market makers and all ECNs

Premarket and postmarket order routing to ECNs

CONS

Slow. Both having to choose preference versus broadcast and having to type in specific market makers combine to slow down the process dramatically. Although the Nasdaq SelectNet specifies a 27-second time limit to fill an order, when an order is broadcast, market makers have the option to not fill the order. Getting your SelectNet preference order filled can oftentimes be like trying to catch a moving target if the market maker does not opt to fill your order and instead chooses to update his price.

Stacked deck. This is an interesting flaw with SelectNet. Market makers have full access to all limit books and Nasdaq Level 3 and order flow, they have more inside market information than the average day trader. You can often assume that if a market maker—a skilled market maker—takes your SelectNet order on the bid or ask, the market maker sees something you don't, and vice versa. There is usually a nasty aftertaste on getting filled on a SelectNet order. Generally, traders usually get filled just as a stock makes a reversal. This doesn't apply all the time, but the aura of having a stacked deck working against you is there.

ARCA

ARCA is short for *Archipelago* and serves as both an order-routing system and an ECN. ARCA was developed by Townsend Analytics and is currently accessible through RealTick™ software platform day trading brokers. ARCA is a very interesting system and will take some time to understand completely.

ARCA can be seen on Nasdaq Level 2 as ARCA limit book. RealTick™ users with a direct feed from Townsend Analytics will also see something on their Level 2 screen that reads ARCHIP. ARCHIP is the active order routing that displays a live order.

As an order-routing system, ARCA will try to fill your order by initially trying to match it with other ARCHIP orders. For example, you may wish to buy 1000 shares of EGRP at 29³/₄ with ARCHIP, and there may be 1000 shares of EGRP on ARCA at 29³/₄ ask. In that case, you should get filled immediately. If ARCHIP does not see a matching ARCA order at your price level, it will then search for a matching order on any available ECN. If still no orders exist at your price level, ARCHIP will begin SelectNet-preferencing each market maker on the inside bid. ARCA will repeat this process until it reaches your requested price-limit level. When ARCHIP finally realizes there is nothing available, chances are your limit order has been surpassed, and at that point ARCHIP will display your order in the ARCA limit book. Normal Nasdaq Level 2 will only show the ARCA inside orders, whereas RealTick™ users with a direct Townsend Analytics feed will continue to see the ARCA limit book on Level 2.

This may seem rather confusing at first glance. So let's look at an example.

Let's assume you want to get 1000 shares of EGRP up to a $26^3/_4$ limit. Let's also assume the inside bid and ask are $26^1/_2 \times 26^9/_{16}$.

EGRP

Bid 26-1/2		ASK 26-9/16	
GSCO 26-1/2	10	MSCO 26-9/16	12
MASH 26-1/2	10	NFSC 26-9/16	10
NFSC 26-1/2	6	NITE 26-9/16	8
PERT 26-1/2	5	ISLD 26-5/8	20
USCT 26-7/16	18	MASH 26-5/8	4
WARR 26-7/16	9	PERT 26-11/16	10
SLKC 26-3/8	10	SLKC 26-3/4	10

In this example you would key up your order to buy 1000 shares of EGRP, limit $26^3/_4$, on ARCA. ARCA would display your order on the RealTick™ screen above GSCO as ARCHIP $26^9/_{16}$ bidding for 1000 shares (displayed as a 10 size on Level 2). This tells traders that you are looking to buy 1000 shares of EGRP up to a $26^9/_{16}$ limit.

ARCHIP would start on the inside ask price level, which is $26^9/_{16}$. First, ARCHIP would look to find a matching ARCHIP at $26^9/_{16}$. In this example, there is none. Next, ARCHIP would look to find a matching ECN. In this example, there is none. The closest ECN is at $26^5/_8$ on ISLD. Finally, ARCHIP would start SelectNet-preferencing MSCO at $26^9/_{16}$. If MSCO decides to fill the order, you will get your 1000 shares from MSCO at $26^9/_{16}$. Order executed.

However, let's assume that many buyers at this time are competing for the inside ask price at $26^9/_{16}$. These buyers are using SOES limit orders in a frantic pace to get filled. Let's assume MSCO has decided not to fill your order, but rather uptick. NFSC sells his order on SOES and upticks. NITE gets taken out also with SOES orders. The Level 2 screen would now look like the following:

EGRP

Bid 26-1/2		ASK 26-9/16	
ARCA 26-9/16	10	ISLD 26-5/8	20
GSCO 26-1/2	10	MASH 26-5/8	4
MASH 26-1/2	10	PERT 26-11/16	10
NFSC 26-1/2	6	NITE 26-3/4	12
PERT 26-1/2	5	NFSC 26-3/4	10
USCT 26-7/16	18	MASH 26-3/4	4
WARR 26-7/16	9	MSCO 26-13/16	10
SLKC 26-3/8	10	SLKC 26-3/4	10

Since ARCHIP found no matches at your original buy limit price of 26⁹/₁₆ for 1000 shares, ARCHIP realizes that your order has now become the inside (best) bid and automatically places your order in Archipelago's limit book, known as ARCA. You have become the inside bid.

At this time, you can either cancel the limit order and reenter your ARCA order at a higher price limit or decide to keep your order on the inside bid, waiting for a possible wiggle to get filled. At this point, you might well ask, "Why did the other orders get filled at $^9/_{16}$ while my ARCHIP order just sat there without a fill until the upticks and I became the inside bid?" This leads us to the flaws of ARCHIP. Since ARCHIP goes through several processes looking for a matching order on the opposite side of your order, you have to assume this will take time. The direct route is always the best route. With ARCHIP, the fastest fills are simply ARCHIP to ARCA. When that match is not possible, the wait begins. As ARCHIP searches to find a matching ECN order at your limit price, it takes precious seconds away. If an ECN order is not available, it then takes on the SelectNet-preferencing route to each market maker. Here is a major delay. Understand that ARCHIP will SelectNet-preference each market maker for the full 27 seconds before moving on to the next market maker unless the original market maker fills the order or upticks. This is very time-consuming and often allows direct SOES or ECN users to completely bypass your ARCHIP order and get fills while ARCHIP may be busy preferencing each market maker. Therefore, the biggest flaw in ARCHIP routing is the SelectNet preferencing and the slowness of fills.

ARCHIP Monster Fill

We described earlier how monster key and monster fills got their names. They are terms used for a front-of-the-line pass when trying to get a priority fill on your order. ARCA has a monster key capability. Let's understand that market makers are in business to get the best price possible on their own fills. If a market maker is on the bid, he wants the cheapest price he can get to buy stock. If a market maker is on the ask, he wants the highest price he can get to sell his stock. Therefore, when you enter your ARCHIP order *above* the ask price when buying or *below* the bid price when selling, you have the priority and the monster fill. This is no real secret; this explains why a group of ARCHIPs trying to buy a stock will try to outbid each other to get the monster fill. The bottom line is that he with the highest bid or lowest ask will get the monster fill to buy or sell, respectively.

There are disadvantages to going with the monster fill. You are obviously taking a larger risk by offering a higher, if not the highest, price for a fill. On a strong-moving momentum stock, the fill itself can be the reward as the stock shoots through momentum ticks, way above your purchase price, and you are nicely in the money. However, if you happen to catch the end of the momentum run and get stuck at a high price just prior to the reversal and sell-off, you are pretty much toast. This leads to our subject of "chippies." Chippies are usually less experienced traders who tend to have predictable reactions to whichever way the short-term trend *appears* to be going. They can exaggerate the movement in a stock up or down powerfully in the short term, which is great if you are on the right side of the run. If you happen to get executed on a monster fill just before a chippie panic sell-off (where chippies will monster-fill to sell in a panic), you are stuck, and it can be rather painful in the short term.

Chippies

The unfortunate aspect of this trick is that many newer traders are coming into the market every day and trying to monster-fill when they are buying or monster-fill when they are selling. This can cause much more short-term volatility in the stock as market makers realize they can get higher prices to sell stock and quickly uptick to meet monster-fill buy prices or get cheaper stock to buy and quickly downtick to meet monster-fill sell prices. The main trigger is the ARCHIP display on RealTick™ screens directly fed from Townsend Analytics. While normal Nasdaq Level 2 does not show ARCHIP order routing, but instead only the ARCA best bid and ask limit, this special RealTick™ shows all the ARCHIP orders on the Nasdaq Level 2 screen. When the market is nervous or choppy, so are chippies. It only takes several ARCHIPs trying to monster in or out of a position to cause a domino-effect reaction from other chippies, and the next thing you know, there is panic. Market makers and experienced day traders know the powerful short-term effect that chippies have on the market and exploit this to their advantage, usually by placing size on ECNs with or against the chippies for immediately exaggerated volatility. We will get into more details on this interesting phenomenon later.

So let's summarize ARCA:

PROS

Easy to use. ARCHIP will order-route for you and then place your order on ARCA if no matches have been found.

Monster-fill function. Highest bidder to buy or lowest ask to sell will take priority.

Premarket and postmarket accessibility. ARCA can route to all ECNs with one click.

Full access to market makers and ECNs.

CONS

Slow. This is the biggest flaw with ARCHIP, as it SelectNet-preferences each market maker for 27 seconds.

Chippies. Since ARCA is the easiest to use, most new traders will use it and react to any moves.

ECNs

ECNs, or electronic communication networks, are simply electronic limit books. ECNs are available for literally every stock on the

Nasdaq stock market. Many consider them electronic market makers. They have a bid side with all the prices that traders are willing to buy shares at and their respective sizes, and they have an ask side that contains all the prices that traders are willing to sell shares at and their respective sizes. Only the inside (best) bid and ask (price with respective sizes) will be displayed on Nasdaq Level 2. However, certain ECNs allow their users to view their limit books, which display all the existing orders in the limit book for any Nasdaq stock. All ECNs are first-come, first-served and basically what you see is what you get, and this is why they are growing in popularity among day traders and even investors alike. We will cover the most widely used ECNs in this book. The nice thing about ECNs is that they provide liquidity through volume, and the more widely used a particular ECN is, the more liquidity it provides. This reiterates our point of the markets being a multidimensional playing field with each new ECN. There is no need to panic and look up every ECN limit book. ISLD, ARCA, and Instinet are the three major ECNs that have dominant market share. Still, there are other ECNs that are growing, like REDI, BTRD, BRUT, and STRK; and the list goes on as more ECNs arise.

ISLD

The ISLD (Island) ECN is the ECN of choice with day traders due to its speed and liquidity. Most day trading brokers offer direct access to the ISLD ECN. ISLD is very fast with fills, usually executing in a matter of 3 to 10 seconds, depending on your Internet connection speed. ISLD generates 10 percent of the daily volume on the Nasdaq.

ISLD is represented on the Nasdaq Level 2 screen as ISLD and will only display the inside bid and ask prices in the limit book, along with a cumulative size for the inside price level on both sides. As a limit book, ISLD will show existing orders not viewable on Nasdaq Level 2, which shows only the best prices. To access this limit book, go to http://www.isld.com/ and click on the ISLD viewer for a full limit book on any particular Nasdaq stock you are trading. Brokers like CyBerTrader have realized the need for this limit book and have already equipped their software to include the ISLD limit book, in addition to Nasdaq Level 2.

Most day trading brokers have direct access to the ISLD ECN with the click of a button. However, if your broker does not, then you can use SelectNet to preference ISLD. Even though the direct route is always faster, this is the next best way to go.

The ISLD limit book has any particular Nasdaq stock and appears very much like a Nasdaq Level 2 screen. However, the orders shown are just orders placed by traders waiting to get filled. Orders on the bid and ask, along with their individual respective sizes, are displayed. This, once again, adds a new level of depth to the playing field, whereas most traders may only see ISLD's inside bid and ask on Level 2 but have no clue that there may be big buyers or sellers on the ISLD limit book.

ISLD's greatest assets are speed and liquidity. ISLD generates 10 percent of the volume on the Nasdaq daily. What you see is what you get on ISLD—and instantly. We are talking about executions inside of 3 seconds, which is faster than SOES in most cases. The only downfall to ISLD is the partial fills. You can get stuck with some pretty odd lots (e.g., 43 shares instead of 500) on ISLD, whereas ARCA only accepts full round lots of 100 shares. To avoid these weird fills, traders can place ISLD orders several levels up or down in the limit book. This is assuming you are motivated to get out of a stock immediately. In other words, when you place a limit order using ISLD, you will get filled up to your requested shares and price level. If you extend your price limit, ISLD will continue to fill as much of your requested size up to your price limit. For example, suppose you want to sell 500 shares of LOOK, which is quoted at $32^3/_{16} \times 32^3/_8$, and the ISLD limit book is showing 100 shares at $32^3/_{16}$ bid, 238 shares at $32^1/_8$, 100 shares at $32^1/_{16}$, and 300 shares at 32. You could place your 500 shares to *sell* on ISLD limit 32, and it will fill all the levels on down to your 32 requested price, resulting in the following fills: 100 shares *sold* $32^3/_{16}$, 238 shares *sold* $32^1/_8$, 100 shares *sold* $32^1/_{16}$, and 62 shares *sold* 32. The last fill at 32 means someone else got stuck with 62 shares at 32, pretty funny.

The ability to place a blanket order (an order set at a limit several levels away from the inside) like the one above is a skill that will come in very handy, especially in stocks that are moving on panic, either buying or selling. It is much quicker to place a blanket order than to have an order cross-lock the market or to become the inside limit and have to cancel and reenter the order.

Cross-Lock Market Rejections

This brings us to note the meaning of a "cross-lock market" rejection on an ISLD order. This is not a very hard concept, but it is one you have to give some thought to. Let's remember that the Nasdaq Level 2 screen has the official inside bid and ask prices for any respective stock. ISLD's inside bid and ask prices (or those for any other ECNs for that matter) can never be greater than the current inside bid and ask prices. Therefore, if you place an ISLD order to buy at a higher price than the inside bid on ISLD (assuming the ISLD inside bid is the same as the Nasdaq inside bid price) and there is no ISLD ask, then you are cross-locking the market.

Let's take an example. Say AMAT is $93^{1}/_{4} \times 93^{3}/_{8}$. ISLD is showing 500 shares with an inside bid $93^{1}/_{4}$, but the inside ask is $93^{1}/_{2}$. If you wanted to bid to buy AMAT at $93^{5}/_{16}$ on ISLD, then it would show up as the new inside bid price in the ISLD book and on Nasdaq Level 2. This is legal. However, if you wanted to bid to buy AMAT at $93^{7}/_{16}$ when AMAT is displaying $93^{1}/_{4} \times 93^{3}/_{8}$ on Nasdaq Level 2 and ISLD is $93^{1}/_{4} \times 93^{1}/_{2}$, you would get a cross-lock market rejection. This is because you *cannot* place an inside bid order with ISLD that is higher than the inside ask on the Nasdaq Level 2. Another way to explain this is that ISLD only routes to ISLD. If you place a bid order on ISLD, this order cannot exceed the inside ask price on Nasdaq Level 2, unless you are buying directly from ISLD either at or above the ask. Therefore, in our example, you could actually buy AMAT at $93^{1}/_{2}$ directly from ISLD. You just couldn't bid any higher that $93^{5}/_{16}$ on ISLD. A very simple way to avoid this would be to simply SOES $93^{3}/_{8}$ for the fill.

The same cross-lock market applies when you are selling. If you want to place a limit to sell shares in AMAT at $93^{1}/_{4}$, you would get filled. Let's assume someone already sold on ISLD and although AMAT is still displaying $93^1/4 \times 93^3/8$, the ISLD best bid is now $93^1/16$. You could not place an ISLD sell limit under $93^1/4$ because that is technically the Nasdaq inside bid price and you cannot be the inside ask. Once again, if you really want to execute on ISLD, then you could sell at $93^1/16$ below the bid, but if you really want the $93^1/4$ fill, you are better off SOESing a market maker at $93^1/4$.

Let's summarize the pros and cons of ISLD:

PROS

Fast executions, usually in 3 seconds.

Liquidity, accounting for 10 percent of Nasdaq volume daily.

What you see is what you get.

Premarket and postmarket access to ISLD limit book.

CONS

Odd fills. Many times can equal multiple commissions trying to refill remaining lot.

ISLD boys. Can be good or bad, depending on if you know the "game."

The (Notorious) ISLD Boys

The term *Island boys* (ISLD boys) is used to describe the large sizes on ISLD that often flash on the bid and/or ask on Nasdaq Level 2. Sometimes the size is real and will hold firm when the ISLD boys get hit. Oftentimes, the sizes are simply flashed to nudge or add to the momentum (buying or selling) and disappear, a bluff. When the actual ISLD limit book is observed, the large block on Nasdaq Level 2 often shows up as a gang of smaller lots at a price level. This particular form of bluff was taken straight from the pages of the market makers, as they have been known to do the same thing with INCA.

When there is buying momentum, you can often see large ISLD bids chasing up the price, and vice versa on selling pressure. This will cause an almost automatic reaction among traders and market makers in the direction of the size. The advent of the ISLD boys has also caused stocks to be very choppy.

This is not to imply that all ISLD sizes are fake. When a large block is placed just right, it can add fuel to the existing momentum, or in many cases cause a momentum reversal, especially when the selling subsides and there is a pause as the gap gets tightened on the bid side in the case of a reversal off a short-term bottom. For example, a strong ISLD trader may watch a stock like DIGL as it breaks 17 and stalls at the teeny ($17 \times 17^1/_{16}$)—a teeny is $^1/_{16}$ as the buying pressure quickly dissipates. He may throw 4000 shares on the ask at $17^1/_{16}$ to shake out the weak day traders as they panic in typical knee-jerk form, causing the stock to retest the 17 round number as it sells back down. The panic continues as traders monster-bid out, only to see the stock stall at $16^1/_2 \times \, ^7/_8$ (a wide spread). A well-placed ISLD bid at $16^9/_{16}$ for, say, 5000 shares *into the selling* above the $^1/_2$ momentum tick support can result in two things: (1) a nice fill right above short-term support and (2) a momentum reversal as buyers come back into the stock attempting to lean on the ISLD size. Therefore, let's assume our ISLD trader gets hit for 2000 shares at $16^9/_{16}$. If he has timed his bid well, then he is willing to take a full 5000-share lot and wait on the bid. Once market makers and traders sense there is a real buyer, you will often see more bids at the $^9/_{16}$ level, and before you can blink, the stock will reverse and retest 17. The ISLD trader took a risk and got 2000 shares at $16^9/_{16}$ and can quickly sell into the strong momentum tick at 17 for a quick $^3/_8 \times 2000$ shares = \$750.

Let's say our trader in the above example was even more aggressive. Once he was filled at $16^9/_{16}$ for 2000 shares, he joined at the bid with three more market makers as the ask got lifted. He may aggressively place another 5000 shares on the inside bid as the stock moves up with panic buyers, as he knows the chance of getting hit with shares during a panic-buying phase is very small. Otherwise, obviously, he would cancel and resubmit the bid. This implies that there is an active block buyer in this stock, causing more buying to force the buyer to chase the stock higher. Of course, our ISLD boy could care less, because he has no intentions of buying more stock. For example, for $16^9/_{16} \times 16^7/_8$ (best bid/size × best ask/size), ISLD boy gets filled for 2000 shares. As the bids tighten more, he will chase the bid for 5000 shares on the inside higher: $16^5/8$–5000 × $16^7/8$–1000, $16^{13}/16$–5000 × $16^{15}/16$–500, and $16^{15}/16$–8000 × 17–1000. At this point, he knows that 17 is a strong momentum round-number tick and his chances of getting hit are even less, and so he may increase his size to 8000 shares to flush more buyers at the 17 tick. Last time around, the stock stalled at $17^1/16$. This time there are buyers at $17^1/16$, and to ensure that sellers do not panic on the $17^1/8$ tick, our ISLD boy may continue to squeeze the bid higher with 5000-share bids at $17^1/16$–5000 × $17^1/8$–500. This should inevitably pop the stock to the $17^1/4$ momentum tick, triggering more buyers. He may eventually look to pare out his 2000 shares, 500 at a time, between the $17^1/4$ and $17^1/2$ momentum ticks, averaging a $17^3/8$ sell price on 2000 shares. He has just scored $3/4$ × 2000 = \$1500 on that trade.

There are many variations on this theme. ISLD boys don't often show their cards that easily. Many times they will fade into the selling, buying smaller lots and even testing the bids with 100 shares to see if selling pressure is drying up. (More detail on this technique is presented after this section.) Once the ISLD trader has his position, he will frequently try to reverse the momentum or squeeze with size, often bleeding out into buyers. Does this sound familiar? It should, because *this is what market makers do!*

Oftentimes, traders keep asking us who the ISLD boys are and do they communicate with each other? *ISLD boy* is just a figurative term that implies a trader or a group of traders using size on ISLD to play the momentum. Going back to the question of whether these ISLD boys "communicate" with each other? The answer is yes. However, this does not mean there is a network of ISLD boys who call each other up on the phone. Traders that are fluent with ISLD can distinguish and feel the real buyers and the bluffers. When a good ISLD trader sees a real buyer or a run starting, he will often join in.

Therefore, in the above example, when one ISLD boy is so apparent in his intentions to hold a level and willing to get hit for 5000 shares at $16^9/16$, other ISLD traders will often join in the fun. Before you know it, the 5000-share inside bid becomes 12,000 shares, which causes more buying momentum as market makers frantically try to cover shorts and day traders frantically try to buy into the panic. This is quite an amazing phenomenon to watch on Level 2. It is the song of the ISLD boys. If you know the game, then you can be part of it. If you do not, then you will often be part of the crowd or the puppets being manipulated by the hands of the ISLD boys or the market makers.

Make no mistake. It takes tremendous skill (absolute familiarity with the stock and timing) and oftentimes tremendous capital to play ISLD like a market maker. This is a fast game of guts and glory. We have seen some legendary moves by a handful of traders using the ISLD ECN and risking up to 50,000 shares to reverse a momentum trend. If they guess wrong, they are stuck in heavy shares. If they guess right at the saturation point, they reap huge profits as the buyers pour back in at a fever pitch. If you want to talk about risk versus reward, this is the top of the game.

The Strange 100-Size Inside Bid-Ask on ISLD

We often hear traders griping, "Who is that little guy trying to buy 100 shares on the bid, sheesh!" or "Who in his right mind is trying to sell just 100 shares on the inside ask? cheapo!"

Things are not as they seem. We mentioned earlier that in order to feel out the extent of a selling or buying session, market makers and ISLD traders will test the waters with a 100-share inside bid or ask. This is done on purpose to bait and measure. Since 100 shares is a small number of shares, anyone who places the 100 size, say, at the bid, is testing to see if there are still nervous sellers out there, and vice versa for buyers when they place 100 shares on the ask. Be aware of the 100 shares on the inside; it means that it is a test. If no one snags the 100 shares, oftentimes it may signal the end of the buying or selling, and a momentum reversal is in store.

For example, let's go back to the DIGL example. Suppose our trader was not so aggressive as to throw 5000 shares on the inside bid to tighten the spread at $9/_{16}$ into direct sellers. Instead, he is willing to pay the ask price rather than the inside bid just for safety's sake, but he wants to make sure there are no more sellers. Once again, DIGL wiggles back from $17^1/_{16}$ to $16^1/_2 \times 16^7/_8$, and there is a pause in the selling. A few trades go off at the bid on time of sales at $16^{1}/_{2}$, but it looks firm. Just to test the waters, our ISLD trader may try to tighten the spread to $16^{3}/_{4} \times 16^{7}/_{8}$ with a 100 size at $^{3}/_{4}$, making him the inside bid. If no one sells to him at $16^{3}/_{4}$, the coast is clear, as he may SOES in at $16^{7}/_{8}$ to get his fill for 1000 shares.

Once again, the other ISLD boys and market makers are always watching. As our trader tests the sellers at $16^{3}/_{4}$—100 with no takers, the other ISLD boys and market makers may already be trying to get in and are already making their moves since the sellers appear cleared. The downside of this is that our ISLD trader is up against the best, and although he may be the one testing, the other traders and market makers may beat him to the punch on the fill.

The moral of this story is to watch those 100 sizes on the inside. Now you know what the true purpose of the small lot placed on the inside really is.

Instinet and INCA

Unless you are trading out of a day trading room or are a licensed professional, you will rarely be able to use an Instinet terminal. We want to clear up a misconception about Instinet and INCA. Instinet is a worldwide network connected by Instinet terminals usually available to market makers, institutional traders, and the occasional day trading room. Many of the online brokers have Instinet terminals only at the order desk. Traders have a misconception that INCA is the same as Instinet. This is far from the truth. Instinet is completely hidden from Nasdaq Level 2. It is like a market unto its own, and it applies to Nasdaq and listed securities. Instinet is also known for large blocks being traded back and forth. Instinet only routes to Instinet. It's that simple. However, when a trader cannot execute on Instinet because there may not be interested parties, then the trader has the option to "reflect" on Nasdaq Level 2, and that shows up as INCA to allow for greater exposure.

Unlike the ISLD book, where the inside bid and ask are always displayed on Nasdaq Level 2, Instinet never has to show anything other than what the Instinet trader chooses to reflect on Level 2. Instinet also has a nonrefresh function that allows a trader to display one size constantly at a price level until he is completely filled. For example, a market maker may want to sell 10,000 shares of KLAC, and rather than display 10,000 shares on the inside ask, which would tank the stock, the market maker could place the order on INCA at 500 shares on the inside ask and choose to not refresh until he sells all 10,000 shares. This gives the illusion of a smaller size than actually exists. Every trader has seen this happen, the never-ending shares on the inside.

Traders can access INCA by SelectNet-preferencing INCA. Traders cannot place INCA limit orders unless they have an Instinet terminal.

Many times there are discrepancies between Instinet and the other limit books, especially ISLD. This allows a sharp trader to access both ECNs when an arbitrage opportunity arises, usually in the premarket and postmarket. For example, ISLD may be showing $43^1/_4 \times 43^3/_8$ on COVD, while Instinet shows $43^5/_8 \times 43^3/_4$. One could buy from ISLD at $43^3/_8$ and immediately sell on the Instinet terminal at $43^5/_8$ for a quick $^1/_4$ profit.

Since market makers also have access to Instinet, large blocks on Instinet terminals can also cause market makers to mysteriously step off their bids, especially when the block is selling below the Nasdaq Level 2 inside bid price. While this is happening, the average day trader has no clue that there may be a 50,000-share Instinet seller on a stock he just got on the bid for cheap on Nasdaq Level 2, as he scratches his head, wondering why all the market makers are bailing to lower bids!

The Most Effective Order Routing

Now that we have an understanding of order routing and ECNs, we will go into the most effective order routing based on your situation. Once again, for any of this to make sense to you, you must have a day trading broker (e.g., CyBerTrader or MB Trading) equipped with point-and-click order-routing execution with SOES, SelectNet, ISLD, and/or ARCA (and REDI if possible). Browser-based brokers will not work since they are usually sent to a market maker to fill.

The goal of order routing is to get yourself the best possible fill, whether you are buying or selling. Order routing gives you the control, as opposed to forwarding your order to the broker's market maker, where the market maker decides how to fill you. Your destiny should always lie in your own hands and not in the hands of a market maker.

When there is little immediate volume on a stock, the order routing per se is important but not as crucial since you have time on your side. However, when there is volume and price movement (also known as *momentum*) in a stock, you have little time to think out your actions since seconds to minutes can mean the difference between a profit and a loss. This is where effective order-routing skills will play a major role.

If you are on a RealTick™ software platform and are starting out, we advise you to start with ARCA as your order-routing tool. For CyBerTrader users, we advise the Smartroute function, which will automatically search for the most effective order routing on your behalf.

Both of these automated smart routing functions are fine for beginners and great to use if you have the time to spare. Time to spare means there is no immediate momentum in the stock, allowing you to take your shot at an easy fill. However, when there is momentum in the form of buying or selling pressure, you do not have the luxury of time to spare. Therefore, more advanced order-routing skills will need to be implemented.

When there is momentum, we emphasize this basic order-routing rule of thumb:

ISLD → SOES → SelectNet preference → INCA (or any other ECN) → Smartroute (for CyBerTrader users) *or* ARCA (for RealTick™ users)

The first option any trader should consider when trying to get into a stock is ISLD on the inside. ISLD is fast, and what you see is what you get. If there are no offers on ISLD, then use SOES (up to the displayed tier size) for fast fills directly from the inside market makers. If the market makers do not have enough shares to fill your requested size and you see other ECNs (INCA, REDI,

BTRD, ATTN) at your limit price, you can SelectNet-preference them directly for a fast fill. We have Smartroute and ARCA as a last resort for traders who either are not up to par with order-routing skills or decide to simply monster in. However, we must also mention that Smartroute and ARCA should be used when you first start off with RealTick™ to get familiarized with order routing since they are smart order-routing functions that will take the burden of order routing off your hands for the price of time delay. Smartroute (for CyBerTrader users) is faster than ARCA because it implements SOES as an option, whereas ARCA does not. Remember that when ARCA cannot find a matching ECN order at your price limit, it will proceed to each SelectNet-preference market maker, which can take up to 30 seconds per market maker. It can be very burdensome to be stuck preferencing a market maker as other traders are filling $1/16$ above the inside limit by routing directly to ISLD or another ECN. Chances are you will wait the 30 seconds and end up with no fill since the market maker will see there are motivated buyers above his inside ask, and he will surely uptick his ask, leaving you in the dust empty-handed. The smart routing functions can be used in a "monster" sense to get priority fills if you place the high bid (to buy) and low ask (to sell), which usually means paying above the ask to ensure the fill. The bottom line here is that the *direct* route is always the fastest versus any monster smart routing function.

Panic Momentum

There will be times when you will want to get filled on a stock immediately, regardless of price, due to some fundamental change like news. The problem is that you are not the only one who wants in—and in fast. Everyone wants in! There will also be times when you want to get out of a stock, regardless of price, because you know the faster you get out, the less of a loss you will take. IPOs are prime examples of this when the momentum quickly reverses. The problem once again is that you are not the only one who wants out—and out fast. Everyone wants out! These situations are what we call panic momentum. They are fast and furious spurts of buying and selling, usually in the lower-float stocks, which means there is the additional problem of a lack of liquidity, which in turn means the price will move in wider price spreads and swings (mere seconds can mean a 2-point drop or gain in the stock price, and spreads can move in $1/2$-point increments!). The bottom line here is major volatility. These are situations where order routing can be the difference between success and failure.

Panic Momentum Buying

Suppose you get in a situation where you need to get into a stock as fast as possible ahead of the crowd. Here's what you do:

1. Route immediately to the ISLD inside limit book ask up to your share limit and price limit.
2. If there are no offers on ISLD, find an ECN and SelectNet-preference the ECN (e.g., INCA, REDI, BTRD).
3. If there are no offers on the ECN, then SOES the market.
4. If SOESing the market doesn't work, monster-bid Smartroute or monster-bid ARCA above the ask.

The goal here is to get in *fast* since you know the stock is ready to jump because of the huge flow of buyers lining up trying to outbid each other and market makers quickly stepping off the inside ask to try to sell shares at higher levels.

Let's take an example with PPRO:

PPRO

Bid 67-1/4		ASK 67-1/2	
ISLD 67-1/4	5	ISLD 67-1/2	12
GSCO 67-1/4	5	MASH 67-1/2	10
MASH 67-1/8	10	PERT 67-3/4	8
INCA 67	20	INCA 67-3/4	4
PERT 67	10	NFSC 67-7/8	5
USCT 67	5	MASH 68	10
WARR 66-3/4	10	MSCO 68	5
SLKC 66-1/2	5	SLKC 68-1/4	5

Assume there is panic momentum buying in this stock and you want 500 shares for the ride. Remember that you will only get a few seconds to react, and many times you will only get one shot to get in before the stock runs away from you. First and foremost, you have to make a quick decision about how high a limit to set in order to ensure that you get shares and how many shares you want. For example's sake, let's say you are looking for 500 shares at a $67^3/_4$ limit. Here are the possible scenarios:

1. Your first instinct might be to try to route directly to ISLD at $67^1/_2$ for 500 shares. This is a case of the quickest draw gets the shares. If you are fastest, you get your shares. However, if you don't get filled, your order will be rejected and you will need to reexecute. In cases of extremely fast momentum, that will be too long. Therefore, since you know you want 500 shares up to $67^3/_4$, you are better off trying an ISLD bid at $67^3/_4$ for 500 shares. This will automatically go to the ISLD book and sweep up everything available up to $67^3/_4$ for 500 shares. Obviously, it helps even more if you have the ISLD limit book up, but sometimes the situation will not allow you to take the time to key in the symbol.

2. You can SelectNet-preference INCA for 400 shares at $67^3/_4$ and go the direct route up to your limit while everyone else is fighting at the lower levels to get shares. This is a case of taking the shortcut right to the finish line while the rest of the pack is fighting with one another to get shares at the lower levels.

3. You can monster Smartroute or ARCA at $67^3/_4$ to 13/16 for 500 shares to get priority ahead of the pack to get filled on shares up to your limit price. Naturally, you are paying more to assure yourself a fill.

4. You can SOES the market for 500 shares. This is very risky, as a market order has no limits. The SOES market is slightly different since it must be on the inside ask. The question is where the inside will be. The fill will come from a market maker and gives you a good shot at getting filled since SOES has priority over SelectNet, which beats out ARCA, which will SelectNet-preference each market maker.

Any of the above in that priority should get you a good shot at getting a fill, depending on your timing. Nothing in day trading is an exact science. Everything is a percentage game. Order-routing execution skill is key in tipping the odds in your favor.

Panic Momentum Selling

Now we will reverse the situation and assume that you are long 500 shares in a stock where you need to get out immediately as panic momentum selling steps in. When you get in a situation where you need to get out of a stock as fast as possible ahead of the crowd, these are your steps:

1. Route immediately to the ISLD inside limit book ask up to your share limit and price limit.
2. If there are no offers on ISLD, find an ECN and SelectNet-preference ECN (e.g., INCA, REDI, BTRD).
3. If there are no offers on the ECN, then SOES the market.
4. If SOESing the market doesn't work, monster-bid Smartroute or monster-bid ARCA above the ask.

Once again, your goal here is to get out *fast* because the stock is tanking and the sellers are building up fast on the ask. This is like a mad dash to the exits in a movie theater while it is burning down.

Let's take the same stock, PPRO:

PPRO

Bid 67-1/4		ASK 67-1/2	
ISLD 67-1/4	5	ISLD 67-1/2	12
GSCO 67-1/4	5	MASH 67-1/2	10
MASH 67-1/8	10	PERT 67-3/4	8
INCA 67	20	INCA 67-3/4	4
PERT 67	10	NFSC 67-7/8	5
USCT 67	5	MASH 68	10
WARR 66-3/4	10	MSCO 68	5
SLKC 66-1/2	5	SLKC 68-1/4	5

You have 500 shares long in PPRO, and you need to get out fast. Unfortunately, everyone else wants to get out fast too. Remember that you will only get a few seconds to react, and many times you will only get one shot to get in before the stock runs away from you. First and foremost, you have to make a quick decision about how low a limit you will set to get out (don't be cheap!). Remember that in panic situations, it is most important to shoot first and get out and ask questions later. Let's say you want out and are willing to take 67 as your final limit. Here are the possible scenarios:

1. Your first instinct might be to try to route directly to ISLD at $67^1/_4$ for 500 shares. This also is a case of the quickest draw gets the shares. If you are fastest, you get your shares. However, if you don't get filled, your order will be rejected and you will need to reexecute. In cases of extremely fast momentum, that will be too long. Therefore, since you know you want 500 shares out, down to your 67 limit, you are better off trying an ISLD bid at 67 for 500 shares. This will automatically go to the ISLD book and sweep down everything available up to 67 for 500 shares. Obviously, it helps even more if you have the ISLD limit book up, but sometimes the situation will not allow you to take the time to key in the symbol.

2. You can SelectNet-preference INCA for 500 shares at 67 and go the direct route down to your limit while everyone else is fighting at the lower levels to get shares. This is a case of taking the shortcut right to the finish line while the rest of the pack is fighting with one another to get shares at the lower levels.

3. You can SOES the market for 500 shares. This is very risky, as a market order has no limits. The SOES market is slightly different since it must be on the inside ask. The question is where the inside will be. The fill will come from a market maker and gives you a good shot at getting filled since SOES has priority over SelectNet, which beats out ARCA, which will SelectNet-preference each market maker.

4. You can monster Smartroute or ARCA at 67 for 500 shares to get priority ahead of the pack to get filled on shares up to your

limit price. Naturally, you are paying more to assure yourself a fill. The problem here is that you may not be the only one on ARCA, as everyone is trying to get out a monster bid, which may cause you to get stuck in line waiting to get out. Market makers can smell all the SelectNet orders to get out and will oftentimes step way off the inside bid just to shake out more day traders in the panic.

Panic selling is much tougher than panic buying, in that market makers can smell panic and can easily (and often do) step off their bids, adding more fuel to the fire with less exits. The most obvious problem is that if you don't get a fill in panic buying, you have lost nothing, whereas if you don't get a fast fill in panic selling, you will continue to lose more. In other words, you can't lose what you don't put in the pot. ARCA is a *last* resort in this case. This is the problem with chippies which we mentioned earlier. When too many traders use ARCA to monster out, the market makers are given a nice, big, blinking neon sign that says "Going Down," and they will take full advantage. The fills are very elusive and very much like jumping into a 9-foot pool of water only to have the water move out of the way. When everyone goes one route, it is usually best to find another. Like the analogy of a burning movie theater where everyone is heading toward the fire exits, it may be more beneficial to find a window.

Momentum Ticks

An interesting phenomenon, called momentum ticks, happens with a stock's price as it accelerates on volume. Traders have witnessed this phenomenon, and astute traders are well aware of the momentum ticks. When a stock starts to accelerate in price and volume, there are certain ticks that either stop the momentum dead in its tracks or catapult the momentum to the next level. These momentum ticks go in this order: the round number, the $1/2$, and the $1/4$. On a larger spectrum based on round numbers, the next levels of momentum ticks are 5 and 10. Momentum ticks provide the most liquidity and give an excellent indication of the short-term strength of the momentum. The round number, also known as the whole number, tends to give the best liquidity and gives a trader a feel for the short-term strength of the momentum. For example, when CMGI ticks $92^7/8 \times 92^{15}/16$, momentum may be accelerating until the 93 round number ticks. Let's say 93 has 20 market makers with a 10 size each and by all accounts that price level looks thick. When 93 ticks, usually it tends to get taken out, and a new burst of buying sets in and accelerates the momentum like a catapult. Once the 93 momentum tick breaks through, the next momentum ticks are as follows: $93^1/4$, $93^1/2$, $93^3/4$, and 94.

The round number is the strongest and most liquid of all the momentum ticks. This is very important when trading a thin-float stock. For example, trying to sell 1000 shares of IIXL at $39^3/4$ can very well cause market makers to step down to a 39 bid as you get filled on, perhaps, 300 shares at $39^1/2$, if you are lucky. However, if you wait for buyers to pop IIXL to tick the 40 momentum tick, there is often enough liquidity to sell the full lot into the 40 momentum tick buyers. The round number is the most liquid momentum tick, and that is where you should concentrate on selling the heaviest of your shares. The $1/2$ momentum tick is the second most liquid, and the $1/4$ momentum tick is the least liquid. This is very important.

The strength of a stock's momentum can be measured by how strong a stock ticks through a momentum tick. When a stock breaks through a round-number momentum tick, you should expect the next momentum tick to hit in order to continue the momentum. If the stock stalls at a teeny, then there is a chance that the momentum is looking to reverse.

Teenies

A way to gauge when the short-term momentum may be coming to an abrupt end is by observing the teenies. Teenies are what traders refer to when talking about $1/16$ in a stock price (e.g., $37^1/16$, $37^3/16$, $37^7/16$, and so on). Consider teenies to be like speed bumps. Experienced day traders and especially market makers like to sell the teenies on momentum buying pops when they feel the momentum is peaking. We know the momentum ticks have liquidity, and if a stock is strong, it will often chew through them. However, in order to get to the next momentum tick, the stock has to climb through the teenies. Market makers will often try to sell the teenies to squeeze out an extra profit and also to curtail the momentum before the next momentum tick. By gauging how strong the teenies hold, a trader can get a heads-up on the slow-down of the momentum. Remember that momentum buying can turn into momentum panic selling at the drop of a dime, and it is advantageous to get out at the peak of momentum buying.

When a momentum tick breaks on a stock, especially the round numbers, always observe the teenies. Market makers are known for shorting the teenies if they feel that a momentum run is played out and running tired. Oftentimes, you will see stocks break the round number only to find one market maker at $1/16$ initially who is selling. The stock may stall as the buyers for the $1/16$ tick disappear. Before you can blink, the sellers start lining up at the $1/16$, and now you have a wiggle (a short-term retracement or pullback in a stock) in place as the buyers head toward the exits, trying to get out of the stock.

There are two advantages to measuring the teenies. If you are long the stock, then you know when you need to be getting out. If you are not long the stock, you can wait for the wiggle rather than chase the stock, only to get filled at the peak of buying prior to a wiggle. The bottom line is that measuring teenies allows you to anticipate and react, rather than blindly predicting short-term tops and bottoms. We do not predict; we react.

How to Use Momentum Ticks to Maximize Profits with Order Routing

Now that we have gone over momentum ticks and teenies, let's put them to practical use. The goal of any momentum trade is to get in and out into the buyers *while the buyers are still there.* Therefore, you should be exiting at the ask and many times above the ask. The best way to exit a moving stock (moving up and fast) is by placing a limit order at the momentum tick on the ISLD limit book to sell. Many times, if the momentum is very strong, you will get filled above the ask.

We have seen some really stupid moves as anxious traders try to sell into a stock's rally only to get stuck. The worst kind of execution is using ARCA to sell below the bid into buyers. For some reason, ARCA tends to jam as it tries to find an ECN or a market maker to preference, as each is quickly upticking, which confuses ARCA. Meanwhile, the stock is rising fast while your ARCA order is still trying to fill at a lower price. We have seen amateurs get stuck trying to cancel ARCA, only to get filled as the momentum quickly reverses and heads lower while the slick ISLD sellers have already cashed out at much higher prices on the momentum ticks into the buyers. This is just bad amateur order routing.

The basic rule when exiting on the momentum ticks is to place your sell order on ISLD on the momentum tick. Do not be premature and load down the ask. Loading down the ask means piling your sell order on top of existing sell orders, especially existing ISLD sell orders. Sizes of 5000 shares or more on the inside ask tend to bring momentum buyers to a crashing halt, often causing an immediate reversal even before the momentum tick. Timing is very important. The key is to *wait* for half the offers to get taken out and sneak your sell order in when the momentum tick is just about taken out. This ensures that you do not hurt the momentum by showing your hand too early, especially if you are playing larger blocks.

Speaking of larger blocks, remember that the most liquid momentum ticks work from the round number, the $1/2$, and finally the $1/4$ ticks. Although this is subjective to the actual stock, as stocks have different floats and rhythms, the basic rule of thumb is that generally you want to dump any lots over 3000 shares on the round-number ticks or else *pare out* (break your sell order into manageable pieces) on the lower momentum ticks ($1/2$, $1/4$) if you can't get a round-number momentum tick. If you show your offer on the momentum tick too soon, there is a very good chance you could adversely affect the momentum. Remember that buyers come in when there is an impression that the shares are scarce and limited. It only takes a few sellers to show up on the ask and banish the illusion of limited shares available to buy, now creating the impression that the buyers are limited, causing sellers to panic to get out of the stock before a further pullback.

Let's take a quick example with PPRO again:

PPRO

Bid 67-7/8   ASK 67-15/16

MSCO 67-7/8	5	PERT 67-15/16	8
GSCO 67-7/8	5	MASH 68	10
MASH 67-7/8	10	PERT 68	8
INCA 67-3/4	20	INCA 68	4
PERT 67-11/16	10	NFSC 68	5
USCT 67-1/2	5	MASH 68-1/16	10
WARR 67-1/4	10	MSCO 68-1/8	5
SLKC 66-1/4	5	SLKC 68-1/8	5

PPRO is a thin mover at these levels. Let's assume you have 1000 shares of PPRO and you want to lock in your profits. The *ideal* method is to:

1. Wait for the 68 momentum tick and buyers to take out the 68 ask until there is only one market maker left selling at 68.
2. Place your full 1000 shares to sell on ISLD at 68.

With this method, you are taking advantage of the most liquid momentum tick, the round number, 68. This round-number momentum tick should give you enough liquidity in the form of buyers to exit a full lot. You do not want to weigh down the ask by placing your sell too early. Selling too early on this stock means placing your sell order at 68 before the round number is actually hit. By waiting for 68 buyers to fill and take out the market makers at the ask down to one market maker, you are ensuring that you are not loading the ask by piling on an extra 1000 shares, which may stifle or even reverse the momentum.

PARING DOWN LOTS

One of the skills that good day traders employ is paring down their lots in a stock, especially a thin-float stock. As noted earlier, paring means to break your order into several pieces, rather than keep it as one chunk. Instead of trying to shove 5 pounds of beef through a meat grinder, you should be piecing out smaller portions to ensure that the meat grinder doesn't get jammed or damaged, and likewise to ensure your executions fill without panicking the market makers. Many times you cannot buy a full lot in a stock without affecting the stock's price, nor sell a full lot without hurting the stock. Paring also helps to maximize gains with less risk on fast uptrending stocks, and it helps to minimize losses on a fast retracement on wiggling stocks by downsizing your risk since your position is decreasing. It helps to buy you time and maintain some semblance of control in a panic situation. The least of your worries in a panic situation is commission costs. They should not even be part of the equation. It is better to pare down in a falling stock at the expense of multiple commission costs rather than try to sell a whole lot and scaring off market makers to ridiculously low levels, where you finally get a fill prior to a bounce.

When a stock starts to pull back and you are not sure whether it is a wiggle or the beginning of a trend reversal, you should consider paring down so that you lessen your exposure. This buys you some time with less risk, because you have fewer shares. In the event of a trend reversal down, you can then exit your remaining shares. However, if the pullback was just a wiggle, then the stock should trend back higher, and you have not taken an unnecessary stop on your full lot. For example, suppose you own 1000 shares of CTXS at $68^1/_2$, and it starts to pull back to 68. You may start to get nervous because the 3-minute chart may still show an uptrend, but the 15-period support is 68. This could possibly be signaling a breakdown, but it is too soon to tell. To protect yourself, you could pare down 300 shares at 68 using ISLD or SOES, which brings your holdings to 700, which allows you to give CTXS more time to consolidate with less risk. If the consolidation plays out and 68 holds support and starts to trend higher, you have prevented yourself from getting wiggled out. If CTXS shows the 5 period breaking down through the 15-period support at 68, then you can pare down another 300 at the respective momentum ticks, with a final stop at $67^1/_2$ to prevent a larger loss. Let's assume CTXS breaks down and finds support at $66^1/_2$. By paring down, you took a loss of 300 shares at $^1/_2$ (when pared out at 68), 300 shares at $^3/_4$ (when pared out at $67^3/_4$), and finally 400 shares at 1 (when pared out finally at $67^1/_2$), which results in a loss of $775; this beats taking a full stop at $67^1/_2$, resulting in a greater loss of

$1000. Stop losses sting, but in this game they are a necessary factor. The key is taking the lesser of two evils, which means to take a smaller stop loss than a larger one. If you had a problem with taking stop losses, you may eventually have panicked out your full lot at $66^1/2$, which would have meant a loss of $2000. Everyone can agree losing $775 hurts a lot less than losing $2000.

When a stock is moving higher, you can also pare your shares into the buying on the accelerating momentum ticks to maximize your gains, yet locking in profits at the same time. Ideally you want to be out of the stock near the peak of momentum buying, but you may not know where that peak is. Therefore, by selling into the buyers at each progressive momentum tick, you take advantage of not selling out your full lot too soon while protecting yourself against a fast retracement by keeping fewer shares. Take the same example with CTXS, of which you own 1000 shares at $68^1/2$. If CTXS starts to break to the upside at $68^7/8 \times 68^{15}/16$, you can look to sell 500 shares at the 69 momentum tick. Let's assume CTXS clears the 69 momentum tick and the teeny and heads higher through $69^1/4$. At this point, you are watching the teenies at $69^5/16$ and $^7/16$ as they disappear, which tells you that buying pressure is strong here. CTXS ticks the $69^1/2$ momentum tick as you sell another 300 shares into the buyers. At the $69^9/16$ momentum tick, there is one market maker who steps in as the buying pauses. This tells you to watch that teeny, as momentum may be slowing down on this pop. Once two more market makers join at the $^9/16$ teeny, this is your signal to take the rest of your profits on the scalp, and you ISLD out at $69^1/2$. Your timing was perfect, as CTXS quickly retreats back to retest the 69 momentum tick and bases at $69 \times 69^1/16$ for a consolidation. In this example, you maximized your profits by waiting to sell the other 500 shares at $69^1/2$ in addition to the 500 shares sold at the initial 69 momentum tick, bringing your gains to 500 shares at $^1/2$ (when selling at the first 69 momentum tick) and 500 shares at 1 (when selling two lots at the $^1/2$ momentum tick), giving you $750 rather than $500 by unloading all your shares at the 69 momentum tick.

The goal of paring is to downsize your risk on pullbacks and maximize your gains on upticks.

CHAPTER 6

Types of Plays

The following is a rundown of the various types of fundamental catalyst plays that you will need to familiarize yourself with as you make your way up the learning curve. There are reasons for the moves in these plays, and the reasons are fundamental. Couple the fundamental reasons with your technical tools, and you can make very consistent profits. A seasoned trader can recognize every one of these types of plays on the fly. Take your time to review and spot these plays throughout the day. Make a note on each of your trades about which category your trade falls into as it relates to the list.

Note also that there are the story stock plays that adopt instant volatility, volume, and definite price trend based on a news catalyst. Many of these stock plays can be found here too.

CNBC

Honestly, CNBC is usually a laggard indicator when it comes to momentum. However, this is not to say it can't bring in more momentum on the mention, because it can. With CNBC's dominant viewership among day traders, the mere mention of a momentum stock in play can send it running on massive volume. Usually this is temporary, and therefore you must only take these pops for scalps and get out before the inevitable pullback. The real measure of strength is after the pullback. If the stock is indeed very strong, it will in many cases pop on the CNBC mention, pull back, coil, fill the gap (of the CNBC mention high, but even better if it's the high of the day), and break to new highs. Therefore, there are two ways to play CNBC stock mentions: Either play the initial momentum for the scalp (fast and risky) or wait for the pullback, coil, and gap-fill for a safer entry. CNBC also gets daily guest CEO interviews on its popular Powerlunch segment. You can get the list of guest CEOs by going to the CNBC Web site, www.cnbc.com, clicking CNBC-TV, and then clicking Guest List. Usually, when a guest is scheduled to appear on CNBC, the underlying stock will start to be bought premarket and/or on the open and slowly rise into the segment. In most cases, the stock sells off during and after the interview, unless the CEO does a spectacular job and unveils some news or developments not previously announced. The way to play is to buy on the open and/or postopen and sell into the beginning of the interview to lock in profits before the pullback. In addition, a short opportunity presents itself during the interview on the pullback. Use the 3-minute moving averages charts to short when the lines cross over to indicate breakdown during the interview. Once again, if the stock pulls back, coils, and fills the gap to new highs, then a breakout situation is imminent and deserves the long-side scalp.

NASDAQ MOST ACTIVE

This list can be pulled from your day trading broker datafeed and is an excellent way to get an idea of what is strong for the day. Go to www.yahoo.com, click stock quotes, and click Most Actives (under U.S. Markets), and you can pull up the most actives and percentage gainers and losers of the day.

WWW.ISLD.COM

This is the home page for the ISLD book. It has a nice feature that you should always check, starting from premarket. This feature is the top 20 most active stocks on the ISLD list. This list has real-time volume rankings on stocks that are trading through ISLD.

Premarket, this is an excellent tool to see where the action is. Stemming from premarket action, this list will also foreshadow where the action may lie on the open. During the market day, it will show you where the momentum is with the day traders since ISLD is the ECN of choice for hyperactive day traders.

BARRON'S

Barron's is the premier weekly financial periodical with a huge following. Any significant mention in *Barron's* has a direct effect on the stock on Monday morning. This is called the *Barron's* effect. The gains are usually seen on Monday on greater than average volume and usually slip when volume slips back to normal average daily volume.

BUSINESS WEEK

The Inside Wall Street column in *Business Week* usually features several stocks and causes some nice momentum on above-normal volume. *Business Week* is usually delivered on Friday morning on the East Coast and Monday morning on the West Coast. However, you can get an early read before the subscribers by logging onto www.businessweek.com on the World Wide Web and clicking on the Inside Wall Street icon. Personally, we like to go long on any mention of rumors of buyouts (by "unidentified" sources) for the spike. However, most of our money is made shorting the same stocks into the close on either Friday or Monday. The reality is that very few of the buyout rumors or valuations by the infamous unidentified sources ever pan out and are safer on the short side after the initial run-up.

NEWS STOCK MOVERS

In most instances, news is the main catalyst for stock movement. The most widely used news service is Dow Jones, and therefore, that is the service you want to get. Note, however, that some of the lesser known services such as Businesswire and Bloomberg tend to release news stories before the Dow (also known as the *Wire*), and that usually presents a nice opportunity to get in early "before the news hits the main wire," as traders say. When these opportunities present themselves, train yourself to take advantage of them.

When a stock releases news, a trader must determine one thing. Does this story have "legs"? In other words, will this story move the stock and by how much? We will go over most of the best kinds of story stock movers and how to play them. Always keep in mind that the effect of good news usually lasts from a few minutes to a few hours and in rare, rare cases more than one day before the trend takes a hard, quick reversal. Always anticipate the reversal due to the inevitability of profit takers. Playing these stocks is a lot like playing musical chairs, and the last one in is usually the last one standing. Remember that news only emits an initial knee-jerk reaction that may last minutes to hours. Do not ever hold a stock based strictly on news; always temper the fundamental with the technical tools, such as 3-minute moving averages charts, to maximize the upside and cut losses.

Contracts (Tech Stocks)

Revenue-generating contracts, strategic alliances, and/or cash investments—these items can result in a very nice pop for the smaller company once the press release hits the wires. If you can pull the information on Businesswire *before* it hits the Dow Jones broad tape, you can get a very nice head start on the trend. The best contract news involves revenue-generating deals or alliances or cash investments for a smaller company with big name bellwether companies like Microsoft, Intel, Cisco, IBM, etc. For example, when GMGC announced an alliance with Microsoft, the stock jumped more than 120 percent inside a few hours. One added bonus is when CNBC also reports the news (expect another instantaneous pop) or if CNBC schedules an officer of the company for an interview. Usually, a nice window of opportunity to short near the end of the day or near the intraday high can be found by way of profit takers. However, be very careful to cover for a fractional gain since there will also be many buyers jumping in to benefit from an anticipated morning gap, especially if an officer is scheduled for an interview on CNBC the next morning.

These stocks are a tough overnight short because they are fundamentally strong and the stock rise is somewhat justified.

Biotech Alliances/Phase I, II, III Trials/Discovery News

These stocks will pop in a mad rush, only to give back a good part of the gains once panic buyers realize that fundamentally the company will not realize any material benefit (revenues) or even a marketable product for a number of years. Biotech stocks are very volatile due to the emotional aspect involved. When key words like *cancer, AIDS, vaccine,* and *disease* are used, people get very sentimental and get filled with all kinds of delusions about being the next Pfizer or Merck. Stocks that discover a "holy grail" gene or some historic findings will often run very hard until the end of the day, and then the profit takers come to their senses and take the money off the table. When the stock starts to fall, investors tend to get a sudden slap of reality, and they panic to lock in their profits, break even, or cut their losses. This is what makes these biotechs so volatile.

A perfect example is GERN. When GERN released news that it had discovered the holy grail of cancer genes, the stock jumped from 7 to 17 in the same day, only to drop back down to 10 three days later. Another example is NYMXF. It had made a historical discovery in regard to Alzheimer's disease which made the stock run from 6 to $12^3/4$ in a single day. The next morning, the stock was gapping as high at $13^7/16$ premarket, only to free-fall to $9^7/8$ just 20 minutes into the trading day. In both these cases, there was no real fundamental reason for the stock to retain its full gain since the companies would not recognize any revenues from their discoveries for years to come. Therefore, it is very important to carefully read the press releases and ask yourself whether the company will recognize any immediate revenues from the discovery. These stocks are excellent short candidates.

FDA Approvals

FDA approvals also mean a fast run-up in the price of a stock. Usually if the approval is announced before the market open; it guarantees a gap up in price at the open, likewise if the approval is announced during a stock halt. If you can get in early enough once the stock resumes, you might be able to catch a nice run-up. However, it is usually tough to get in early on these plays. We prefer usually to take the short side on FDA approvals. The law of gravity will set in, and the stock will always pull back to a more reasonable level from anywhere within a few hour to a few days. This is, for the most part, a contrarian stance and usually feels crazy during a buying frenzy. Most people will jump into a stock that receives an FDA approval with hopes of making a killing. When the trend turns, they will be flushed out in a panic even faster. Even when a stock receives FDA approval, the company would most likely need, at the very least, two quarters to launch the product and even longer to see any real material effect reflected on the balance sheets.

In these biotech run-ups, the pattern is very evident. We like to usually short into the end-of-the-day strength (after the profit takers), anticipating a nice premarket gap and then a free-fall plunge. You might ask why then do we not wait until the next morning to short into the strength? In many cases, this is an even better way to tip the scales in your favor. However, the opportunity to actually short on the open may not present itself since the premarket run-up gives the illusion of strength, only to collapse at the opening bell, making it much tougher to short the downtick. Is it safer to wait for a morning run before you short? Yes. However, we have to weigh the possibility of a gap down in the stock's price premarket and consider a small short position to hold overnight.

Lawsuits

Class-action lawsuits, patent infringement lawsuits, and competitor or antitrust lawsuits are usually bad news for a company and are best played on the short side. When the suits are resolved in favor of your company, it is obviously best played on the long side, short term. *Short term* is the key wording here. Usually the effects of the lawsuits are felt only for a day or two, so keep the plays intraday and based on technical 3-minute trends.

Upgrades and Downgrades

Be very wary of upgrades by brokerages at or near their 52-week highs! The public may be duped into buying these overpriced stocks, but the smart money is selling into the strength. Let's take some time to explain the way a brokerage benefits from these upgrades. When a stock gets downgraded, people naturally will sell. Meanwhile, the trading department will usually be accumulating big positions all the way down. When the trend turns, the traders will sell into the strength. However, the big money comes when their analyst upgrades the stock. Once the analyst upgrades, the retail brokers (also known as the *distribution system*) contact their clients to inform them of the upgrade and advise them to buy shares. Guess who they are buying from? Exactly. Directly from the trader's inventory! Therefore, usually the people who get in on an upgrade are the ones holding the bag when the music stops playing. Does this happen all the time? No—but it happens enough. How do we know the traders from the brokerage are selling into the upgrade? Our Level 2 screen will often show the brokerage's market maker on the inside ask all day, and this is the smoking gun.

Many times an upgrade by a brokerage would imply that the brokerage's marker maker is or should be buying the stock also. However, many times in reality, the trader will be selling at best ask, and the upgrade usually provides liquidity for the trader to unload his inventory! Upgrades that are followed by the market maker buying heavily at the best bid are genuine and worth jumping into on the long side. Likewise and vice versa with downgrades.

We will usually play the long side on an upgrade if we see the upgrading broker's market maker supporting the bids on a steady uptrend, or we will step in on momentum when we see blocks being covered by the upgrading brokerage as they uptick on a steady uptrend. On downgrades, we will always go short for a fractional scalp, especially when the major investment houses put out the downgrade. Keep in mind that when the downgrades do come out, the traders will have usually unloaded the bulk of their inventory prior to the downgrade announcement.

Earnings Warnings

Usually, by the time the warning is announced, the stock will already have been punished, and therefore earnings warnings actually provide a better buying opportunity as a dumper stock. Premarket, market makers will gap down the warning stock to a point where they feel the risk is safe to take the bid and ask spread. Understand that there will be a lot of selling. The only way to play is to make sure you have a 3-minute consolidation and support, with blocks being covered on the bid. Spot the firm sellers on Level 2 and watch their spreads as they uptick. If they uptick as they cover blocks, that is usually a decent sign that selling pressure is letting up and an entry will be safe. Always remember that you want to make sure you have a minimum of a consolidation first, and a breakout from the consolidation would be even more favorable. The pitfalls of playing an earnings warning is the possibility of multiple downgrades during the day or next several days. For this reason, we recommend that you look to take scalplike gains intraday and be wary of holding fresh dumpers overnight.

Takeover Rumors

First and foremost, do not believe the hype. Takeover, shmakeover. The only thing we are interested in with takeover rumors is the momentum that follows. Stocks moving on takeover rumors have great momentum and can be very profitable if played right. Usually takeover rumors will surface near the beginning or middle of the week and climax into the end of Friday before the weekend. Never hold a full-lot position into the weekend on a takeover rumor. Rumors rarely (we mean *rarely*) ever evolve into the actual takeovers; and to many a naive holder's disappointment, the underlying stock usually crumbles on the following Monday when no takeover materializes. You will only want to play the momentum and uptrend for point gains while the sheep clutch their shares, waiting and praying for a lottery-type win over the weekend. Sheep get slaughtered.

Split Announcements

When stocks announce a split, they usually gap on the news and then start to rise within a 10-day period into the split date. This is a tried and proven formula, meaning stocks soon to split should always be on your radar.

Sympathy Plays on IPOS

Usually when an IPO turns out to be a spin-off of an already existing public company (parent company), the parent company will
pop upon announcement of the IPO. The company will also usually pop a week into the IPO. However, ironically, when the IPO
opens, the parent company will usually fall. This is a rather strange
but very played-out phenomenon. Some examples that immediately come to mind are DBCC, which ran from 14 to 33 into the
IPO opening of MKTW and then proceeded to tank to the teens,
and NAVR, which ran from 9 to 14 into the IPO opening of
NETR and then proceeded to tank to the 8s upon the open. The
list goes on and on. The choice here is obviously to play the
momentum on the long side into the opening of the IPO spin-off
up until the day before the spin-off occurs. On the day of the IPO,
usually on the open, it is wise to short the parent company and
make sure you use the 3-minute moving averages trend charts to
find a decent entry on a consolidation breakdown.

Earnings

There is a simple rule of thumb in regard to earnings. Do not hold
a stock on earnings release. Usually a stock will make a run-up five
days prior to the release of earnings. Play the momentum up to the
day of earnings and then stay out. There are obvious exceptions to
this rule, but in the long run, this rule will save you. The simple
reality is that holding a stock into the actual earnings release (usually after the bell or premarket the next morning) is nothing more
than a straight gamble. In this game, a gamble is a 50:50 chance,
and the odds are inherently not in our favor, so why take the risk?
In addition to playing the earnings momentum up to the day prior
to earnings release, you can also consider playing after the earnings release. Usually, if earnings are strong and an upgrade
accompanies them, play them like an opening gap and trap, and
wait for gap fills. A *gap and trap* is when a stock rises premarket
and immediately sells off on the market open. Traders will buy a
stock at the open because the gap implies buying strength only to
see the stock tank after they buy. If accumulation is setting in, you

will know it from the steady 3-minute moving average uptrend with a nice, tight trading channel.

Flavor-of-the-Moment Movers

There are always themes that tend to drive momentum. The way to interpret the flavor of the moment is by watching the top Nasdaq gainers and looking for strong-moving stocks and their respective sympathy lower-tier movers. This can be played out in a tier-type fashion. However, rather than looking straight for semi equipment maker strength or box makers, we are speaking more of less obvious plays and their themes. For example, Linux operating system companies were showing strength in the fall of 1999, led by RHAT. Understanding that Linux may be hot, traders quickly searched for new Linux momentum plays in the form of CORL, EDFY, and ADSP. When the flavor of the moment was B2B (business-to-business Internet), CMRC led the pack as it made an incredible move from 70 to 350, sparking momentum to look for other B2B plays in ARBA, VERT, PPRO, and ICGE. And who could forget the Pokemon craze led by KIDE, bringing along movers (some were only one-day wonders) like GRIN, TMAX, and TOPP. You get the idea. Momentum moves fast and is fickle. The best way to stay on top of this is by being in touch with the markets through the various chats and top Nasdaq gainers.

Gap Plays

As a day trader, you will rarely opt to hold positions overnight unless you are swing-holding in a swing account. However, there are times when a stock is so powerful that you are compelled to hold it overnight in anticipation of a gap after-hours or the following morning. Our criteria for gap plays are very simple. When a stock closes at or just short of its intraday high on volume, then we consider it a potential gap play. The main thing to remember on gap plays is that you must manage your risk by tempering your shares. We highly suggest only a small lot and enough shares so that you can stomach a 50 percent retracement on the gains for the day in case the stock gaps down. An even better deal is if you already have a gain in the stock and wish to hold it overnight for the gapper. The existing gain already gives you a cushion for the potential retracement. For example, you are looking at CNET as it closes at the high of the day at 66 (+4) on strong volume into the close. You would consider a morning gap play as long as you could stomach a 50 percent retracement, which would be −2 points. If you already own CNET from 65, then you already have a 1-point cushion of safety for the retracement. If you entered at 66 into the close, then you go in fully aware of the risk of a gap down. If you normally trade 1000 shares of CNET, a good risk may be to take 300 shares overnight with a downside of −600. This is a decent risk. You would not go into CNET with 1000 shares or more, because it is just too much risk. Always trade to preserve capital and protect your downside.

SCANNERS

Another way to find stocks throughout the day is with the assistance of market scanners. A scanner allows you to enter in criteria (e.g., stocks hitting new highs or new lows) as it filters the market, looking for plays that meet your criteria. Tools like scanners can make a good trader better, but they cannot make a bad trader into a good trader. They are tools and only tools. One of the best intraday scanners currently on the market is Stormtracker. We recommend checking it out at www.stormchasertech.com. We have also found a wonderful tool for end-of-day scanning called the Big Easy Investor. Its Web site is www.bigeasyinvestor.com. Simply download the software, unzip, install, and run. This package will scan the entire market for potential plays the next day. The vast number of criteria and its ease of use are absolutely amazing. We particularly like the big screening and the three-price break scans coupled with stochastics reversals through 20 bands with volume. You can use the ever-expanding criteria for scans or create your own combination. We highly recommend these products for all traders who are looking to put potential plays on their radar for the next morning.

INTERNET STOCKS

The advent of the day trading movement has brought on greater concentrated and focused short-term buying, resulting in big momentum. When talking about big momentum, the Internet stocks reign supreme. Nowhere else can you make 3 points in 2 minutes, or lose 5 points in 5 minutes. It is high risk and high reward. Different levels of risk are associated with the different types of Internet stocks. They are a special breed of stock and deserve special attention when trading.

The whole Internet stock craze in our opinion has been accelerated by the actions of the hyperactive day traders. Not all Internet stocks are the same. There are discrete differences in these stocks, which we shall detail right now. The more volatile and thin an Internet stock, the greater the risk and potential reward. If you maintain the defensive attitude of trading to preserve capital, then you will always be on your toes.

As discussed at the beginning of this book, the market can be broken down into sectors, and within the sectors you have a totem pole that starts from the generals, also known as the Tier 1 leaders, on down. The Tier 1 stocks are always important to keep on your market minder, as they are the bellwether for the overall trend and strength in their respective sectors. The Tier 1 stocks are usually the most heavily traded and are usually linked to indexes such as the Nasdaq 100, the S&P 500, and/or the various sector indexes. For this reason, these stocks are also included in program buying and selling. They may hibernate, but they rarely die.

In the Internet sector, we use YHOO, AOL, EBAY, and AMZN as our Tier 1 indicators. As mentioned earlier, if you overlay a 3-minute moving averages price chart of each Tier 1 stock, you will see a very interesting phenomenon. The stocks literally move together, barring any significant news that may cause an initial knee-jerk divergence, but the trends remain literally identical.

CHAPTER 7

Playing Initial Public Offerings

Initial public offerings (IPOs) are dangerous. Let's clarify this. Initial public offerings on the open are extremely dangerous. They are fast and illiquid. Very much like the stock market open, there is also no intraday trading history of the stock. In fact, there is no history, period! This makes an IPO open even faster and more chaotic than the market open. The risk-reward ratio is very high. In a best-case scenario, you can get a decent fill, catching the right side of the trend as the underwriters step off the asks, allowing buyers to take the stock higher. Depending on the float, you can make 2 to 10 points on the open in a matter of minutes. On the other hand, you could find yourself buying shares as the momentum immediately reverses on you, locking you into the equivalent of standing under a falling 2-ton knife. Trying to get out anywhere near the bid is nearly impossible, as other unfortunate traders are panicking, trying to get out way under the bid price. Market makers will step off the bids to limit their exposure, causing the stock to literally implode. Depending on the float, you can lose 2 to 10 points on the open in a matter of minutes also.

Market sentiment and sector conditions weigh heavily on how strong an IPO will be. Usually, you can expect the market makers to gap a stock above its initial pricing range in an effort to get the best price on the open for the shareholders, who are free to sell in the open market. Many factors are involved when assessing an IPO to play.

EVALUATING THE IPO

Business

Aside from Internet and tech companies, most other IPOs are pretty stagnant on the open unless they are very highly oversubscribed. We tend to favor high-tech IPOs on the Nasdaq and preferably Internet companies. In all honesty, fundamentals mean little as far as an IPO is concerned. Profitability, growth, and branding are the three criteria that may attract investors. As day traders, we only care about price volatility—and in the case of IPOs, rising price volatility—and we take fundamentals with a grain of salt. Alliances or equity ownership stakes by well-known public corporations are a definite plus that will attract more interest.

Float

The float is the amount of shares that will be available in the aftermarket. The fewer shares available to the public, the better the price volatility and momentum. We prefer stocks that have a float of 4 million shares or less on the IPO. This usually ensures that there will be some lateral upward movement in the stock if the volume can support the run. The higher-float stocks take more volume to move, very much like the difference between a speedboat and a cruise ship in a race. However, there are always exceptions to the rule in cases where an IPO has major hype and interest and is very oversubscribed. *Oversubscribed* is a term used by the underwriters, indicating that demand for the IPS is so many times greater than the float. Therefore an IPO that is five times oversubscribed implies that there is five times the float in demand before the IPO is issued in the open market. There is no exact indicator showing what the demand for an IPO is, nor how oversubscribed an IPO may be, as everything is an assumption.

Underwriters

The major brokerages have large distribution chains in their retail and institutional clients. We have found that not all underwriters are the same in supporting their IPOs in the aftermarket. In fact, we have found the lack of support by underwriters rather disturbing.

Usually an IPO will peak as underwriters sell into the buyers and step way off on the bid to protect themselves when the panic buying turns into panic selling. When an underwriter goes out of his way to step in and hold the bid firmly against all sellers, that underwriter deserves respect and a solid reputation. As of this writing, we would have to say that MSCO (Morgan Stanley) is the undisputed king of underwriters. MSCO has built a strong reputation for eating (accumulating shares at the bid) a lot of shares in the aftermarket to support his companies. The best examples that come to mind are RBAK, BRCD, CMTN, and ARBA. We remember very well how strongly MSCO supported the bids on the respective aforementioned IPOs. In the case of ARBA, MSCO had opened the IPO around $54 as the buyers came in. Typically, the lead underwriter would shamelessly sit on the ask and sell as many shares as he could at the peak of buying. However, in the case of ARBA, MSCO would step on the inside bid at $56 when sellers started to take profits. Instead of cowering and dropping the bid, MSCO sat firm at the bid, buying up over 50,000 shares at $56 until the other market makers and traders realized that MSCO had the courage and tenacity to support the IPO. From that point on, every time MSCO upticked his bid price, the IPO would be 2 points ahead of him as traders jumped over each other trying to buy shares before they peaked. At every top, MSCO upticked his bid and held the bid firm, buying any shares that came up for sale. MSCO continued to drive the shares of ARBA to $90 into the close and at the highs of the day. This was an example of what a strong firm underwriter can do for an IPO.

As for other brokers, we have no respect or sympathy for the lack of support they often provide their IPOs. The next best possible IPO underwriter would have to be RSSF (Robertson Stephens), which supported the IPOs GSPN and QSFT very firmly on their opening days. RSSF can sometimes move up to MSCO's league on certain IPOs, and so we always keep RSSF's IPOs on the radar.

GSCO (Goldman Sachs) may be the undisputed king on Wall Street as far as investment banking and institutional clientele, but their support on IPO aftermarkets has much to be desired. GSCO tries to pick a range and spend most of the afternoon selling shares in that range. The company is not stupid by any means, as it will lift and fade if extenuating buying comes in, and it will allow fertile opportunities to take place. However, it cannot be relied upon to heavily support its own IPOs in the wake of heavy selling.

FBCO (Credit Suisse First Boston), PRU (Prudential), HMQT (Hambrecht and Quist), MLCO (Merril Lynch), COWN (Cowen), BEST (Bear Stearns), and PIPR (US Piper Jaffrey) are questionable at times and will only support their IPOs based on market conditions. Usually, these underwriters can be found selling into the buyers, rather than supporting their IPOs. Any IPOs with these underwriters as the lead always send up red flags.

The irony is that CNBC and other media will only report how "successful" an IPO is based on the initial pricing and where it opens. Rarely does the media ever report on how horrible the aftermarket action is on an IPO. This is once again a sign of the lack of insight on the part of the media and the public, as underwriters literally have a license to kill, only to be praised on the success of an IPO based on the opening price and not the aftermarket price action, where underwriters often flagrantly fail to support price levels.

PLAYING AN IPO

We cannot state enough times how extremely dangerous it is to play IPOs on opening day. Understand that there are actually three periods that are used to base the action on an IPO in the opening day. You have the open, the aftermarket, and finally the last half hour. The most volatile and dangerous time to play an IPO is right at the opening. The action is fast and furious, and usually underwriters gap up the opening and sell right into the overzealous buyers, taking the IPO lower. There is no way to anticipate the bottoms on IPOs, as they can be pulled out from underneath, like a rug. The only reason to play the open is that by some chance the IPO turns out to be an insanity momentum runner on the open. These IPOs either run hard straight out of the gate and continue to make new highs or start off with giant gaps, sell off, and then fill the gap of the highs to move to new highs on strong volume.

Too often, traders mistake the exception IPOs to be the rule. It is a very dangerous mistake to assume an insanity IPO trades the way IPOs normally trade. Some examples of exception IPOs include ARBA, FDRY, RHAT, CRDS, and NTOP. These IPOs were, by all standards, insane. They gapped ridiculously high and continued to run higher.

Very similar to playing a market open, you are looking for the same criteria. Either you are looking for strong buying and market makers lifting on the open, allowing the price to move higher, or you are looking for a gap fill where underwriters support an initial pullback and new buyers take the IPO back to the opening highs and break it out to new highs. These kinds of plays are rare indeed and depend highly on market strength and most importantly on underwriter support.

Let's also be honest here. Most IPOs are total duds. They gap on the open, tank, and then stay in a range the rest of the day. Therefore, never go into an IPO thinking that it will be a momentum runner. Anticipate all IPOs being flops until they prove otherwise. Although we mentioned that there are three periods to an IPO, the reality is that the open is usually when the most momentum occurs. After that, it fizzles, condemned to a choppy range and nothing more. Bottom line, don't get your hopes too high.

When you are playing the open, you must always limit your shares, because the worst-case scenario is that you get filled and the IPO tanks, leaving you stuck with all the other passengers. Trying to get out of a falling IPO is an exercise in futility. Do not ever waste your time trying to SOES or SelectNet a market maker on a falling IPO. The only route out is to bid the ISLD book as low as possible and hope to sweep any orders to your limit price. You can lose several points in seconds on a falling IPO. And vice versa. If you catch the right side of the momentum, you can sell into the ISLD book buyers, oftentimes above the rapidly upticking ask. We highly recommend you do not sit on any IPO stock through the open. The key is to get in, ride the trend, and get out while there are still plenty of buyers. More than ever, you want to sell when there are buyers, not sell when the buyers are dried up and everyone else is panicking to sell too.

The only IPOs that we suggest playing are thin-float tech companies (on the Nasdaq, of course) that fill the gap on the open. This means the IPO sells off on the open, bottoms quickly, and then heads back to the initial highs and breaks to new highs. Always keep an eye on the underwriters to see who the ax may be. The ax will be the underwriter that either holds the bids or sells the asks consistently, putting a lid on the momentum unless he gets squeezed from sheer volume. Always lean on the ax when taking an entry. Use the momentum ticks for exits into buyers. Taking the same momentum tick philosophy onto a larger scale keeps increments on resistance and target points to 5 and 10. This means that you should always expect resistance at the 10 round number, and then the 5 round number, and then the 10, etc., as an IPO rises.

Here is an example of an IPO that we featured as a trade alert. On December 2, 1999, HMQT was the lead underwriter of 3.1 million shares of the IPO PFSW. The company is an electronic transaction services software company for both traditional and Internet-based commerce. The IPO opened shortly after 11:40 a.m. EST at around $38\frac{1}{2}$, made an intraday high of $40\frac{1}{2}$, met with strong resistance at the 10 round-number tick 40, and sold off strong to the $36\frac{1}{2}$ range. At that point, we noticed MLCO and HMQT were holding the bid at $36\frac{1}{2}$ and eating a ton of sellers' shares. Their initial support caused traders to reverse and start buying again as MLCO continued to lift his bid to 37 and then $37\frac{1}{2}$. At this point, a trade alert to consider a buy PFSW 38 limit at 11:44 a.m. was issued to us, pointing out that MLCO and HMQT were initially supporting the run and that momentum was shifting back again fast to retest the 40 round-number tick. Members quickly stepped in at 38, taking shares from the ISLD sellers. The traders that tried to SOES or SelectNet up to 30 had no luck, as the market makers were upticking too fast. The 40 tick tested and thinned out, as market makers ran for cover, taking the asks higher through 41, 42, 43, and 44. Traders were told to lock in some profits into the buyers, as we were ready to test the 45-tick resistance. The 45 ticked through at 11:47 a.m. while most traders locked in profits. PFSW ticked slightly above 45 and reversed hard, and traders who failed to sell earlier into buyers were trapped with other profit takers and panic sellers, causing the stock to reverse momentum and collapse back under 40 by 11:57 a.m.! Traders that played this correctly gained up to 7 points (38 to 45) in a matter of 3 minutes! From here the IPO stayed in a 40–44 choppy range the rest of the afternoon as the momentum fizzled.

This is a nice example of a well-played IPO open. However, if you were unlucky enough to buy at 45, you would have been stuck without much of an exit, as the ISLD bids dried up until the 41–42 range in a matter of minutes. This is the reward and this is the risk. They are proportionate in the IPO game to the extremest of degrees. New traders should watch and only play after the criteria we mentioned above fit the bill. The best way to learn to trade IPOs is to watch the seasoned traders play them first. Learn from their successes and errors. IPOs are unpredictable and require the highest level of momentum on the fly, trading with flawless order routing capabilities.

QUIET-PERIOD PLAYS

Quiet period is a period of 25 days, starting from the day of the IPO, during which a stock cannot release any financial information nor can brokers make any formal initiations of coverage. The stock is free to trade without any fundamental change after the IPO for this period. Understanding that most brokerages will release upgrades the day after quiet period, traders will usually take positions 5 to 10 days before the end of quiet period for the run-up and possible gap on the upgrades. This has been a recent phenomenon due to so many IPOs in 1999, which peaked during the spring of that year. We recall KOOP, which stood at $14 five days prior to quiet period and ran to a high of $48 on the day after quiet period when buy recommendations came from the respective brokages. WITC was another stock that ran from $13 to $33 into the day after quiet-period coverage. Naturally, as the public becomes more aware of this, the dramatic rises tend to dissipate as everyone tries to step in front of each other for the anticipated run. In any case, recent IPOs should always be kept on radar 5 to 10 days prior to the end of their quiet period in anticipation of a run-up. We don't recommend actually holding the stock until the end of quiet period, but rather entering and selling the run-up just prior to the end of quiet period.

CHAPTER 8

Determining Your Style

The greatest skill you will attain as a day trader is the ability to adapt to changing market conditions. To put it another way, the best day traders are masters at adapting to changing market conditions. The fine line between stubbornness and conviction is as clear as night and day to them. Just as people can be divided into mostly left-brain analytical thinkers and right-brain creative thinkers, traders can be broken down into swingers and scalpers. We do want to make clear that you can be a scalper that also swing-trades or a swing trader that also scalps. However, most traders lean more toward one or the other style. You need to determine which style fits your temperament and character. We define swing trading as taking a position in a stock intraday and holding through wiggles and/or taking a position for several days like a short-term investment. We define scalp trading as getting in and out on momentum. Swing trading can reap greater rewards, but the risks are also greater in that larger stops need to be implemented in order to distinguish between a wiggle and a trend reversal. Scalp trading is fast and the least risky as you are not exposed for any extended period of time. Any extended wiggle calls for quick stop losses. Scalping is essentially self-explanatory, and so we will take this time to go over true swing trading.

SWING TRADING

In the beginning, day trading meant trading for one-eighths intraday and *never* holding a position overnight. Day trading has evolved since then. The days of the ⅛ scalps and SOES bandits are long behind us for the average day trader. The tools and charts have evolved as more and more traders rely on technical indicators. A form of day trading has also evolved, known as swing trading. Swing trading can be viewed as a hybrid form of trading—partway between day trading and investing. Swing trading refers to holding a stock for an extended period of time, usually several days. Swing trading is short-term investing with stops and targets. It involves more risk than scalping in that one has to stay exposed to the markets in a stock position for a longer duration of time. The stops on swing trades are larger than scalps in order to allow for the trend to work itself through any extended wiggles and resume its destiny. The gains on a well-placed swing trade can be huge. However, if stop losses are not implemented when swing trades turn sour, the losses can be just as bad as, if not worse than, the potential gain. Risk versus reward once again is the key formula in this equation. Swing traders have to think and act like investors but tempered by day trader skills. The day trader skills come in the form of the ability to read technical indicators and to take the necessary stops or profits as they arise. Therefore, while an average investor may sit and wait to reap large gains on a position, she will also take substantial hits when reversals occur. Swing traders look to lock in large gains while not taking the kind of substantial pullbacks that an investor would sit through.

Double Accounts

Swing trading involves a different paradigm in thinking from the intraday scalping mentality. For many traders, it is very hard to hold a stock through an extended wiggle, much less a pullback. This is what makes swing trading so much harder to stomach than taking the quick scalps and nullifying your exposure in the market. The most effective technique to deal with this problem is to have a separate swing trade account.

Remember the days when you would purchase a stock and only look at it every week or so and be pleasantly surprised at the gains or slightly ticked off by the losses? Yet in the long run your stock seemed to accelerate nicely in value. Most of society still invests for the long term and is not affected by short-term intra-day volatility in a stock.

Can you imagine how the average investor would react if she truly knew the intraday tick-by-tick movements of her positions? Seeing a 52,000-share INCA seller tanking MSFT on the ask, knocking off billions in market cap in a matter of seconds, would wake up most investors. It would be a rather eye-opening experience. It would be safe to say that many would be slightly rattled at the volatility of the movements. A sense of nervousness might hit their stomachs.

Chances are you are not part of the general investor society if you are reading this book and day trading. You are part of the crowd that knows the volatile nature of the stock market and has insight into the moves and swings of the markets. This is wonderful knowledge to have. On the other hand, you are more prone to the effects of the tick and intraday indicators. All this knowledge can cloud your judgment when it comes to holding overnight positions. Every tick becomes an emotional struggle when quick stop losses are your nature. Swing trading plays against this and can make life very hard to bear if the swing starts off at a loss.

The reality is that most day traders find it hard, if not impossible, to hold a swing trade since it requires that they relinquish much of the control to the markets. The hardest part about swing trading is sitting in front of the screen and having to watch each tick. Investors do not have to do this.

We have a very simple solution. As suggested a few paragraphs above, open a swing trade (short-term investment) account that is separate from your day trading account. Watch your intraday day trades tick by tick if you wish. Don't watch your swing trades tick by tick. This is not the purpose of a swing trade. When swing trading, you are leaving your stock to either hit a target or hit a stop. If you have the right technical indicators measured in your favor, then you should pull out ahead; if not, then your stop will get hit. You have assessed that the risk and the odds are in the direction of your swing trade. You should have conviction enough to stomach the pullbacks (not tick by tick). However, you are *not* stubborn enough to *not* implement a *stop* loss or take a *stop* when your technical indicators reverse. Always remember the difference between conviction and stubbornness. Everyone wants larger gains. The real question is whether you have the stomach to handle the intraday wiggles and pullbacks in order to ride the trend for those larger gains. If so, then you may want to add swing trading to your portfolio (in a separate account, of course).

CHAPTER 9

Preparing to Trade

PAPER TRADING AND RISK CAPITAL: GETTING STARTED

Day trading has a terribly expensive learning curve. In other words, you will most likely lose a lot of capital before you start making consistent profits. Therefore, we can't emphasize enough to start off by paper trading. At first, do nothing but observe the Level 2 screen and time of sales on your stocks. Observe how the market makers move, and try to identify the ax and anticipate his actions. Observe how a stock reacts when news hits the wire. Watch how the market makers are jockeying for position and how a stock will run depending on the legs and how it will pull back. One needs to paper-trade first and foremost to develop a frame of reference and ideal patterns. The key is to observe enough stock movements to be able to anticipate on some level how a stock will react to certain news and the type of trends that develop. Trade on paper and execute hypothetical trades and compare your results. Keep accurate notes in your trading journal so that you can familiarize yourself with setups and patterns that will lead to profits in the near future with real money.

Even better than paper trading are trading simulators. These demo mode simulators allow you to actually watch the stocks and place buy and sell orders in real time without playing with real money. The simulators are the next step toward going live trading.

The only drawback with the demo mode simulators is the unreal fills. Paper trading and simulators are great for training so long as you understand that the key is to base your buy-sell entries on the technical indicators. The rule of thumb is that you should not go live trading until you have an 80 percent winning streak on the simulators. That percentage will drop tremendously when you go live with cash. The goal of paper trading and demo mode simulators is for you to test your skills in reacting to technical trends. They give you the benefit of a sure fill and mental solace, as money is not on the line. When you go live with cash, both of those luxuries go right out the window.

Expect to start with a minimum of $20,000 and preferably up to $50,000. This is risk capital and should not be the last of your money. When you start off trading live with real money, you should play smaller lots of 300 to 500 shares and spend this initial time getting acquainted with order routing. Don't even consider trading 1000-share blocks until you have become consistent and profit for at least 14 straight trading days. You should also try to get your account over $30,000 (and upward of $50,000) before going into 1000-share blocks. Too many traders start with $10,000 accounts, make a few trades, and lop off their capital by 40 percent in a few days. That's a very hard position to be in, because now your leverage has dropped and you are forced to play smaller-share lots, not to mention the negative attitude you've just developed which makes it even harder to take a loss fast. Eventually, this can destroy your capital and trading career. The key is to *start small* and then build up to larger sizes as you get more comfortable and disciplined. Initially, you are trying to master order routing, which is something you can only learn from actual trading. Therefore, start off with 100–300-share lots and trade as if you were trading 1000 shares. Look for those 1-minute stochastics bounces and take the $1/4$- to $1/2$-point scalps. Do not jump into stock and give up the $1/2$-point gain just because you are trading 200 shares. Imagine you are trading 1000 shares because you are training for that moment. You are giving up a nickel now in commission costs to make a dollar in the long run when you play the full lots with confidence. You won't make any money on these little scalps with such small lots, but that is not the purpose in the beginning. You want to trade to get comfortable so that you can eventually work 1000-share lots and even more. You can't build a building without a stable foundation.

MENTAL PREPARATION

Trading is 75 percent mental. Your confidence, which is built on your experience, composes your mental framework. Pay careful attention to these words: The only thing that matters is your *own* profit and loss statement at the end of the day! What do these words signify? Ego. Get rid of it.

There is a fine line between stubbornness and conviction. Day traders are in essence moving targets that are not attached emotionally to any stock. They are (or are supposed to be) objective, and while having conviction in the tools and trend at a given moment, day traders will not hesitate to take a stop, without even a second thought when a trade turns bad.

Do not kick yourself over missing a trade or taking a profit too soon. These kinds of self-recriminations will inevitably lead you to think that the market is playing against you personally and will cloud your judgment. Furthermore, whereas a day trader may usually take scalps on momentum, if she starts kicking herself for taking profits too soon, she may convince herself to stay in longer on the next trade, which may sour. This is an example of ego leading to stubbornness.

The best way to manage trading anxiety is to get familiar with the stocks you are trading. This is why we recommend having a basket of stocks that you follow every day. The more familiar you become with a stock, the less you are taken by surprise. Familiarity breeds confidence. Remember that. Familiarity breeds confidence, and the more stocks and patterns you are aware of, the more confident you become. This is all part of the learning curve.

One of the most common questions we are asked by traders is, "Where should I take a stop?" Contrary to some opinions, we are firm believers that you should be watching and keeping stops manually rather than automatically. And this is never a question you should be asking when you are trading. Your stop should be predetermined before you enter the trade. To do otherwise is to put the carriage in front of the horse. This doesn't cut it. You need to know your stops beforehand instead of jumping in and wondering what to do once you enter a stock.

Stops are very subjective to your own style of trading. The key is getting in and getting out. The best liquidity is when there are buyers. If there are panic buyers, then chances are you can get out at the ask. Remember, the trend can change and reverse at the drop of a hat—so *fast* is key.

Take profits where they are on the table. Cut losses fast. Use stops based on 15-period moving average support on the 3-minute chart. We are sure you've heard people tell you to cut your losses fast and ride your winners. Easier said that done, right? But, of course, with your luck, the second you sell, the stock comes right back up, and this time you don't want to get shaken out so easily, right? The position pulls back $1/4$; you wait. It pulls back $1/2$; you wait. It then drops 1 full point, and you start to panic and sell it after a full $1^1/2$-point drop—and then it comes back again. Sound familiar? How do we combat this? As it turns out, most traders take stops too late or too soon. Whenever you find yourself in a trade that backfires, watch the 1-minute stochastics. Chances are you may be near a stochastics bottom. If not, then take an immediate stop and look to reenter the position on the bounce. If it's too late, keep your cool and wait for the stochastics reversal to exit into the buyers on the bounce.

Understand this: Every trade is a speculation, *period.* There is an imaginary scale that measures the odds of your success, depending on:

1. Your positioning
2. The trend

An even scale of 50:50 odds is simply not compelling enough for us to take a position. That is a gamble in our book. The scales must be tipped at least 80:20 in our favor. When we see this opportunity, we immediately understand that we are 80 percent more likely to hit a $1/4$-point gain than to hit a $1/4$-point loss. Therefore, we take the position—we take the speculation.

Can it prove us wrong? Sure. The stock could pull back as soon as we take a position. That means that our odds were not correctly figured and we exit as soon as possible with our $1/4$-point loss.

Now what if it starts to bounce back after we get out? When we exit, we immediately refigure our odds and wait for a trend to emerge. We don't care at what price we get in at so long as we get in when the trend is hot. This is called *trading*.

For example, our indicators show that COMS is a good play and has bottomed out at $37^1/8$. There is a lull in the action, and we feel that our position at $37^3/16$ is a safe bet. However, as soon as we get filled at $3/16$, the stock pulls back. We immediately pull the plug at 37 even as the stock pulls to $36^3/4 \times 36^7/8$. Within seconds, the stock runs to $37^1/4 \times 37^5/16$. Our indicators show a strong trend, and we decide to take a position (higher than our original position). We get filled at $37^3/8$ as COMS continues to run to 40, and we sell for a $5/8$ gain. In the above (true) example, we had to strip our mind of the attitude of taking a loss and paying more for the stock than we originally paid on the first trade. Some people might ask us, "So what was the advantage of taking that loss when you could have stayed in and made a $3/4$ point?"

We simply reply, "Hindsight is 20/20. There was a good chance that the stock would have continued to pull back another full point. We don't take those risks. We cut our losses fast. The fact that a stock pulls back tells us that our calculations were somewhat flawed, because a trade should be moving forward and be profitable every time (ideally). Failure of this happening causes an automatic reaction—take the quick loss. Reevaluate, tighten parameters, and reenter."

Never trade just to make a trade—even veteran traders can identify with this temptation. It takes tremendous discipline to stay away from frivolous trades due to boredom.

Don't let winners turn into losers! You need to realize that when you become an investor, you lose in the game of day trading. The hardest mindset to master is the ability to learn to take quick losses and quick gains. When a position turns against you, you need to have the intestinal fortitude and the focus to make getting out your number one priority. Always remember that the goal of the game is to preserve your capital, and not to make a fortune. Logically, the more winning trades you have and the fewer losing trades, the better your chances of preserving your capital and making money.

Forget the notion that you are going to make a killing in the markets by trading. Too many people come into day trading with that idea. With that kind of thinking, it is easy to decide to stay in a losing position, hoping that it will turn around. And though the stock continues to lose strength and drop in value, the amateur trader continues to believe that the stock will come back and she can at least break even. But the stock continues to drop, and eventually the trader realizes that the small loss she didn't want to take has turned into a large loss that she is forced to take. In the end, the trader is left with a bad trade, a bruised ego, and a large capital loss. A capital loss not only hurts your wallet but also restricts your ability to purchase more shares, therefore restricting your future income.

Even the best traders have losing days. Rather than dwell on them, these traders simply look upon them as drawdown days where they give back some profits. This is normal, and you should never dwell on any single trade or trading day. However, if you find yourself in a series of losing days, the worst damage is usually done to your confidence. Your losses may signal defeat mentally as well as put more pressure on you to get wiggled out more often. The worst mental hurdle when encountering losing days is the money factor. If you are focusing too much on the money and the paper losses in a wiggle, then you need to immediately stop trading and regroup your thoughts. If you are kicking yourself for plays that you did not make, then you need to stop. If you cannot control yourself from jumping into anything that moves, then you need to stop. Take a day off. For the next few days watch, but don't play. Watch Level 2 and the charts. Go back to the basics and paper-trade or use a simulator. You will be surprised how the clarity comes back when the money is not on the line. This allows you to focus on the trade and not the money. Trust us when we say this will help immensely. It sounds simple and it is, but until you take the time off and watch, you will not know the incredible stress load it takes off your shoulders when money is not a factor. When you finally go back to live trading, start with fewer shares. We suggest $1/2$ lots to get back into the groove to continue to relieve pressure about losing money. As you regain your confidence, you should eventually return to the full-lot sizes that you were playing. This is the best way to heal yourself from the mental anguish that accompanies a losing streak.

THE INFAMOUS AND EXPENSIVE LEARNING CURVE

Trading is the world's most expensive speculator sport. Learning to use Level 2 to enhance your profit potential also carries its own learning curve. Most people will often fail to fund themselves adequately through this period and will walk away in disgust. All the successful traders will tell you their own horror stories about their learning curve and how much it cost them. Consider it tuition and a cost of doing business. We will relay our own learning curve breakdown from our own personal experiences. Keep in mind that you can dramatically cut down on your "tuition" by spending a tremendous amount of time just paper trading and watching the Level 2 screen. The following is our evolutionary breakdown of the stages you will go through.

The Newbie Stage

This stage is the beginning of your journey as a trader. Up until now, you have been taught to invest in stocks with excellent fundamentals. You have followed the textbook guidelines for investing your money and have considered yourself a long-term player. You watch CNBC, read *The Wall Street Journal,* and have a retail or discount broker. You might have been making some money investing or losing your shirt. In either case, your attention is drawn to day trading. The concept of being able to sit in front of a computer making huge profits with a few keystrokes really appeals to you. The allure of the easy money from playing the volatility in the stock market compels you to investigate. You notice the intraday swings in all stocks just by seeing the highs and lows in *The Wall Street Journal.* Gee, you could really make some quick cash by buying 1000 shares and then selling them for a quick fractional gain, repeating this all day. Theoretically, this sounds good. So you set up an Internet brokerage account and begin trading. First you will start with delayed quotes and lose some money. Second, you will invest in real-time quotes and eventually lose more money. At this point, you hear about this gizmo called a Nasdaq Level 2 screen that lets you see the inner workings of a stock's price movement. Third, you sign up for Level 2 service and have no clue how to interpret it. So you test it out.

As you learn to read the Level 2, you realize that you are getting shaken out on every other trade for lots of little losses that add up to bigger losses. You are trying to maintain your discipline of keeping very tight mentals top losses and never letting a small loss turn into a big loss, but this results in your selling into a panic only to have the stock recover right after you get out. You doubt yourself a lot and get panicked easily. You struggle to maintain a trader's mentality only to end up as an investor (holding a losing position in hopes of breaking even one day), or you will cut your losses like a trader only to wish you had been an investor because you wouldn't have missed out on the rebound and recovery.

The Crossroads Stage

Needless to say, you are frustrated at this point. You probably have lost a good $20,000–$30,000, have lost your self-respect and confidence, and have finally arrived at the crossroads. At this point, you will:

1. Give up and curse the day you ever pulled your life savings out of your mutual funds to throw away on trading!

Or

2. Become obsessed and continue to trade the rest of your capital away and then move to Alaska before your wife finds out you raided the retirement account.

Or

3. Temporarily stop trading, step back, reevaluate your trades, find the patterns and reassess your errors, and paper-trade

until you derive a system that consistently puts the odds in your favor. As you are paper trading, you are also reconstructing your self-confidence. When you start trading again, you find yourself anticipating moves and making profits!

If you decided to go with option 1 and quit, then it is probably the smartest decision you ever made, because you are not cut out to be a trader. Option 2 is the mark of a gambler, and you will eventually end up losing everything. Option 3 is the sign of a true speculator and a potentially successful trader. The key is control. The gambler has none, but the speculator always maintains control. This control is what gives a successful trader the conviction of taking a position against the herd and profiting handsomely when there is blood in the streets. Control is what keeps a speculator from panicking.

The Education Stage

At this point, everything seems to come together. It literally hits you one day—wow! You start to notice how certain stock plays set up (e.g., biotech run-ups or tech stock contracts and earnings disappointments). You experiment and paper-trade these patterns successfully. You start to be able to interpret the action on the Level 2 for the few stocks that you follow religiously (your basket) and attain the "feel." You see the synergies with the futures moves and your basket stocks. You focus on your basket and compare the moves with other Tier 1 leaders and 3-minute chart patterns. Your earlier mistakes seem to repeat themselves, and you notice the pattern and the similarities. There is a level of clarity that emerges from your mistakes. You gain familiarity with rhythms and patterns as you step back and watch. Eventually, you build a solid foundation of knowledge based on experience and familiarity with your basket, and you continue to strive to discover more setups and patterns and indicators. You start to gain confidence in your trades.

The Trader Stage

You are now trading very profitably and have learned when to take a small loss and when to hang in there for the big bounce and payoff. You can jump in and out of trader versus investor mentality at the drop of a hat. You find that you are getting shaken out a lot less and that you often are able to anticipate and mimic the ax market makers for big profits. Your emotional threshold has grown tremendously. You have arrived. At this stage, you have achieved your highest level of control. You thrive on panic and usually take a contrarian position against the herd, ending up with consistent profits. You have finally arrived! Welcome, fellow trader!

If you survive to the trader stage, you will have your own horror stories about your personal learning curve. Most traders we speak with have learning curves that have cost them between $15,000 and $70,000 and up to two years in time. If you have what it takes, you will make it. The markets have a way of weeding out the weak hands—it's the law of the jungle. (*An aside:* We have a series of roundtable discussion logs where members of our company share their own learning curve horror stories in our archives section.)

THE TRADE JOURNAL

Your brain is an amazing organ with an incredible ability to retrieve memories and experiences as if you just relived them. If you ever kept a personal diary, you know how resourceful the mind can be in remembering, as you reread each entry, exactly what happened that day as your diary fills in the details.

That is why one of the best tools that a new trader can use is a trade journal. It allows you to measure your progress and review your trades. As the saying goes, hindsight is 20/20. Making errors is part of the learning curve, as long as you review your errors and learn from them. Trading journals take an extra effort to maintain, but they will help your progress immensely if done properly. The learning curve consists of making as many errors as possible and learning from them. A trader learns more from a bad trade than a good trade, especially in the beginning. So let's go over how you should format your journal and use it. Keep in mind that you should keep things simple.

The basic journal format should have the following headings in the following format:

Day/Date

Monday 10/23/99

Trade	Reason	Gains/Losses	Win	Loss	Comments
Buy CSCO $78^{1}/2 \times 1000$	Stochastics reversal 20 band				
Sold CSCO $78^{3}/4 \times 1000$		$+^{1}/4 \times 1000$	+250		Sold momentum tick
Sold CSCO 79×1000		$+^{1}/2 \times 1000$	+500		Sold momentum tick
Buy AMZN $72^{1}/16 \times 500$	Momentum break				
*Sold AMZN $71^{1}/2 \times 500$	Stopped/ 3-minute breakdown	$-^{9}/16 \times 500$		−281.25	Bad entry
Buy RHAT $87^{1}/2 \times 200$	3-minute breakout				
Sold RHAT $89^{1}/4 \times 200$		$+1^{3}/4 \times 200$	+350		Consolidation/ break
Sold short RHAT $88^{1}/2 \times 200$	100 band stochastics				
*Covered RHAT 90×200		$-1^{1}/2 \times 200$		−300	3 minute strong
Gross totals			+1100	−581.25	
Net profit-loss			+518.25		

*Got wiggled on AMZN and RHAT. Both good stops but bad entries. Entries stunk because I ignored the 3-minute trends. Next time, pay better attention to the 3-minute trend for breakdowns or breakouts. Also entered AMZN on a spoos breakout, bad timing. Oh well.

One look at your entry page should let you summarize your trading for that day. The comments should be able to pinpoint exactly where the errors came across. Going back and reviewing your trading journal should instantly bring back the feelings that you were experiencing before, during, and after the trade. Spend the most time on your losing trades, because in this game, it is a matter of cutting down on them. Pose these questions:

1. How did you lose on the particular trade? (For example, was it a wiggle? A trend reversal? A stochastics breakdown?)
2. What will you do the next time to avoid the same errors? (For example, will you watch the 3-minute trend? The stochastics?)

One extra *major* benefit of a trade journal is the aspect of closure, especially on a bad trading day. You know the feeling you get in the pit of your stomach at the end of a bad trading session. It may take hours to wear off, and it plain burns. The initial anger and then the frustration can be a tough thing to carry with you. Your mind wanders and keeps replaying the trades in your head. You keep telling yourself that you should have, could have, would have, if only—ah, shucks. A trade journal allows you to put your feelings in writing, but more importantly it allows you to analyze where you made errors and this will give you closure. Peace of mind alone is worth the extra effort. This sounds simple, and it really is. We highly advise you to give a trade journal a shot for at least 2 weeks and see the improvement in your trading and your sanity. Never judge your performance on any single trade or trading day. Step back and judge your performance on a weekly basis. This way you can gauge the trend of your trading.

PAY YOURSELF

Once you start becoming consistent with your trading and the profits start to materialize, we highly suggest that you pay yourself weekly. Initially, you should build your account size to a certain level that you are comfortable with. Once that level is achieved, you need to regularly take profits out of the account and store them someplace safe. This is as much mental as it is material for you. When you take money out periodically (no less than once a month, but we suggest weekly), you are giving yourself closure. There is no need to constantly grow your day trading account past a certain level, where most of the money will be sitting idle and where it can easily be given back to the markets on bad trades. The larger your account, the more tempting it is to break your rules and perhaps overleverage yourself on a gambling trade. You do not need this temptation, nor the potential to give back profits. Both Cybertrader and Mbtrading are very efficient with same-day wire transfers. Reward yourself for your efforts—you certainly deserve it.

PART TWO

IMPLEMENTING THE TOOLS

CHAPTER 10

How to Day-Trade Correctly

Now that we have gone over all the tools, indicators, plays, and execution systems, essentially laying out all the silverware, it is now time to use everything we've discussed and learn to dine properly.

The goal of any day trader when starting out is to gain as much understanding as possible of individual stock rhythms and patterns in correlation to the indicators and tools we have described while preserving as much capital as possible. First and foremost, we advise just watching the charts and indicators. There is nothing wrong with watching and learning through osmosis. Speaking of osmosis, a good trading environment where you come into contact (physically or through the Internet) with experienced traders should also help speed your trip across that learning curve. Online day trading chatrooms can be good and bad, as traders can have ulterior motives and hype can run rampant. We naturally have a bias to our own chatroom, where the traders range in skill levels from beginners to experts and they all share being "in the trenches" day in and day out in an effort to profit and learn. This is our idea of a fertile environment—no hype, just substance.

What makes a successful trader? Educational background tends to make little if any difference. In fact, in our experience, we have found that day traders come from all kinds of backgrounds and education levels. What is vitally important is to be able to recognize, adapt, and shift paradigms on the fly and to maintain

129

strong emotional control. These characteristics, coupled with experience with a plethora of stocks and skills from mastering order routing to charting, tend to make a strong day trader. We have found that the most important characteristics in learning the art of day trading are an open mind and a natural desire to learn.

Keep these notes posted in front of your computer:

1. Start trading on paper and then demo mode simulators.

2. Trade small lots to get a taste of real-time executions.

3. Trade to gain a profit every day. Try to keep a personal streak of winning profitable days.

Understand that you will take losses in the beginning. You will learn more from a losing trade than a winning one. You have to fall in order to pick yourself up. This is what builds your character and helps you stick to your rules. In time, you will gain the ability to close the door behind you on a trade and cut your losses fast so that you can catch another trade. Eventually, you will come to a point where you have reached the bottom of your learning curve. This is a point where you question yourself as a trader and you have given up a significant portion of your initial capital. When you reach this bottom, either you will quit or you will begin to trade carefully and precisely by the rules with your tools. You are no longer reckless but calculated as you bide your time for entries. This is where you turn your trading around. As you build your track record, you will gain faith in yourself as a trader. You will be willing to take stop losses to give up a nickel to gain a dollar. You discover that it is not the win-loss record that matters—it is the profit-loss statement. Proper money and risk management will allow you to pull consistent profits even when your losing trades outnumber your winning ones. Your goal is to continue to consciously implement the tools to make careful trades so that your actions become subconscious. You want to develop that autopilot so that decisions can be made on the fly. You have already figured out in your head the charts on your basket of stocks, and you are literally one with the market. You adapt like water to the conditions, and you flow with the trend. You develop that sixth sense that great traders call the "feel." This is when you know that you have crossed the learning curve, and it will show on your daily profit and loss statements. This molding process can take anywhere from 4 months to 2 years. It all depends on you and how hungry you are to learn and how adaptive you are. So let's get started.

START OFF WITH ONE BASKET OF STOCKS

Pick a basket of stocks and watch stocks religiously. Typically, your basket should consist of stocks that have nice volume and intraday high and low ranges on the average of 2 points (e.g., CSCO usually has a 2-point range between its intraday high and low). A basket of stocks picked from the Nasdaq 100 is preferable since those stocks are directly affected by the NDX futures and program trading.

When starting off, pick only two or three stocks for your basket, and make sure you have either a lead Tier 1 general stock in the sector if you picked a Tier 2 or a matching Tier 1 stock to confirm trends if you picked a Tier 1 general. For example, if you choose LCOS (Tier 2) for your basket, then make sure you have YHOO as your Tier 1 lead indicator.

This would be a typical basket of stocks: CSCO, AMAT, LCOS, and SUNW. CSCO is a Tier 1 networker play that responds nicely to the futures and moves in parallel with LU (confirmation Tier 1 stock). AMAT is a Tier 1 semiconductor maker that also responds directly to the futures and moves in parallel with NVLS and KLAC (confirmation Tier 1 semi equipment maker stocks). LCOS is a Tier 2 Internet play that moves with YHOO as a Tier 1 stock and that responds in its own way to the futures. SUNW is a tier 1 computer box maker that moves with the futures and moves in a parallel with IBM (Tier 1 box maker).

This sample basket has some nice Tier 1 generals and a Tier 2 in different cross-sectors of the market. There stocks constitute a manageable group since they are tech stocks and on the Nasdaq. We like to watch both spoos and NDX futures. But if you are limited in your desktop space, then the NDX futures would be your primary futures lead indicator for your basket.

NOW THAT YOU HAVE YOUR BASKET STOCKS, WHAT NEXT?

On your basket stocks, you are simply looking for scalps and swings based on the indicators. These stocks are old friends and should be your consistent money makers during the trading day. You should at the very least have them up on a market minder, and you should have at least two of your basket stocks on Level 2 all day every day. You should be able to know the rhythm of your basket stocks and how they trade. With this knowledge, you will be scalping your daily targets with them. Remember that you do not need to make a hundred trades on your basket stocks. You should be waiting like a sniper, watching for the right opportunity to arise. It only takes a few scalps to hit daily targets. If your daily profit target is $500 a day, you only need two $1/4$-point scalps on 1000-share lots. The surest way to make a quick $1/4$ point is to play the stochastics reversals. On strength days, you can take a half lot and swing some of your basket stocks higher. There is no one way to trade. You need to find what works for you.

Let's once again go over the tools you will be intimately close with for the rest of your day trading career:

1. *One-minute stochastics.* This measures short-term momentum through a magnifying glass to illustrate short-term overbought or oversold conditions; 20/80 band reversals are normal; 0/100 band reversals are best for oversold and overbought indications, respectively.

2. *Three-minute moving averages chart.* This measures medium-term trends and is like watching a stock from down the block. The chart depicts the trend and leaves out the wiggles. This tool allows you to interpret the trading channel that gives you resistance and support prices and most importantly the direction of the stock. This tool is also used for risk assessment on entry price, based on this simple rule of thumb: The farther away from the crossover (breakout), the higher your risk.

3. *S&P 500 futures and Nasdaq 100 futures on their own 3-minute stochastics charts.* These charts give you a visual of the trend of

the futures, which act as lead indicators for the stock market (the undercurrents), and most importantly give you the oversold and overbought indications. The charts are like the 1-minute stochastics minus the wiggles.

4. *Tier synergy.* This refers to the Tier 1 general stocks for the respective stocks in your basket. These stocks act as a father or a brother to your basket stock. If your basket stock is a Tier 2 stock, then this Tier 1 stock will act like a father and will usually move first, giving you a heads-up on an anticipated movement in your Tier 2 stock. If your basket stock is a Tier 1 stock, then this stock acts like a brother and confirms the move in your stock, as well as confirming money flow into the respective sector.

Intraday basket plays are one of the most consistent forms of scalping out profits for an experienced day trader. Once you have a basket of stocks that you religiously watch and trade, this form of trading will be your cash cow. Under the premise that a stock will usually set an intraday high and an intraday low, correct positioning long and short will allow you to scalp gains many times throughout the day.

How is this possible? If you take a look at price history (intraday high, low, and close) for any stock for a consecutive string of days, you will find that less than 15 percent of the time will a stock ever close at the intraday high or the intraday low. This leaves you with an 85 percent chance of making a profit, provided you can spot and play the intraday high or low on a stock. When a stock is trading at its intraday high, traders will often want to take profits, causing a pullback. When a stock is trading at its intraday low, bargain hunters will often buy, closing it on a bounce. We reiterate, *rarely does a stock close at its intraday high or intraday low.* To tip the scales more so in our favor, we must make sure that our basket of stocks fits this description historically and displays a nice amount of volatility and trading volume. What to look for: patterns, Tier 1 leader, spoos, 1-minute stochastics, and 3-minute moving averages for trend.

Here are your *necessary* tools:

1. Nasdaq Level 2 screens (at least three)
2. A 1-minute stochastics chart
3. A 3-minute moving averages chart
4. S&P futures on a 3-minute stochastics chart
5. Nasdaq 100 futures on a 3-minute stochastics chart

We like to dedicate at least one Nasdaq Level 2 screen to be linked to a 1-minute stochastics chart (list item 2) and a 3-minute moving averages chart (list item 3). This allows us to key in one symbol and have all the information pop up on the charts without having to fumble and key the symbol into each chart.

Always check to see if there is news on your basket stocks. If you do not have access to Dow Jones, you can use Businesswire for free at www.yahoo.com. Click on stock quotes and enter your stock symbol, and recent news should be listed. Remember that news will cause an initial knee-jerk reaction, popping the respective stock into its own range. The stock will then resume its move with the rest of the sector within its range.

OBSERVING YOUR BASKET STOCK ON NASDAQ LEVEL 2

Find the ax marker maker of the moment. You can spot him because he will hold the bid or ask when volume surges. Make a note of the ax. Remember that on the Tier 1 stocks, the ax can change during the day, depending on who has the big institutional orders. Watch to see how the ax moves and tightens and widens his spreads.

Watch the spreads and the speed of the momentum ticks. Do those market makers tend to fake a lot? Do you see momentum ticks holding a resistance? Are momentum ticks slow? Where does the spread fill the gap? How is your stock and the sector reacting to the futures? If the futures are rising, your stock should be rising with the sector. If your stock actually sells off or stays steady on futures rises and falls when futures retrace, then your basket stock is weak. If your basket stock rises with the futures and consolidates or wiggles minimally on futures pullbacks, then your basket stock is strong. Always confirm with another Tier 1 general stock in the same sector to make sure your stock is not diverging but moving with the sector. Therefore, your basket stock should be indicative of the sector. The longer you watch your basket stocks on Level 2, the clearer they become. The fast wiggles and gyrations look slower and more manageable. In fact, the more you watch, day in and day out, the more comfortable you become with their moves. Your confidence level should rise.

Initially, you should only paper-trade to get comfortable. Eventually, work yourself in with smaller lots to continue to maintain your comfort and confidence levels. Remember that you are not initially looking to make big profits. In fact, you should try to take scalps even on small shares, knowing that as you get more comfortable scalping $1/4$ and $1/2$ points on 200 shares, you will automatically be trained to take the same scalps on 1000 shares. You are trying to train that autopilot inside your mind. This can only be done through constant repetition until you can literally take $1/4$ to $1/2$ scalps on stochastics bounces with your eyes closed. Congrats, there is your money maker! You may cringe at the idea of just taking $1/4$ to $1/2$ scalps, but that is more than the average spread trade for a market maker (usually $1/8$). As you get proficient with order routing and scalping, those 1000-share scalps can turn into 5000-share scalps. They add up!

BUY SIGNALS

As the legendary Chinese warlord Sun Tzu said, "Every battle is won before it is ever fought." Understand that if you select the right stock and the right entry, your battle is already won. Trading should be free flowing and fluid as it flows with the trend. Good trading is simply a matter of finding the right entry points on the right stock and letting the momentum and trend carry you forward. Therefore, the real battle lies in the preparation and selection. With this understanding, let's pinpoint the best entries that you should look for.

There are two kinds of technical buy signals that you are looking for, 3-minute moving average breakouts and 1-minute stochastics reversals. You should try to enter a long position on a 3-minute moving average crossover, also known as a breakout. As we mentioned earlier in the charts section, the closer you are to the point of crossover, the less your risk. The best kind of 3-minute breakout is one that occurs after an extended consolidation (anything over an hour is considered extended). When you make your entry, use the 15-period moving average line as your trailing stop if you are looking to swing the position.

If the 3-minute moving average trend is up and the stochastics is reversing, you may opt to wait for the stochastics to fall and then go back up over the 20 band for an entry for the scalp. Scalps should be taken on the way of the trend. In other words, if a stock's 3-minute trend is steady up, you should be looking to take scalps on the long side. And if a stock's 3-minute trend is steady down, you should be looking to take scalps on the downside (shorts).

Whenever you take an entry, you need to also be aware of the futures, tier synergy, trend, and ax.

For a Buy Signal

For scalps, watch the 1-minute stochastics chart:

1. The buy signal triggers when the %d falls under the 20 band and reverses, going back through the 20 band with a crossover through the %dslow band. The crossover point is your entry for the scalp.
   a. The *best* buy signal is the zero band reversal where the %d reverses off the zero band and crosses the %dslow band (for confirmation).
   b. Even *better* if accompanied by the 20 band reversal up on the 3-minute stochastics for the futures (S&P 500 and/or Nasdaq 100).
   c. Even *better* if a Tier 1 general also makes the same move to confirm sector reversal up.
   d. Even *better* is if the 3-minute moving average is in an uptrend that confirms that the pullback that caused the %d

to fall in the first place was only a wiggle and not a trend reversal.

e. Even *better* if the ax starts bidding support and upticking— lean on him.

For intraday swings, watch the 3-minute moving averages chart:

2. The buy signal triggers when the 5- and 15-period lines cross over to the upside (breakout) led by the 5 period.

a. The *best* buy signal is after an extended consolidation period where the 5 and 15 period are in a steady consolidation range for at least 1 hour.

b. Even *better* if the futures are rising on the 3-minute stochastics (S&P 500 and/or Nasdaq 100).

c. Even *better* if a Tier 1 general is also in an uptrend on the 3-minute stochastics.

d. Even *better* if the ax is bidding and holding 15-period supports—lean on him.

e. Even *better* if your stock is in a strength sector that holds gains with small wiggles on futures pullbacks and makes new highs on futures bounces.

If you can have a combination of any of items a through e on the stochastics scalps or items a through e on the intraday swings, then the odds are more in your favor. Naturally, the best entry is when you can get a stock to meet all the above requirements before you enter. Make sure you meet at least two of the requirements prior to your respective entry. Remember, this is a percentage game, and the more indicators you have in your favor, the better your percentages. Always make sure you are aware of the above criteria before you enter a stock. They are fundamental, and you need to base the majority of your trading on them.

SHORT SIGNALS

We would estimate that 90 percent of the market participants do not ever short stocks on a regular basis. Theoretically, shorts should be just as common as longs, and it is well understood that stocks fall faster than they rise. So why is shorting so rare among day traders? We believe it is a mental problem, as most day traders are accustomed to going long on stocks that are breaking out or uptrending. More importantly, unlike a long position where your entry can immediately reap gains as you enter on strong uptrend, a short position means you will have to start with an immediate loss on paper because of the uptick rule. It is a direct challenge against another trader who goes long anticipating a continued rise while you go short anticipating a short-term rise (just enough for you to get shares) and an eventual fall. Shorting a stock usually means you lose the battle (short-term upticks), yet eventually win the war (stock breaks down). Most traders cannot swallow these kinds of odds. This is one reason that we feel most traders do not like to short—being upside down on an entry. In addition, most traders are not skilled enough to anticipate a top until it happens, nor do they have the conviction to hold a short until that top is reached. Money can be made on the long side and even faster on the short side. We particularly love to take the short position due to the basic principle that selling is always inevitable, while buying is not. The universal law of "what goes up must come down" applies to virtually every stock. Usually, stocks fall faster than they rise, thanks to the inevitability of profit takers.

The ideal short position is near or at the intraday high, without question. However, when you are sitting at the intraday high, it can be a gamble as to whether the stock will trend higher. In fact, an intraday high can only be determined after a stock makes a slight pullback from the high. Therefore, most times, it is wiser to short slightly under the intraday high. The most useful tool is the stochastics oscillator. The ideal short should be executed when the oscillator is riding the 100 band and then starts to go back down.

This is not to say that many traders do not attempt to short. They do. But picking the wrong stock to short and being a weak short can lend more momentum toward a short squeeze, especially in the thin, fast rhythm movers. If you get caught in that squeeze, it can be very painful and can make you feel like you never want to short a stock again.

Whenever you take a short entry, you need to also be aware of the futures, tier synergy, trend, and ax.

For a Short Signal

For scalps, watch the 1-minute stochastics chart:

1. The short signal triggers when the %d moves above the 80 band and reverses, going back through the 80 band with a crossover through the %dslow band. The crossover point is your entry for the scalp.

   a. The *best* short signal is the 100 band reversal where the %d reverses off the 100 band and crosses the %dslow band (for confirmation) and then breaks out.

   b. Even *better* if accompanied by the 80/100 band reversal down on the 3-minute stochastics for the futures (S&P 500 and/or Nasdaq 100).

   c. Even *better* if a Tier 1 general also makes the same move to confirm sector weakness.

   d. Even *better* if the 3-minute moving average is in a downtrend and futures pops are met with resistance at the 5 band while futures pullbacks make the stock fall to lower lows.

   e. Even *better* if the ax is shorting the ask—lean on him.

For intraday swings, watch the 3-minute moving averages chart:

1. The sell signal triggers when the 5- and 15-period lines cross over to the downside (breakdown) led by the 5 period.

   a. The *best* short signal is after an extended consolidation period where the 5 and 15 period are in a steady consolidation range for at least 1 hour and then break down.

   b. Even *better* if the futures are slipping on the 3-minute stochastics (S&P 500 and/or Nasdaq 100).

   c. Even *better* if a Tier 1 general is also in a downtrend on the 3-minute stochastics.

   d. Even *better* if the ax is bidding and holding 15-period supports.

e. Even *better* if your stock is in a weak sector that hits a lower-resistance 5 band on a 3-minute moving averages chart when futures bounce and that makes new lows when futures slip back down again.

If you can have a combination of any of items a through e on the stochastics scalps or items a through e on the intraday swings, then the odds are more in your favor. Naturally, the best entry is when you can get a stock to meet all the above requirements before you enter. Make sure you meet at least two of the requirements prior to your respective entry. Remember this is a percentage game, and the more indicators you have in your favor, the better your percentages. Always make sure you are aware of the above criteria before you enter a stock. These criteria are fundamental, and you need to base the majority of your trading on them.

SHORTING NEWS STOCKS

Stocks that make strong moves on a news item are an excellent shorting opportunity. The main fundamental theme to remember on shorts is that volume is the lifeblood of momentum and price acceleration. Always check the average daily volume and then compare it with the current volume on the day of the overblown run-up. When volume dies, so does the stock.

Another constant that appears to be predictable is that end-of-the-day profit taking occurs on stocks that make big gains throughout the day. The logic is very simple in that most traders do not want to keep a position overnight. They want to end the day "flat," meaning all cash. These profit takers usually show up during the last 15 to 30 minutes of the trading day, depending on the market conditions. On the flip side, many buyers will also show up at the end of the day in anticipation of a "morning gap" (having a stock open higher than where it closed the prior day). Therefore, as a short, you are looking to gain from the profit takers and yet avoid the end-of-the-day morning gap players. This makes shorting more of an art than a science.

The question is, how does one gauge whether the profit takers will outnumber the morning gappers? The answer lies with the overall market indicators. As a rule of thumb, we like to take firm short positions slightly off the intraday highs on stocks when it appears that the market itself is either pulling back or going negative. This is usually enough for the traders to be panicked into locking in their profits for the day. Another, lesser, concern is based more on fundamentals: How old and how significant is the news that propelled the stock gains in the first place? Significance of news is a major factor that will convince a trader or investor to hold onto a stock in anticipation of further stock appreciation.

We feel that the best shorts are run-ups on biotech stocks based on research news, clinical findings, and FDA approvals. These biotech stocks will usually rocket up on news and sell off even faster when the profit takers come in. The reason traders are so quick to jump on and off biotech stocks is that news, while significant, will not affect the bottom line for months or years to come, and so the stock is usually considered dead money until revenues and profits are affected. For the record, GERN has always been a great hype gap on news and then shorts the open-type play. It rarely fails. GERN will usually base near the 9–11 range, and then some cancer cure press release will come out and gap the stock near 20 on the open. It will then fall back to the 12–14 range eventually as volume dies back down to normal range.

One example that comes to mind is a short we had on RBOT. This particular biotech company got FDA approval to market the world's first robotic arm used for invasive surgery. The stock immediately shot up from 7^1/$_2$ to 10 before slightly pulling back and trading in the range between 9^1/$_2$ and 10^1/$_2$. Later, CNBC's stock editor started talking about the FDA approval in greater detail throughout the day, causing the stock to gain more exposure and buyers to run the price up to the $12–$13 range. We stepped in with our short at $12 about 30 minutes before the end of the day. The stock made one last pop to $13 before the profit takers showed up in force near the last 5 minutes of the close, causing the stock to close at 11^1/$_2$. We decided to hold the short overnight, anticipating a sell-off instead of a gap due to the Dow closing in negative territory at −60, the S&P futures closing at −4, and more worries in the market over the Pacific Rim markets. The next morning the S&P futures were gapping down another 4 points, and sure enough most stocks followed the trend and gapped down on the open. We finally covered our short 3 minutes into the open at 10½ before the stock rallied to 11¼ and pulled back to close around 10. However, we felt that the negative market sentiment was enough to convince traders to lock in a profit off the open if there was no rally as anticipated, and there wasn't.

The basic principle is to position our short at or near the intraday high with a stochastics 90/100 band reversal. This tips the scales in our favor and gives us an advantage. We cannot stress enough that positioning is the key element in successful trading. One key point to remember is that as volume dies, so does the momentum, and that takes the price back down. We suggest that you go to www.yahoo.com to find the average daily volume in the stock. Normally, these run-up stocks are moving on momentum of over 10 to 20 times the average daily volume. Taking a short position in these stocks is not a bad idea so long as you know that the volume will eventually drop back down and so will the stock.

THE ANATOMY OF A SHORT SQUEEZE

Two words strike fear into the hearts of traders who take short positions in an overbought stock: short squeeze. For a trader who is long in a stock undergoing a short squeeze, it is a beautiful thing. Outrageous valuations, fad of the moment, and high short interest (usually by weak-handed amateur traders) are a deadly combination for shorts. A short squeeze occurs when a stock makes an unusually strong run, which brings in many skeptical shorts (traders who take short positions in anticipation of a pull-back), only to get stopped out, which adds to the buying momentum, taking the stock's price even higher. Usually the move seems like an overreaction, and this invites short sellers into the run. The danger arises when the run continues to extended higher highs as the initial shorts get panicked out of the initial positions. As the shorts take stops, this adds more buying momentum into the stock, taking the price to higher levels. The initial shorts realize that a short squeeze is brewing and will become converted longs, adding again to the buying pressure. As the stock continues to make new highs, more short sellers come, take positions, and get squeezed out. Let's not forget the day traders who come in and add major fuel to the fire, exaggerating the squeeze and often carrying it beyond comprehension. The market makers are very key in this. If the market makers also realize a short squeeze is in the works, they too will hold firm bids in an effort to squeeze more shorts out of their stops. It is quite an amazing phenomenon.

When a stock rises strongly on good news, a favorable play is to short at or near the intraday top and/or 52-week high since this is where we expect the profit takers to come in, especially on stocks where the actual fundamentals leave less to be desired. Market makers are aware of the shorts, and instead of jumping to lower bids as the profit takers sell their shares, the market makers (usually led by the ax) will jump to higher and higher bids, thereby pushing the stock higher. As the stock continues to rise fast, the undercapitalized shorts are forced to cover and try to reenter, at which time the market makers might continue to push the price higher since they are guaranteed that the shorts will take their shares off their hands at a handsome premium when they are eventually forced to cover. As mentioned, usually good news or an upgrade will spark a short squeeze, and this will usually happen with industries that are the fad of the moment. The Internet stocks were the fad of the moment from mid-1997 through 1998. Most Internet stocks had little revenues and negative earnings; however, their valuations were outrageous. Companies like YHOO and AMZN were being squeezed higher and higher and higher, following upgrades. The market makers were relentless in squeezing the shorts. The shorts were also relentless exiting and reentering their bids at a higher price, only to get squeezed higher. It was an amazing phenomenon on Level 2.

Another example: Earnings came out for MANU on March 27, 1998. MANU closed previously at 38 and opened up 8 points higher the next morning. The short interest was close to 30 percent of total float, the p/e ratio was 100, and B. T. Alex Brown

Brokerage upgraded the stock. Day traders were foaming at the mouth trying to short MANU. It felt like every day trader and her relative was shorting the stock—all the Internet threads had short, short, short! Hindsight almost always proves that the herd is wrong. MANU continued to run into the close that Friday, up 15 points to close at 53³/₁₆! The 52-week high was 47, and MANU had sailed past that with a vengeance. The ax market maker was Montgomery Securities, and he kept taking MANU higher and higher as the other market makers followed his lead. MANU continued to run to 57 two days later, and more and more shorts were forced to cover their positions.

A more recent example comes to mind on a stock called ISLD. ISLD was a recent IPO for which BEST was the lead and the ax. Normally ISLD traded to 28 on news stories and would then fizzle back down to the 22 range. Its trading pattern was predictable. This predictability was the downfall and death of the shorts. On Monday, October 25, 1999, ISLD issued a press release stating that it was purchasing Sandpiper Networks for $621 million in stock. This news normally should have caused ISLD to slip premarket, but instead ISLD gapped to near 28. The shorts naturally came in on the open, and ISLD pulled back near 26. Initially, it looked like a repeat of history. However, something very interesting happened. BEST and other market makers would not let ISLD fall under 26. In fact, once traders realized this, they started bidding it higher. This invited the ISLD (the ECN) boys to come in with size until ISLD cracked 30. The market makers held every pullback and continued to frustrate the shorts. ISLD continued to hold the wiggles to 2-point ranges and the bounces to new highs. The shorts were also fueling the bounces by covering the stock, buying it back, and trying to reshort higher. As a result, we anticipated an ISLD short squeeze and issued buy alerts in the low 30s into the close as the price squeezed to the highs of the day and closed near 38. The next morning, ISLD gapped and ran to close near 60 on continued short squeezing. The morning after that, ISLD gapped and ran to 75 on the blood of more shorts. Needless to say, a lot of shorts were slaughtered. What the shorts did not realize is that when ISLD bought Sandpiper, this put it in direct Tier 1 status as an upcoming IPO, AKAM, on Wednesday. This is what fueled the market makers and the longs as the shorts got creamed. We were told to short ISLD finally at 75 when the AKAM IPO came out. We anticipated that the longs would no longer hold interest in ISLD since all the momentum was in anticipation of AKAM, which gapped over $150 on the open. We scored up to 8-point gains on ISLD on the short. However, amateur shorts got creamed on the initial run-up. We will continue to see more short squeezes as more and more of the newbies try their hand at shorting. This is quite a paradigm.

As illustrated, short squeezes can last several hours to several days to several months. In fact, we would go so far as to say that the initial rise of the Tier 1 Internets of today—YHOO, AMZN, and EBAY—was the result of short squeezes in 1997–1998. Once the short squeeze is combined with firm institutional buying, there is simply no stopping the upward momentum. Many who attempted to short YHOO in the $50s can truly attest to that fact.

HOW TO SPOT A SHORT SQUEEZE

Spotting a short squeeze in time can be very lucrative. Most short squeezes start off with the obvious giant run-up on some kind of news or sympathy move. Usually, the stock will consecutively hit a high and pull back, thereby inviting shorts in on the tops and gathering more shorts as the stock pulls back. Even though the action may be fast and choppy, the wiggles are rather controlled and the supports are there. The stock will then enter a consolidation period, allowing for more shorts to come in and take positions as they gain confidence. It is at this point of consolidation that the squeeze can present itself. When a stock is consolidating, there is no real panic, as buyers and sellers are at a stalemate. Eventually, the buyers will come in spurts as the market makers hold firmer bids. Since this is a battle of wills (and *capital*!) between the longs and the shorts, you may see large ISLD size on both the bids and the asks. Both sides are trying to create knee-jerk buying or selling panics. Short squeezes will appear in the form of a breakout, many times filling the gap of the intraday high and forming a handle of new buyers on the price chart. Once the breakout occurs, weaker shorts are panicked into covering, which adds momentum to the fast price acceleration. The key to a strong short squeeze is support. Pops on breakouts will occur and settle in the form of a wiggle. When the market makers or strong ISLD boys come in at the point of the wiggle and hold with size is when more buyers come off the fence and also more shorts come off the fence to cover. Every wiggle is met just under a momentum tick with ISLD boy size or firm market makers not allowing any more pullback. Eventually as more and more traders realize that the stock is not pulling back, they jump right in. ISLD boys attract more ISLD boys. The buying pops become stronger as the short squeeze is full blown. On a 3-minute chart, short squeezes are usually shown with a very firm and steady uptrend even though the Level 2 may be choppy and all over the screen.

So remember, this is the recipe for a short squeeze:

1. Market makers have to hold firm price levels on wiggles.
2. Size (ISLD boys) needs to step in with strong bids at the point of recoil.
3. Traders need to panic and buy.
4. Shorts cover.

Short squeezes can extend to several days, as was the case with ISLD. If you thought intraday was vicious for the poor shorts, the premarket gapping on short-squeeze stocks is amazing, to say the least. Due to the smaller liquidity in the premarket, you will get outrageous gaps in an effort to continue to squeeze shorts out in a panic.

AFTERMARKET SHORT SQUEEZE

What happened to ADSP is another variation on a very strong short squeeze. We discovered ADSP early premarket on November 24, 1999, and issued a trade alert to buy at $5^1/8$ premarket near 9:10 a.m. EST. Since this was the day before Thanksgiving, much of Wall Street was off, and this allowed for the ISLD boys and loose market makers to let many stocks fly. This was the case with ADSP, as it reached our $10 target by late morning on momentum and then blew through to a $13 1/2 intraday high. It then fizzled and closed near 10 9/16. By all accounts, ADSP was pretty much a done stock play. The average volume on ADSP was under 300,000 shares, and it had hit over 13 million that day. Many amateurs were shorting the stock above 10 with the understanding that as the volume died, so too would the stock. It was a good bet.

The clincher was after-hours. The volume skyrocketed to over 14 million after-hours as heavy ISLD boys came in and placed massive bidding pressure, pushing the stock to 19. Apparently, this brought in more shorts. After Thanksgiving, while most traders were gone for the day, the ISLD boys gapped ADSP to 30 premarket. Many took profits on the open where it pulled back to 20. At this point, the market makers held firm and the ISLD boys came in with size. What happened next was an amazing short squeeze!

ADSP ran from 21 to 27 1/2 (where we called a buy alert) and squeezed to 57! The shorts were getting destroyed left and right as a 60,000-share ISLD bid came in on the momentum ticks to stop any profit-taking pullback dead in its tracks. It was quite an astonishing phenomenon. Finally, the stock pulled back from 57 to the mid-30s, where it consolidated and closed for the day.

The irony of this particular short squeeze was that it started strong in the after-hours and premarket and continued after the initial cup and handle formation on the open. This was one very powerful short squeeze. The total volume on ADSP on November 26, 1999, was over 50 million!

There was not much liquidity in the aftermarket on Wednesday. Therefore, the ISLD boys who took a chance with big blocks after-hours were taking a risk, but not a very formidable risk because really no one could hit there for the 16,000-share bids since the market makers went home. This allowed them to control the aftermarket and thus build up the momentum needed on Friday. The reality is that even if you had shares, you would not dare sell into a 16,000-share bidder but rather wait for the next morning to see what would unfold.

STRADDLES AND BOXING YOUR POSITION: A SHORT'S DEFENSE

One of the key defenses a short player can employ is the straddle. A straddle consists of having two opposite positions in the same stock simultaneously. For example, having both a 1000-share short position in ORCL at $31^1/_{16}$ and a 1000-share long position at 31 is considered a straddle. You are basically playing both sides of the trade, locking in your profit or loss with your second position and most importantly becoming immune to volatility.

A straddle allows you to box in your loss or gain on any position and stay protected in a period of chaos and wild momentum. If you are caught in a short that runs and you still feel the short is viable, you may consider taking a matching long position in another account (straddles require two accounts) to limit any more downside.

We like to use straddles as a defensive measure to buy us time and shield us from market maker shakeouts and noise. When there is a tremendous amount of volatility and no clear direction of a trend, it is wise to lock in profits or losses with a straddle position. We like to play straddles on stocks with high volatility and bigger-than-normal point swings. When a trade turns against us in a volatile panic situation and yet we instinctively feel that the trend will turn shortly, we will often consider a straddle position.

For example, let's assume we are playing JBIL, which is trading right at or near its intraday low and down $3^1/_2$ points for the day on no news. We have been watching the ax (GSCO— Goldman Sachs) continue to head-fake traders all morning, taking the stock to new lows regularly. It appears to be a falling knife. However, we notice that the sell-off seems to be slowing down and building some support at $30^5/_8$, which happens to be just $^1/_8$ above the intraday low of $30^1/_2$. The 3-minute chart is starting to bottom, but it's too early to tell. We are stepping ahead of the consolidation, looking for an early bounce. The stochastics is also under the 20 band. We want to play the long side, but we want to protect ourselves against continued selling. In this instance, we are looking to box our long position with a short, much like a market maker would. Let's assume we take a long position at 30⅝ since the 1-minute stochastics is riding the zero band and looking to reverse. Just as we get filled, GSCO steps inside big at ⅝.

JBIL	B:30-5/8			A: 30-3/4 N: -7/8			VOL: 324,500	
MMID	BID	SIZE	TIME	MMID	BID	SIZE	TIME
GSCO	**30-5/8**	**10**	**15:02**	INCA	30-3/4	10	15:02
MSCO	30-5/8	10	15:02	INCA	30-3/4	10:	15:01
PWJC	30-1/2	5	15:01	PWJC	30-7/8	10	15:01
ISLD	30-7/16	15	15:00	SALB	30-15/16	5	14:18
BEST	30-1/4	10	14:45	FBCO	30-15/16	10	14:15
MONT	30-1/8	10	14:38	MSCO	31	10	14:14
HMQT	30-1/8	10	14:35	**GSCO**	**31**	**5**	**15:01**
NAWE	30-1/8	10	14:29	MONT	31	2	15:15
FBCO	30-1/8	10	15:01	BEST	31-1/4	15	13:25
MASH	30-1/16	10	14:25	MASH	31-3/8	10	15:10
LEHM	30-1/16	5	14:20	HMQT	31-1/2	10	15:05
NITE	30	10	14:45	NAWE	31-1/2	10	14:56
DEAN	30	10	13:25	LEHM	32	5	14:10

We figure that JBIL is oversold and due for a bounce, and we are anticipating the bargain hunters. Even nicer, we see GSCO upticking to 30⅝ best bid. All looks good as the buyers start to come back into JBIL, taking positions at 30¾. In fact, we notice an inordinate about of buys at the ask at 30¾, and GSCO is just sitting there with a 10 size. Something fishy is going on here. Suddenly, we notice that GSCO has dropped his best price to 29½ and jumped to 30¾ on the ask! GSCO head-faked us and is planning to take JBIL lower! Anticipating a pullback, we short 1000 shares of JBIL (preferably in another account) at ¹¹/₁₆ and now hold a simultaneous 1000-share long position at 30⅝ and a 1000-share short position at 30¹¹/₁₆. Remember, we anticipated another pullback, *but* we also feel that JBIL can't pull back too much more and will most likely bounce strong. With these convictions, we take the straddle position not only as a means of defense, but also as a way to profit from playing both the long and the short side, profiting from the volatility.

JBIL	B:30-9/16		A: 30-11/16	N: -15/16		VOL: 332,500		
	MMID	BID	SIZE	TIME	MMID	BID	SIZE	TIME
	MSCO	30-9/16	10	15:03	ISLD	30-11/16	10	15:03*
	HMQT	30-1/2	10	15:02	**GSCO**	**30-3/4**	**10**	**15:03****
	PWJC	30-1/2	5	15:01	PWJC	30-7/8	10	15:01
	ISLD	30-7/16	15	15:00	SALB	30-15/16	5	14:18
	BEST	30-1/4	10	14:45	FBCO	30-15/16	10	14:15
	MONT	30-1/8	10	14:38	MSCO	31	10	14:14
	HMQT	30-1/8	10	14:35	GSCO	31	5	15:01
	NAWE	30-1/8	10	14:29	MONT	31	2	15:15
	FBCO	30-1/8	10	15:01	BEST	31-1/4	15	13:25
	MASH	30-1/16	10	14:25	MASH	31-3/8	10	15:10
	LEHM	30-1/16	5	14:20	HMQT	31-1/2	10	15:05
	NITE	30	10	14:45	NAWE	31-1/2	10	14:56
	GSCO	**29-1/2**	**10**	**15:03**	LEHM	32	5	14:10

*We step inside ask to short

**GSCO wants to take this lower

Just as we anticipated, GSCO takes the ask lower, dropping it to $3/4$. At this point, we are only going to concentrate on finding the bottom and covering our short for a profit. Let's assume the stock quickly downticks to $30^{1}/_4$ before coiling. Our time of sales screen shows a string of buyers coming in at $30^{5}/_{16}$, quickly upticking the ask to 3/8. GSCO chases the bid to $5/_{16}$, and several other market makers follow suit. We quickly cover our short at $30^{3}/_8$ for a $5/_{16}$ profit on the short side and concentrate on closing out our long position on this short-term bounce. INCA now jumps on the best bid with a 50 size. Traders take notice and realize that a bottom has been reached, and they raid the time of sales screen with a flurry of buys, taking the price up to $30^{7}/_8 \times {}^{15}/_{16}$.

We see that GSCO is still sitting at the 31 ask and $30^{3}/_4$ bid and notice a lot of resistance at 31 (four market makers). At this point, we realize that there is still buying strength but will not take the chance for the round-number momentum tick to hold. Instead, we decide to take advantage of this and place a limit sell order at the ${}^{15}/_{16}$ ask and get taken out shortly thereafter for a $5/_{16}$ profit on the long side.

JBIL	B:30-7/8		A: 30-15/16	N: -11/16		VOL: 343,500		
	MMID	BID	SIZE	TIME	MMID	BID	SIZE	TIME
	INCA	30-7/8	50	15:04	ISLD	30-15/16	10	15:04
	GSCO	**30-7/8**	**10**	15:04	**GSCO**	**31**	**10**	**15:03**
	PWJC	30-13/16	5	15:01	PWJC	31	10	15:02
	ISLD	30-11/16	15	15:00	SALB	31	10	15:02
	BEST	30-5/8	10	14:45	FBCO	31	10	15:00
	MONT	30-5/8	10	14:38	MSCO	31-1/8	10	14:14
	HMQT	30-1/2	10	14:35	INCA	31-1/4	5	15:01
	NAWE	30-1/8	10	14:29	MONT	31	2	15:15
	FBCO	30-1/8	10	15:01	BEST	31-1/4	15	13:25
	MASH	30-1/16	10	14:25	MASH	31-3/8	10	15:10
	LEHM	30-1/16	5	14:20	HMQT	31-1/2	10	15:05
	NITE	30	10	14:45	NAWE	31-1/2	10	14:56
	DEAN	30	10	13:25	LEHM	32	5	14:10

Not only did our straddle protect us from the volatility, but it bought us enough time to be able to sit back, think rationally (not panic), and watch the action with a level head (since we could not lose any money until we covered or sold) before we implemented our attack. Most importantly, the straddle helped us scalp $+5/8$ on a very volatile stock and protected us from being shaken out. This is a very small scale example of using a straddle. Had you been one of the unfortunate shorts in ISLD on the short squeeze from 31 to 75, you would have held the straddle perhaps for several days and scalped in between to recover locked losses. Specifically in the ISLD short squeeze, you would have been able to lock in a limited loss until ISLD definitely broke down on the 3-minute charts. When AKAM finally IPOed, ISLD started to sell off. Therefore, a straddle would have given you the luxury of being able to stop the bleeding long enough to wait for an obvious trend and then unlock the long and ride the short down.

In addition to being a defense against a short squeeze, a straddle is a wonderful tool to employ when trading momentum madness stocks. Many traders may think that *boxing* (also known as *straddling*) is a waste since you could have taken a stop just as well without tying up capital. And if it comes to just scalps, we agree—you should take the stop. However, we have to assume a few things. You cannot short a downtick, so if a stock tops out and starts to tank, then you cannot get the short because you need an uptick. You miss your entry if you stop out on a short looking to reenter higher. You also have to get perfect fills, and the wiggles can be murder, resulting in many blown stops on momentum stocks. Also understand that momentum is often a knee-jerk reaction and eventually the trend always emerges. At some point during the day, the trend is obvious. The problem is that when the trend is so obvious, entry may be a problem. This is where the utility of the straddle or box comes in. The boxed position allows you to bide your time. It allows you to wait until the trend or momentum becomes blatantly apparent, at which time you can unlock your box on the other side. Remember, every battle is won before it is ever fought. This can be analogized in trading to explain that your entry price is key. Your positioning on the entry can often mean a winning or losing trade. Using straddles affords you the luxury of picking the right entry on the short or long without having to worry about a missed fill.

In summary, the straddle or boxed position allows you to:

1. Limit downside in any trend because your gain or loss is locked.
2. Short the downticks, because you already own the position and by selling the long you activate your short.
3. Bide you time for the obvious momentum or trend to emerge, at which point you can unlock one side of the box to ride for gains.

Market makers straddle spreads to limit risk and maximize gains. There are so many variations on the straddle, such as taking odd lots to favor a trend (long or short), boxing to lock in profits as a hedge, and boxing to scalp and rebox like a market maker. The best advice we can give you when you are boxing a position is to get the short position first since you need the uptick, and then box the long position and look to lock in as little a spread as you can.

CHAPTER 11

Playing Momentum Stocks on the Fly

The highest level of day trading is the ability to play momentum stocks on the fly as they hit your radar. The buy and sell criteria mentioned in previous chapters apply to basket stocks and stocks that you are familiar with. However, momentum is like a loose fire hose with water gushing out full speed. It is wild and often unpredictable when you first encounter it. The runs are often extended. The basic rules of safety in the form of the criteria we mentioned are literally thrown out the window. This is what makes momentum on the fly so dangerous and risky, but oh so rewarding! This is the most exciting and usually the most lucrative form of day trading. However, you must never forget that risk is proportionate to reward. This form of day trading is also the most risky form of day trading.

All too often, traders dive straight into momentum-based day trading and assume this is the only form of day trading—as they get destroyed in the process. Let's drive this point home: You must be able to identify with the rhythms of at least 30 different stocks; master order routing like the back of your hand; be absolutely fluent with the 1-minute stochastics chart, 3-minute moving averages chart, and tier synergy; use the futures on a 3-minute stochastics chart religiously; and have *experience* with all the aforementioned tools.

The toughest part of momentum trading is being able to interpret moves on the fly and make lightning-quick decisions on entry and exit. You need the ability to distinguish between a wiggle and a trend reversal on the fly, and you need to have the skills to order-route effectively to minimize losses and maximize gains.

Whenever you first encounter a stock, it is like trying to interpret a painting that has yet to be painted. It is a matter of filling in the canvas, letting the image materialize. The more you get to know the stock, the more the lines and the color start to come through. The details, the contours, the shades start to fill in, and eventually the picture evolves on the canvas into an image—a readable, viewable image. When you step back, you can see the painting. This is the same thing you are accomplishing when trying to familiarize yourself with a stock. The more you watch and interpret, the clearer the image becomes. With momentum stocks, you do not have that luxury when you play them on the fly the first time. You have to go with what you know about momentum and rhythm and, it is hoped, some past experience with a similar type of momentum play. The safest way to play momentum on the fly is for scalps. The scalps can be large if played right.

GAUGING RHYTHM

One of the key characteristics that successful momentum day traders have is the ability to sense and interpret a wide variety of rhythms. *Rhythm* can be defined as the flow of the spreads on the Nasdaq Level 2 when volume rises, which dictates the speed of the upticks and downticks. *Usually, thinner-float stocks have faster rhythms, and thicker-float stocks have slower rhythms.* Thin-float stocks are considered to have less than 10 million shares. There is one more element to rhythm in addition to the float, and that is the price of a stock. *Usually, the higher priced a stock is, the faster its rhythm speeds up.* A nice example of this is EGRP. In October 1998 EGRP was trading as low as $12 a share with an 11 million share float, which is not necessarily thin by definition. At these low prices, EGRP spreads rarely strayed from $1/16$ between the bid and the ask. It also took tremendous volume to uptick the stock. However, as institutional buying came into EGRP, raising it to the $30 range, traders noticed that the upticks took much less volume as the spreads started to widen. When EGRP propelled to the $50–$60 range, the stock moved much faster on the same float, usually upticking with only a handful of trades in the several thousand share range. The spreads varied from $1/8$ to $3/4$ points when volume came in. When EGRP ran into the $80s going into the split, the spreads averaged $1/4$ to 1 point, and the stock would uptick with the change of the wind (just an expression of how easily it moved on little volume). This is a great illustration of how even a not-so-thin-float stock can move much faster on the same volume at much faster rhythms at higher price levels.

Therefore, a stock that is both thin and high priced will have the fastest rhythm. The higher the price rises, the thinner the rhythm, which adds more momentum to the upside. *A side note:* When overzealous shorts come into the picture underestimating the thinness of these little monsters, they get squeezed very hard, which continues to add to the upward momentum as they eventually cover their plays with great losses. This is a very interesting phenomenon, as anyone who has seen stocks like PHCM rise from $56 to $298 in a matter of weeks can see. In fact, thin stocks with fast rhythm can usually move 5 to 15 points on a volume of a mere few hundred thousand shares. This is both lucrative and dangerous. Risk is very much indeed proportionate to reward.

Another example comes to mind. SILK (a Nasdaq stock) was trading in the $30s in September 1999. If you take a look at the chart, you can see the great ascent it took into the $90 range, often rising 5 to 10 points on volume under 400,000 shares a day. The spreads of the stock usually averaged $1/2$ to $1 1/2$ points during the climb. These momentum stocks are very glamorous to the casual onlookers, who usually kick themselves for not getting on board.

There are also other stocks that have a fast rhythm even with a thick float. These are stocks that used to have a thin float, and market makers usually display the minimum tier size requirements. By all definitions, these stocks should not be so thin, but it is as if the market makers continue to believe the stock is thin and thereby set the minimum tier size requirements on the stock to lend credence to the thinness. Our best explanation is that perhaps the institutional ownership is so high that what small amount of shares is out there trading hands makes the stock a thin mover. Take a look for yourself at stocks like SEBL, AMCC, MCHP, LLTC, and LVLT.

RECOGNIZING RHYTHMS

We are going to take a shot at attempting to explain a phenomenon that most momentum players understand intuitively. That is rhythm patterns. Assuming you have understood everything we have covered in the previous chapters, we will apply that knowledge here.

A typical example of a rhythm pattern on a thin mover is round-number break, uptick to $1/4 \times 5/16$ exhaustion, pause, wiggle back under the round number to $1/2$ support on a wide spread, pause, spreads tighten and then a bounce recoil, retest through round number, break $1/4$-tick exhaustion break point, break $1/2$ tick on volume, and break to the next round number. Once again this is a literal description of a rhythm that traders usually understand intuitively.

Let's break this down and use an example of ADBE (on the Nasdaq) as it traded in the month of September (ADBE has since split 2 for 1). ADBE had a float of approximately 52 million shares (presplit) in September. Before ever playing a thin mover, you should always be familiar with the rhythm. If you had watched ADBE's rhythm, you would have seen the aforementioned pattern every time it would break a new rounder number intraday as it uptrended.

Let's take an example with ADBE priced at $92^1/4 \times 92^1/2$. Since $1/2$ is a momentum tick, we watch as the buyers come in and market makers uptick as the $1/2$ tick quickly disappears. The next momentum tick is the $3/4$ tick, and so on. When ADBE hits *93 (round-number break)*, this triggers strong buying because it is a round-number momentum and the most powerful and liquid tick, allowing the 93 to get eaten up in a matter of seconds. ADBE quickly upticks to the $93^1/_{16} \times 93^1/_4$ momentum tick where you see market makers trying to sell the teenies just above $93^1/_4$ at $^5/_{16}$. Interestingly, the buying is not strong enough to take out the *93¹/₄ tick* as the $^5/_{16}$ gets more sellers (*exhaustion*). At this point, the fast upward momentum takes a *pause*. ADBE starts thinning out at the bid at $93^1/_{16}$, and *93 bidders* disappear as ADBE quickly starts downticking to $93 \times 93^1/_4$, $93 \times 93^1/_{16}$, $92^3/_4 \times 93^1/_{16}$, $92^1/_2 \times 93$, $92^1/_2 \times 92^7/_8$ (*wiggle*), and profit takers and panic buyers turn into panic sellers who panic the stock to the *92¹/₂ bid (support point)*. The spread is now $92^1/_2 \times 92^7/_8$, and there is a *pause* as the selling depletes at $92^1/_2$. The spread is *wide* because market makers do not take unnecessary risks. The wide spread is a means of defending oneself. When there are no more sellers at the bid on the widened spread, then a short-term bottom is made. Suddenly, the *spread tightens* again as bidders come back—$92^5/_8$, $92^3/_4 \times 92^7/_8$ (*coil bounce*). Buyers come back in, taking out the 93 (*retest round number of volume*) tick again as the stock once again returns fast to $93 \times 93^1/_4$. This time $93^1/_4$ (*exhaustion break point*) is taken out by buyers as the stock bulldozes through onto the $93^1/_2$ momentum tick, to the $93^3/_4$ momentum tick, and finally through the *94 (round-number break)* momentum tick. Once again it hits an exhaustion point at $94^1/_2$, pulls back, and repeats the rhythm pattern.

We can break this rhythm down to:

1. Round-number break
2. Exhaustion at the teeny ($^1/_{16}$ above a $^1/_4$ momentum tick)
3. Pause (bidders thin out and ask sellers thicken on Level 2)
4. Wiggle (back under round number)
5. Support (usually on a momentum tick)
6. Pause (spread between the bid support and ask is wide)
7. Spread tightens (on the bid side)
8. Coil bounce back through round number
9. Retest round number of volume
10. Exhaustion break point
11. Repeat steps 1–10 on the next round-number break

This rhythm can account for the majority of the thin-float runners. The benefit of knowing this rhythm is that you can anticipate a better entry point and keep yourself from getting wiggled out at the wrong moment. It is rather sad that when the members of the "crowd" see a round-number break, they automatically jump into a stock and take the move out of context. Usually, we find that when the short-term momentum goes from panic buying at the round-number tick to panic selling at the exhaustion point, the traders in the thick of it are the profit takers from the earlier exhaustion point break and the same panic buyers now trying to take a stop. Initially, many will have the stomach for a $1/4$ wiggle until it turns into a $1/2$ wiggle, and then they cry uncle in a mad dash to get out. It is just when the last weak trader is shaken out that the stock hits the momentum support and recoils and bounces. (We like to use the term *recoil* to describe what happens when a stock bounces from a wiggle. Like a spring that is stretched out and then squeezed back, the spring is coiling. When a spring coils, it is gathering momentum and stretches back harder and faster. This applies to stocks in the same sense.) When we hear traders stating, "Darn, now that I am out of this stock, it will probably go up," it does. This is the "crowd"—the silent majority of day traders who lose in the markets.

Familiarizing yourself with the rhythm allows you to sit back on the round-number breaks and wait for the stock to wiggle back to its support point before you reenter, usually at the expense of overzealous weak day traders. It also prevents you from making knee-jerk reaction moves at the round-number tick. When a stock is toppy on the stochastics, it also allows you to anticipate shorts at the exhaustion points for quick scalps on the wiggles. Most importantly, it puts *you* in control, rather than your emotions, as you have a map to anticipate the short term moves.

CHAPTER 12

The Market Day Breakdown

The equities markets are technically open from 9:30 a.m. to 4:00 p.m. EST. This is what the public believes, and that is fine and dandy. However, we must also consider premarket from 8:15 a.m. to 9:29 a.m. EST and postmarket from 4:01 p.m. to 6:00 p.m. EST. The premarket and postmarket trading occurs (as of this writing) on ECNs only. Market makers cannot be hit outside of regular market hours on SelectNet. For day traders, the markets are technically open from 8:15 a.m. to 6 p.m. EST. During these hours, there are peak times to make money and weak times to lose money. The following is a quick breakdown and description of the period.

8:15–9:29 A.M. EST—PREMARKET

ISLD and most other ECNs open at 8:15 a.m. for most brokers. This is usually the time that the gaps start to form on stocks. This session is very illiquid, as only the ECNs are active. Spreads can be and usually are very wide and move frantically on stocks with news or momentum. Market makers *cannot* be hit during this time period. The biggest danger we see in the premarket period comes from market makers who will uptick their bid premarket, implying a gap in a stock, only to be selling at a discount on the ask through an ECN like INCA. Market makers can do this since they cannot be hit premarket on SelectNet. This allows them to post outrageous bids, tricking amateur traders into thinking they are getting

159

an arbitrage opportunity as they buy from INCA on the ask and then realize they cannot hit the market maker on the bid. For example, let's assume IVIL closed at 28 the night prior. RAMS may be bidding 30 premarket, while the INCA and ISLD ask is 29. An uneducated day trader might buy from ISLD at 29 and think he has gotten a bargain since RAMS is bidding 30. Little does he know that he can't sell to RAMS premarket. Ouch! This has hurt many a day trader as they learn the hard way that market makers cannot be hit premarket. The only bids and asks that matter are the ECNs, and usually they are ISLD, INCA, REDI, and ARCA. Have we made that point clear?

A nice advantage during premarket is that there is no uptick rule for shorting since you are shorting through ECNs. In other words, you can short the inside ECN bid premarket. There is no requirement that you have to short on the ask. This makes things very convenient if you are positive that a stock is moving lower. Premarket is more of a sellers' market. In other words, the odds are in the hands of the sellers that have taken overnight shares and are looking to sell the premarket gaps. We do not prefer to buy much stock premarket because of this. If a stock is gapping, then chances are it will pull back on the open, and we prefer to wait until then. Finally, premarket is also the time to watch how the S&P futures are trading. If the futures are gapping above fair value, then stocks should be gapping, and vice versa.

9:30–10:00 A.M. EST—THE OPEN

The market open at 9:30–10:00 a.m. EST is the most fertile, risky, rewarding, and opportune time of the day. This is pure momentum as traders and market makers look to establish ranges in respective stocks. During this feeling-out period, there is a sense of orderly chaos that allows stocks to exaggerate either way, and price volatility is at a peak. Market makers are also very lenient as they try to get a feel for the trading ranges of their particular stocks. It is in this time span that good traders can often make their daily profit targets, albeit that this is the riskiest time to play also. Since the action is so fast on the open, you must make sure that you have the capacity to play the action without locking up your computer system. Make sure you have a true day trading broker. The riskiest aspect of playing the open is that there is no historical intraday data. This means you must play the momentum on the fly. Remember, use the open only for scalps, and always use the futures (S&P 500 and Nasdaq 100) on a 3-minute stochastics chart as your lead indicator. If played right, a good day trader will make her daily profit target during the open.

The open can be broken down into three basic patterns from the opening bell:

- Strength open—buying, buying, buying, *peak*, profit-taking selling, selling

  We usually see this scenario when the S&P futures are gapping above fair value, causing stocks to also gap premarket. The S&P futures usually hit the ground running on the open, lifting the market and causing stocks to continue to run higher on the open until they peak, at which point the profit takers sell off the stocks. Usually, stocks will pull back, base, and then try to fill the gap again. If a stock cannot fill the gap, then it will trade lower or try to consolidate before breaking out or breaking down. Strength opens are not particularly our favorite types of open since most stocks are already gapping from a strong premarket S&P futures, meaning that stocks will open overextended and continue to overextend on initial strength before giving back—they're like a rubber band that gets to a breaking point and continues to get stretched until it snaps back. Usually, strength days are fruitless for day traders since stocks tend to gap strong premarket, make an extended move on the open, peak, sell off on profit taking, and then stay range-bound for the majority of the trading day. Dow+200 days are simply fruitless for the most part. Day traders need volatility and momentum. Pure strength days do not provide this. Usually the futures will run and ride the 90/100 band on the 3-minute stochastics for the full open period.

- Gap and trap open—profit-taking selling, selling, selling, support, coil, bounce, gap fill

This scenario happens when the S&P futures gap over fair value, causing stocks to also gap (like a strength open). This scenario also can happen when the S&P futures are negative and under fair value, causing stocks to gap down (rather than up). Gap and trap opens give the illusion of the opposite of what actually occurs. In other words, expect reversals from the premarket trend initially. Rather than seeing continued strength (on gap up S&P futures) or weakness (on gap down S&P futures) on the open and more buying, we see a reversal from the get-go. Therefore the name gap implies stocks pricing higher than the previous closing price, giving the illusion of continued rally strength on the open or continued selling pressure only to reverse direction and in essence trap any overzealous traders who jumped in on the open anticipating continued buying, and vice versa in the S&P futures gap-down scenario which traps the shorts. These are the worst times, as you can feel like a real sucker getting head-faked on a large scale. The best way to avoid getting burned is to start each day assuming that all gaps will trap on the open and wait for the reversal. This will allow you to anticipate and not be too quick to jump in, but rather wait for the pullback and avoid getting stuck. Should buying continue on the open rather than profit taking, then you can play it like a strength open. Gap and traps usually start off with profit taking from the start. You may get some buyers that come in, but they are soon overwhelmed by sellers and in essence trapped as panic selling kicks in. You will want to wait for selling to slow down, as many stocks will do a fast reversal and head back toward the initial opening high. This, as noted earlier in the book, is called filling the gap, and that is the best time to enter a stock on a gap and trap open for the momentum scalp. As we also mentioned earlier on filling the gap, the profit takers are out and new buyers are coming in. As a stock breaks its initial opening price, a mini cup and handle formation is formed, causing more new buyers to come in on the breakout and taking the stock to a higher peak. Usually the futures will reverse first, so keep your eyes on them.

- Weak open—selling, selling, bottom, coil, bounce, buying, peak, selling, selling,

  This scenario explains itself, as the S&P futures will usually gap below fair value, causing stocks to gap down premarket. Selling will come in right on the open and continue to take prices lower. Eventually, the first wave of selling will cease, and stocks will try to bottom, coil, and bounce back up. The buyers on the bounce are usually met with more sellers right into their buying as stocks will make a short-lived peak on the bounce and reverse, going lower. These weak opens are usually characterized by a futures sell-off on the open and continued selling into any reversal attempts on the 3-minute stochastics, causing them to stay in the 0–20 band range for the majority of the open period.

The open is the most significant trading period of the day. It frequently sets the tone of the trading day. Usually a stock's intraday high and low are established on the open and therefore create the intraday parameters too. The open is also the easiest trend to play. Many times the ax's motives will be transparent on the open. Keep in mind that usually when a stock runs on the open, it will hit an intraday high, pull back, and perhaps hit an intraday low. Depending on the "legs," one can usually play the open's strength.

In especially tough, jiggly markets, a simple $1/8$-point mental stop is not enough. Safety is the major concern when trading, and there is only safety when there is a definite trend that is taking the stock into uncharted territory at the beginning of the day.

Keep in mind that market makers only make money when there is action—volume. When the volume tends to slow down, market makers tend to cause panic selling or buying through jiggles and head fakes.

If we can measure a short-term top or bottom in a stock, we can theoretically always make money. We include the qualifying words *short term* because bottoms and tops are usually short-lived phenomenon resulting in a trend reversal. Even if we can't catch the absolute top or bottom, it pays handsomely to be close. We are not out for home runs. We take safety into consideration and go for the singles and doubles as we get them. Not all tops and bottoms for a particular stock intraday are the same. Usually, the most evident and powerful tops and bottoms are the first, and they are often present right from the open. A stock will usually run or fall from the open and in essence make its first top or bottom. We always like to play the initial run. We usually prefer finding a top right off the bat since a stock often has a reason to pull back (profit takers), and we can profit from that essential phenomenon. People don't necessarily have to buy a stock, but once a stock is purchased, a sell is inevitable and can't be denied, and therefore shorting the tops is oftentimes easier (in our opinions) than buying into a bottom. We utilize Level 2, time of sales, and most important the 1-minute stochastics chart. We like to qualify short-term bottoms and tops in two categories: finding the initial bottom on the open and finding the initial top on the open.

FINDING THE INITIAL BOTTOM ON THE OPEN:

1. Watch the time of sales and Level 2 screen on the open (9:30 a.m. EST).

2. Highlight the ax and observe where he goes.

3. As the stock continues to fall, you will notice all the market makers rapidly jumping to a lower bid. You might even notice the ax sitting on the best ask, driving it lower.

4. Eventually, selling will subside, and the inside bid and ask spread will widen, signaling a pause.

5. At this point, the trades on time of sales (usually all sellers) will slow, and you will see a trade in between the bid and ask. This will signal a *bottom*.

6. On the Level 2, you probably will see a market maker tighten the spread on the bid side (usually the ax). At this point, the ax might switch to the inside bid, and other market makers will follow him, adding depth and support to that inside bid price.

7. *Your 1-minute stochastics should dip below the 20 band and preferably touch the 0 band and reverse.*

8. Time of sales should show straight buyers coming in at the ask, driving the stock price higher.

9. New buyers come in to fill the gap.

10. The point at which the gap fills (high of the day breaks) is the safest entry point.

The reverse applies when trying to find the initial top.

FINDING THE INITIAL TOP ON THE OPEN:

1. Watch the time of sales and Level 2 screen on the open (9:30 a.m. EST).

2. Highlight the ax and observe where he goes.

3. As the stock continues to rise, you will notice all the market makers rapidly jumping to a higher bid. You might even notice the ax sitting on the best bid, driving it higher.

4. Eventually, buying will subside, and the inside bid and ask spread will widen, signaling a pause.

5. At this point, the trades on time of sales (usually all buyers) will slow down, and you will see a trade in between the bid and ask. This will signal a *top*.

6. On the Level 2, you probably will see a market maker tighten the spread on the ask side (usually the ax). At this point, the ax may switch to the inside ask, and other market makers will join him, adding depth and support to the inside ask price.

7. *Your 1-minute stochastics should break through the 80 band and preferably touch the 100 band before reversing.* Usually, this is the prime time to place a short.

8. Time of sales should show straight sellers coming in at the bid, driving the stock price lower.

9. More sellers come in to load the ask.

Throughout the day, you should be using the stochastics indicator to determine the short-term tops and bottoms utilized by your parameter bands. Again, we like to use the 20 and 80 bands for buy and sell/short signals. However, should the stochastics oscillators hit the 0 or 100 bands, we gladly take the opportunity to pull the trigger on the first sign of a reversal.

Always watch the ax and his movements. Always observe whether he is real or not in his positions, and keep an eye open for block trades, which usually will signal a short-term trend reversal.

Since no system is perfect, we like to make sure that our indicators prove to us that the scales are tipped in our favor before we make the trade. Should there be a divergence in the evidence, then we usually hold our trigger until the opportunity becomes more appealing.

The following indicators are what we use in deciding to go long on a short-term bottom:

1. Stochastics oscillator just dropped below the 20 band and is now reversing, about to recross the 20 band on the way up. The zero band reversal is the best.

2. Level 2 shows the ax increasing his inside bid offer (usually indicated with a "+" next to his name) on some datafeeds.

3. Time of sales shows steady buyers coming in rapidly at the ask.

The following indicators are what we use in deciding to go short on a short-term top:

1. Stochastics oscillator crossed above the 80 band and is now reversing, about to cross below the 80 band. The 100 band reversal is the best.

2. Level 2 shows the ax on the ask taking his offer down (usually indicated with a "−" sign next to his name) on some datafeeds.

3. Time of sales shows steady sellers at the inside bid.

The above indicators are a very simple breakdown of our analysis. Many times, the stochastics might indicate we go long on a trend reversal that follows the short-term bottom. However, Level 2 will show the ax on the inside ask selling. This is where we either wait for our indicators to support each other or take a shot based on our knowledge of the ax's movements and our experience in trading the underlying security.

10:01–11:30 A.M. EST—POSTOPEN

The postopen period is when the initial frenzy momentum that began at the open starts to slow down and stocks start to establish their early ranges. Market makers and traders are more comfortable. Most stocks have established the initial high and low trading ranges. Stocks take a breather, and consolidation patterns start to form. We refer to consolidation a number of times in this book. Imagine a stock to be a bridge made of rope suspended between two mountain peaks and dangling 300 feet in the air. Playing the momentum on the open on any stock is like trying to cross that bridge. It can snap at any moment. There is no stability. As a stock trades past 10:00 a.m., the trading range begins to slow down and clarity sets in. The longer a stock consolidates, you can assume the stronger that bridge becomes. Stability becomes clearer. The stronger the bridge becomes, you can assume the safer it is to cross. This is nice analogy of playing the open versus playing the postopen. The postopen is less risky than the open, and for safety's sake, new traders should consider only watching the open and playing the postopen. The postopen is usually the time to look for the consolidations that we speak of. When these consolidations break (either up or down), this is a good time to lock in intraday swing positions with trailing stops (use the 15-period moving average line as your support and stop/pare down point). Postopen also allows you to get an initial feel for the market strength and sector strength in particular. The strength sectors will have held at or near their highs uniformly, starting with the Tier 1s. For example, the semiconductor equipment makers are showing strength when the Tier 1 generals AMAT, NVLS, and KLAC are all at or near intraday highs. The real test of strength comes when the futures (S&P 500 futures and Nasdaq 100 futures) have their pullbacks on the 3-minute stochastics chart. In other words, any stock can look great when the futures are running up. The true test of strength shines when the futures pull back from the 90–100 band on the 3-minute stochastics. The sectors that manage to hold their gains are considered the strength. Ideally, the strength-sector stocks should move higher on the futures bounces and only wiggle on the futures pullbacks. This would show up as nice, steady 3-minute moving average uptrends with full 1-minute stochastics oscillations and would provide very nice scalping opportunities on 20-band stochastics reversals (buy when the stochastics reverse and go back above the 20 band and futures are rising, and sell when the stochastics reverse and go back under the 80–90 band and futures are falling).

Once you determine the market sentiment, you must start adapting immediately. If the market is strong and futures pullbacks do not dent the indexes or strength sectors, then you can use wider stops on fuller lots because the market strength is your safety net. You can trade harder. If the market is weak or choppy, then you must pare back the size of your trades to protect your downside since there is no real safety net. This is absolutely a key part of risk management you must master to survive.

11:31–2:00 P.M. EST—DEAD ZONE

Dead zone is when the volume and momentum of the general markets dissipate. Traders take off for lunch, and action slows to a crawl. The markets look like a ghost town in general. This is also the most dangerous part of the day. Most new traders get trapped into making overzealous trades out of boredom. This is usually where most traders lose their morning profits. Volume is thin during this time of day, which also means liquidity is thin. This is where you will see head fakes that trap day traders. Market makers or ISLD boys use size to temporarily bid up a stock to sell, and vice versa. There is little follow-through, and the odds are against you. You simply can't kick a dead horse. Most IPOs tend to open during dead zone, and this tends to break up the monotony. However, most IPOs are a losing game, as underwriters gap up strong issues way above the opening prices and sell down into the buyers. We warn traders to sit out dead zone unless there is real volume in a particular stock that may be breaking out of consolidation. In general, dead zone is exactly what the name says—dead. Overtrade and you will know what dead means.

2:01–2:59 P.M. EST—POST DEAD ZONE

Post dead zone is when the volume and liquidity start to return to the markets. The slow Nasdaq Level 2 screens begin to speed up, implying that the momentum is starting to flow again. This is the last hour going into the bond market close.

3:00–4:00 P.M. EST—LAST HOUR

The last hour is characterized by the same kind of momentum that can be found at the open. The main difference is that in the last hour there is intraday history on every stock. Therefore, in a sense the bridge that we spoke of is more stable than when we saw it on the open. The only problem is that the last hour can be very choppy. The bridge may be firm, but high winds are causing it to sway wildly. Our rule of thumb in the last hour is to manage your risk—don't go for any home run hits, but rather try for base hits in the form of scalps. The last 30 minutes—from 3:30 to 4:00 p.m. EST—are the choppiest. We like to look for strength buying coming from buyers who are anticipating a morning gap. This buying momentum is great to scalp and is triggered when intraday highs are taken out on strong volume. This is also the time to look for these morning gap plays with the same criteria. When taking a stock home overnight, there are key rules you must not violate. You must limit your risk and take only a smaller lot. For example, if you normally trade 1000 shares, you should consider up to 500 shares maximum on an overnight hold. You should always be aware that you can swallow a 50 percent retracement on the daily gain. For example, if you decide to take OMKT overnight and it is up 4 points on the day, you should be able to stomach a 50 percent retracement, or 2 points as your downside. If you cannot, then decrease your share size. Finally, the best way to take a stock overnight is when you are already profitable in the stock. This gives you some cushion in the event of a premarket sell-off.

4:01–6:00 P.M. EST—POSTMARKET/ AFTER-HOURS

The postmarket period is usually reserved for traders who are looking to sell their overnight trades after-hours or for those times when news may break on a stock which may have a material effect on its price the next morning. As more and more brokers are allowing postmarket (after-hours) trading, we are noticing that the gaps are often stronger in the after-hours than premarket the next morning. Therefore, we recommend that postmarket only be used to lock in some profits on your overnight holds. If they are truly strong gap candidates, they will already begin trading up in the postmarket.

There you have it—the whole market day broken up. The most fertile times to trade are the open and the last hour. Many of the best traders we know stick to those two periods religiously. As mentioned earlier, the good momentum traders can usually hit their daily profit target on the open and cruise the rest of the day. The main theme to remember here is that *when* you trade is just as important as *what* you trade. Trading more does not equate to reaping more profits. In most cases, it has the opposite effect, known as *overtrading*. Find the fertile periods that you can trade, play them, lock in profits, and relax.

CHAPTER 13

Putting It All Together

We have gone over all the tools and the possible plays. Let's take everything and put it all together and put you inside the mind of an underground trader for two trading sessions. This should give you a very real idea of how you should be thinking throughout the day and the mental discipline you should maintain.

In this scenario, you have a dual-monitor setup with 256 megabytes of RAM and a cable modem connection. Your daily target is $1000. The time is Eastern Standard Time.

MONDAY

8:00 a.m. We turn on CNBC and see that the S&P futures are neutral. The market has been on a tear lately, with the Nasdaq making news highs. The breadth of the market hasn't been that great, however. It seems the momentum has been moving in pockets of strength. I boot up CyBerTrader (or MB Trading, depending on your online broker). I log into the online trading site I belong to so I can check for news, guidance, and potential plays. Say hi to the gang.

8:30 a.m. I go to www.briefing.com to check for morning upgrades, and check for news on our basket stocks on www.yahoo.com. The moderator at the trading site logs on and starts commentary and news. We go to www.isld.com and turn on two Java ISLD books as well as keep a window open with the Island top 20 volume movers premarket.

8:45 a.m.   Several members are mentioning WALK (a Nasdaq stock) in a deal with CMRC. CMRC is a Tier 1 B2B (business to business) stock that has been on fire, and B2B is a strong flavor of the moment. The Island top 20 volume movers are listing WALK as number 1 for the morning. It closed yesterday at $3^3/8$. It is not gapping on strong volume premarket at $9^1/2$. This is obviously a dangerous junker momentum play. Very dangerous here. I am watching Level 2 and notice how well the bids keep filling and the wiggles are small. This makes it more dangerous, as I know that we need a strong shake premarket and then a bounce (also known as filling the gap) to reinforce short-term momentum. I check the float. It's 9.5 million shares, which is pretty thin. The alliance with CMRC gappage is the knee-jerk reaction. I am serious about riding this momentum short term, but we haven't had a pullback so I am wary. I know this is a total junk mover and do not intend on staying in any longer than I have to. These stocks are very dangerous, and premarket makes them triple times as dangerous—big risk and big reward.

9:04 a.m.   The moderator at the trading site issues a buy alert on WALK at 10 limit high risk. I've seen this building from 5 this morning, and the bid looks solid. I see some size to sell on ISLD at 10. I take a half lot of 500 shares filled at 10. This brings in more buyers off the fence. WALK is quickly gapping as the ISLDers pull their asks. WALK is upticking as fast bidders are coming in. It's $10^1/2 \times 10^5/8$ and upticking. I see 9000-share bids, which tells me the ISLD boys are playing this and moving it higher with the size bids. They can pull the plug any minute, so I watch. I have my sell order already keyed up by the ISLD bid, which is currently $10^3/_4$, now × 11. The 11 round-number tick doesn't last long. Premarket is very fast and thin.

9:08 a.m.   The trading site manager mentions to not lose $11^1/_2$. WALK is not ticking the $11^1/_2$ momentum tick. The ISLD boys are still bidding this one higher . This is nosebleed territory for me. ISLD is now $11^1/_2 \times 11^3/_4$, with NCA and REDI bidders. Not many on the ask, which is the best time to be exiting premarket, when the sellers are thin. I still have my sell order in for ISLD at 11. Even though the ISLD bid is $11^1/_2$, I can get out with a sweep order down to 11 if the inside bid disappears fast. I pare out 300 shares at the ISLD bid $11^1/_2$. As we get closer to the open, there may be more buying pressure.

9:10 a.m.   WALK pulls back to $10^1/_2$. I am still riding 200 shares with an ISLD sell trigger ready at 10 limit. The $10^1/_2$ is holding firm as more ISLD boys come in and load that bid. Oh yeah! WALK is running now. It's blasting through 11, $11^1/_2$, 12, $12^1/_2$.

9:17 a.m.   Just as I anticipated—more buyers. The trading site moderator mentions strength at the site. He calls another *buy* alert at $13^1/_2$. More buyers are coming in as we get closer to the open. I always anticipate profit takers on the open, so I am looking to sell into this momentum. WALK is ticking—$13^1/_2$, 14, $14^1/_2$. My exit is coming up on that 15 momentum tick. Here we go—place 200 shares to sell at 15. WALK now being bid up to $14^1/_2$, heavy ISLD boys, 12,500 on the bid. WALK upticking $14^5/_8$, $14^3/_4$ on the bid. Oh no, look at the 15 ask level—big size, 16,500 shares on the ask! I'm not taking my chances. I quickly downtick my sell trigger to 14. The second that the inside ISLD bid downticks, I'm out of here. WALK is now at $14^3/_4 \times 15$. 15 is getting eaten a bit. Oh no, INCA 6000 on the ask! Forget about it! Sell! My 14 sweep order takes me out of WALK at $14^{1}/_{4}$ as the ISLD bid dropped from $14^{3}/_{4}$ to 14 in the blink of an eye. Good thing I didn't try to sell at $14^{3}/_{4}$. I would have been stuck and had to reenter the order, wasting precious time. Nice score on WALK premarket.

$300 \times 1^{1}/_{2}$
$200 \times 4^{1}/_{4}$ Total gains: $450 + 900 = +\$1,350.00$

9:20 a.m.   Well, that was certainly a nice catch. I don't usually play premarket, as it is a seller's game. I guess I got lucky—with some skill. My daily target has already been exceeded, so now I will try to take it easy from here. I will watch my basket stocks CSCO and AMAT. CSCO has been on a nice uptrend, and AMAT along with the rest of the Tier 1 semi makers has sold off. I will keep an eye on LU and TLAB, which are in CSCO's sector, and also NVLS and KLAC, which are Tier 1s in AMAT's sector. From here on I will like my risk. I don't want to blow a nice gift this morning.

9:25 a.m.   The moderator at the trading site gives his morning briefing and mentions a number of stocks to keep on the radar. We played ELCO yesterday as a nice run on earnings. It is gapping this morning to 17 from yesterday's close of $16^{3}/_{8}$. The Tier 1 Internets YHOO and EBAY have slight gaps, and AMZN is also gapping slightly. This will be interesting. My basket CSCO and KLAC are neutral no-gaps. I usually make most of my daily targets on the open. The momentum on the open is ripe and ferocious while market makers track the ranges before clamping down. Any fast profits usually come from the open. I rarely ever hold or swing a stock from the open because it's usually overpriced and too close to the near high range. I'm just looking for some quick ins and outs with money in my pocket.

9:30 a.m.   Market is open, and I am looking for gap fills. Watching ELCO—quick sell-off on the open. ELCO pulls back to 16^1/$_4$ from 17. Watching the spread—as the trading site moderator says, everything on the open is scalps. ELCO now at 16^1/$_4$ × 16^3/$_4$—spread widens; no more sellers. I see buyers coming in. It's upticking fast—16^1/$_2$, 16^3/$_4$ bids and the ask is lifting. I see RAJA market maker selling and holding the levels. If ELCO breaks 17, it will have filled the gap.

9:35 a.m.   ELCO testing 17 RAJA at the ask; the buyers are coming in. The trading site moderator issues a buy alert on ELCO at 17^1/$_2$. I'm going in. It's currently bidding 16^7/$_8$ × 17. The ARCHIPs are bidding and pressing the 17 ask. This is a gap fill. I am sure it will break once RAJA steps off the ask. I'm not going to take my chances and bid with the ARCHIPs at 17. Instead, I see ISLD offering 2200 shares at 17^1/$_4$. I route directly to ISLD for 500 shares at 17^1/$_4$ and get filled. RAJA steps off at 17^1/$_4$ and jumps to 17^1/$_2$. ELCO immediately pops, and ARCHIP bidders follow straight to 17^1/$_2$. I already have my sell order ready. Since there is momentum, I am watching the momentum ticks now. Currently, I have my ELCO to sell 500 shares at 17^1/$_2$. Watching that momentum tick—17^1/$_2$ gone. RAJA upticks to 18. I quickly uptick my sell order to 17^3/$_4$; buyers coming off the fence. ELCO is in breakout mode from the mini cup and handle gap fill. Here comes the 18 momentum tick. I'm not going to push it, since I already made daily goal here. I see 18 ticking; market makers thinning out. This is my exit, not being greedy. I place my sell ELCO 500 shares at 18 ask into the buyer. Yeah! Out in 3 seconds. It upticks; now 18 bid. I'm out, and frankly that's all I care about. I've been greedy before only to let a profit slip on the wiggle; not anymore. ELCO's now at 18^1/$_4$ × 18^1/$_2$. This is only momentum, and the 1-minute stochastics is already toppy at the 90 band. This can reverse any moment now. There's ELCO at 18^1/$_2$, momentum tick buyers. Up to 18^9/$_{16}$—there's size and more sellers at $^9/_{16}$. Momentum always dies on the teeny, and it looks like all the bidders are drying up here as the sellers are now holding the $^9/_{16}$ and quickly downtick the stock. ELCO back to $17^3/_4$. Panic sellers caused the bidders to dry up. I'm out of there. Next!

500 × $^3/_4$ Total gains: +$375.00

9:40 a.m.   I am watching AMAT and CSCO. The futures are starting off on an uptick and rising. CSCO is at the high of the day at 95. I hate it when stocks hit their highs early on. I check the stochastics. CSCO is already at the 90 band and rising. This is overbought territory, but, heck, it's momentum. I check LU and it's trading at the high. CSCO 3-minute chart shows a nice run on the open, a wide trading channel on the open, with $94^1/_4$ as support. This is momentum. 95 is testing—and testing hard. The NDX futures are at the 80 band. I decide to pass on this one. Going to let CSCO breathe and wait for a futures stochastics pull-back. I am up $1^1/_2$ times my daily goal; will play it safe. I usually go 1000-share lots, but taking it slow and safe here. The markets are holding up well. I keep reminding myself that this is the open and just an adjustment time for market makers.

10:00 a.m.   Postopen and I am looking for some consolidation. WALK has pulled back to the $9^1/_2$ range, and the 3-minute chart is not pretty; it broke down. What a pull-back from premarket highs. Glad I am out. WALK may be looking to consolidate at the 10 momentum tick. Looking at CSCO and it's holding a tighter consolidation range. There is news with RBAK and CSCO, interesting. CSCO is holding in the $94^3/_4$ × 95 range near the high of the day. The spoos are starting to pull back from the 80 band here. I'm going to let it breathe and see how well CSCO holds up in the futures downdraft. Amin, sniper mode here, sitting and watching. I know the tighter and longer the consolidation, the stronger and more stable the breakout. The trading site moderator alerts us to watch AMZN on the radar. I just flipped on my charts for AMZN. It has been testing that 95 momentum tick. This is one tricky stock, as it tends to break momentum ticks to a teeny under $1/4$ and $1/2$, to wiggle almost a full point, and then to coil and bounce. Keeping it on the radar.

10:10 a.m. There's AMZN again knocking at 95. This is unusually strong momentum. It breaks 95, and the 3-minute chart looks good. It's coming out of consolidation and breaking that 95 resistance. I'm going in here. The 1-minute stochastics on the 50 band reversing up, so it's not too toppy. I also see the spoos and NDX futures are turning back up on the 3-minute stochastics. I'm in ISLD at the $95^1/4$ tick for 300 shares. I am now watching the momentum ticks. AMZN always wiggles, so I will give myself 1 point for the wiggle. AMZN support based on 15-period 3-minute moving averages chart is $93^7/8$. AMZN upticking to $95^1/4$, $95^3/8$. There is strong size to sell at $3/8$ on INCA for 8000 shares. Oh brother, the chippies are going to panic! I am in on a small lot compared with the usual 1000 shares, so I am going to stick to my stop loss of $93^7/8$.

10:15 a.m. Great, AMZN retraced to $94^1/4$! This is getting a little close for comfort, but it's only 300 shares, so I am going to sweat it out. YHOO and EBAY are holding up well on the day, and they are the Tier 1s. AMZN tends to switch from Tier 1 to Tier 2 and sometimes has a mind of its own, especially since the split. The 3-minute chart tells me consolidation is here again; the support is lifting $94^1/4$. AMZN takes a dip to 94 and tests. I know there is always a knee-jerk reaction at the round-number momentum ticks in both directions. If it breaks $93^3/4$, I am stopped out. Damn, there goes $93^3/4$! I sell out AMZN at $93^1/2$ on ISLD.

$$300 \times -1^1/2 \qquad \text{Total loss} = -\$450.00$$

10:18 a.m. Oh no! I just checked the 1-minute stochastics. Like a panicked fool, I stopped out when AMZN was *reversing* on the 20 band! Damn! AMZN bouncing, now at 94 × 94¼. It's upticking fast. I'm going to wait it out here. It couldn't break 95⅜ the last time, so until it does, I'm out. Show me, AMZN, that you've got the strength to break and then you will convince me. I am sure the other traders are thinking the same thing. Fill the gap and I'll be back.

10:20 a.m. Here we go. AMZN testing 95 again. It breaks—95¼, 95⅜. There's the resistance. I already have my buy screen up for 300 shares of AMZN at 95½ if ⅜ can break. Checking AMZN 1-minute stochastics, I see it's on the 60 band and still uptrending. YHOO is breaking new highs; this is good. Come on, AMZN— ⅜ upticking.

10:23 a.m. The site moderator issues a buy alert on AMZN at 95½. That's a good call. I'm in at ⅝ on ISLD for 300 shares. AMZN is upticking fast; the sellers are moving out of the way. I can't believe I got wiggled out. Oh well. AMZN coiled and is moving fast on new buyers coming off the fence. It's breaking here. YHOO is at the high of the day, and momentum is sneaking into AMZN too.

10:25 a.m. AMZN is testing the 96 momentum tick. I check my stochastics chart; and it's getting toppy here, 90 band, but it hasn't turned. I am ready to release this baby at the 96 momentum tick while the momentum is fresh. I place my sell order at 96 on ISLD for 500 shares into the buyers. I am out in 3 seconds flat as AMZN upticks to 96⅜ and reverses on the wiggle. Nice play.

300 × ⅜   Total gains: +$112.50

11:00 a.m. The momentum is slowing down in the markets. As the trading site moderator calls it, this is dead zone, where the volume decreases as traders go to lunch. I have already been a victim of dead zone, making stupid, unnecessary trades based on a few upticks that looked like an uptrend or breakout. Will sit on my hands here. The semi makers are strong. Dow and Nasdaq up nicely today and holding well against the spoos' downdrafts. Market is in a hold and wait mood. There is strength in this market and not much choppiness. OK for small shares. I am still up nicely past my daily target, so I'm not sweating for any dumb trades.

11:19 a.m.   Traders talking about RMKR. I pull up the charts. This is a recent IPO, and I remember how strong DLJP was unloading this one. It broke out over that 20 resistance that I remember. Hmmm, the moderator at the trading site issues a buy alert at $20^{7}/_{8}$. Nice call, as it upticks to $21^{1}/_{2}$ before the wiggle. The 3-minute moving averages chart looks interesting. I see a PUP formation breakout coming. The 5 period has been steady holding the 21 range, and the 15-period support is rising. No way I could catch that trade alert. I'll sit back and wait for the wiggle.

11:25 a.m.   RMKR wiggled off $21^{3}/_{4}$ and pulled back to $20^{3}/_{4}$ on panicked sellers. The stochastics pulled back to about the 50 range. Not perfect, but looks good since the 3-minute chart is still showing that PUP breakout. I'm in this time for a scalp. Taking 1000 shares RMKR at 21 through ISLD. The wiggle proved to be just that—a wiggle. Buyers coming back in upticking and stochastics reversing up through the 60 band. Man, this one is a choppy stock!

11:30 a.m.   RMKR at $21^{1}/_{2} \times 21^{3}/_{4}$. It seems to like the 21 base and basing at $21^{1}/_{4}$ firm in the wiggles. This one looks like its coiling here again. I have my sell order keyed up for 500 shares to pare out starting at $21^{1}/_{2}$. I am not nervous because when the panic is over, RMKR basing nicely as the 3-minute chart continues its breakout— just a matter of time.

11:50 a.m.   RMKR bouncing through 21$^1/_2$, I let 500 shares go
              into the strength when I see there is only one lonely
              market maker left at the $^1/_2$. It's testing 21$^3/_4$ on the ask;
              buyers are coming in. Here comes the 22 momentum
              tick. Stochastics around the 90 band can reverse here
              any time. This is my exit.

11:52 a.m.   RMKR ticking 22. I place my sell order right into the
              buyers at 22 on the ask. I am out in the blink of an eye.
              RMKR upticks hard to 22$^1/_2$ and wiggles again.
              Enough with that jibe—I'm out and happy.

              500 × $^1/_2$
              500 × 1   Total gains: +$750.00

That puts me at two times my daily goal. I'm going to
take a break and try to keep my profits. This is dead
zone, and where most trader lack the discipline to stay
out of trades. I've been bitten before, and it wasn't pretty. Time to fire up the Sega Dreamcast and play some
NFL2K. I'll be back later to catch any potential action.

1:00 p.m.   The site moderator says to put BEOS on the radar.
              This is one I played on the last major run-up from 9
              to 15 about 3 weeks ago. I'm familiar with the rhythm.
              It moves like an Internet stock and tends to move with
              the Linux plays since it's an alternative DOS maker.
              RHAT and CORL have been very strong today. I'm
              pulling up the charts. Stochastics above 70—looks a
              bit high. But wait, the 3-minute moving averages chart
              shows a pretty tight trading channel—12$^1/_4$ is the 15-
              period support, and the 5-period resistance is 12$^3/_4$.
              Current price is 12$^1/_2$ × $^9/_{16}$. This shows promise. My
              downside on this is a $^1/_2$ point, no need to go heavy. As
              I recall, this one is choppy, and chippies can panic
              because of the fast spreads.

1:01 p.m.   The site moderator issues a buy alert at 12$^3/_4$. There go
              the chippies, not going to get anything under 12$^3/_4$. I'll
              let the newbies fight it out under. This one has nice

potential. I'm going for the ISLD ask at 12⁷/₈ for 400 shares, and am confident my downside is 12¹/₄ max, which is support. I'd rather pay more than try to be cheap and miss the fill.

1:02 p.m.   VOLP is the ax on this one, and he is holding the momentum ticks for a pause and upticking. Here we go 12³/₄, 13 momentum tick. VOLP is kind of firm here, but the buyers are strong. The other market makers all upticked. I have my sell order for 400 shares set and ready to fire if I see any heavy selling on the teenies. Buyers chew through 13; VOLP upticks to 13¹/₂, and immediately buyers take it to 13¹/₂. I up my sell price to the 13¹/₂ momentum tick for 400 shares; not pulling trigger yet though.

1:04 p.m.   Wow, the buyers are chewing this one up! The momentum ticks aren't lasting. Looks like 13³/₄ going to test. Wow, not for long! Here comes the 14 momentum tick. Don't want to push my luck here; placing sell order at 14 on ISLD for 400 shares. I'm out before you can say bang. Oops, that didn't last long now ticking 14¹/₄, 14¹/₂, 14³/₄. Holy moly, look at this thing go! The stochastics is too toppy here; now it's at the 95 band—too toppy. I left some on the table, but who cares. What a run! It broke the 15 momentum tick and found resistance at the teeny at 15¹/₁₆. VOLP clamped down, but it was the 6000 SHWD ask that killed the momentum. It's downticking fast here, 14¹/₂ and now 14; looks like short-term support. Stochastics has reversed now from the 100 band. This one is choppy.

$$400 \times +1\tfrac{1}{8} \qquad \text{Total gains: } +\$450.00$$

1:33 p.m.   BEOS hits 16, damn! I got out of that one too early, but it was just a momentum play for me. Hmmm, that 3-minute chart didn't waver or give a sell signal. Oh well. It's slowing down here, and I'll wait for a consolidation before another scalp or a gap fill to the high of the day. This one really has some volume and interest today.

1:49 p.m.   BEOS fills the gap through 17. Going in here at $17^1/4$ for 1000 shares. I'm filled on ISLD. Oh, phooey! There's a seller at the teeny $7/16$. Come on, BEOS. All we need is for the $1/2$ momentum tick to catapult this pop. Damn, stochastics looks toppy at the 95 band. The 3-minute chart is in a decent uptrend but may be stalling as the stock is $1/2$ point above its 5-period resistance. The $7/16$ is holding pretty tight. Oh no, more ISLD sellers at $7/16$! Bad entry—I downtick my sell size to 600 with a monster bid at $16^3/4$ on ISLD. I see ISLD bidders at $17^1/4$, but they are not going to last. Time to pare down here before the momentum dies. This jerk at $7/16$ is firm, and now there are two more market makers there; momentum's turning, and fast. Bidders are stepping off. Go, go, go! Out 600 shares of BEOS on ISLD $17^1/8 \times 300$, 17×300. I know that 17 is not going to hold, and the stochastics is too toppy. Bad entry here. Sellers taking out 17, and the market makers smell the panic and drop bids to $16^1/2 \times 17$. Yuck. I don't believe this! There are $16^1/2$ sellers on this one with a $1/2$ spread, sheesh, amateurs! This is not good, because the spread is actually filling on the ask side! BEOS is now $16^1/4 \times 16^1/2$. The 3-minute moving average support is $15^3/4$; looks like I am stuck for a while on this one. Ouch! I took too many shares too high on the stochastics chart too close to a top. I really thought the $1/2$ tick who hit would have catapulted the momentum to $3/4$ and possible 18. Oh well, no crying over spilled milk. The panic sellers are overreacting. Let's hope they come to their senses. 16 is gone now. BEOS is $15^3/4 \times 16$.

1:56 p.m.   BEOS is filling the spread on the bid side now. $15^7/8 \times 16$ and the stochastics is bouncing off the 20 band reversal. The 3-minute chart is looking like it may reverse here. The 16 momentum tick is very tough. I'll give it another minute or two for the stochastics to play out and then bail. Good thing I downsized when

I did. OK, 16 breaks; now it's $16 \times 16^1/_4$. Not many takers on the ask. The stochastics is climbing. Let me give it a little more time. I just want to cut my losses here with the least amount of damage. If I can get the $16^1/_2$ momentum tick, I'm out of here. Damn, there's that seller at $16^7/_{16}$ again holding the teeny! I'm out of here. I spotted an ISLD bidder for 500 shares at $^3/_8$. Bang—sold 400 shares of BEOS at $16^3/_8$. The 3-minute chart is breaking down. I'm out of there. Going to go grab a soda.

$300 \times -^1/_8$
$300 \times -^1/_4$
$400 \times -^7/_8$ Total losses: −$374.00

2:30 p.m.   Bond market closes in a half hour. Markets have been holding pretty steady. The Tier 1 stocks YHOO, EBAY, AMAT, INTC, and CSCO are all range bound. There is not much action here. Spoos just took a dip under the 20 band and are reversing. Looking at AMAT, which is up 4 points today near the high of the day, along with KLAC up 4 points near the high of the day, and NVLS up $^1/_{16}$. Wait a minute! NVLS is a Tier 1 stock just like AMAT and KLAC and usually leads them. Hmmm, something is up. I check the news; there is no news. Pulling up charts and Level 2. If the rules of tier synergy play out, then NVLS is a laggard and should move up. There is no news, so there must be a large seller in the stock today holding the price down. NVLS is $84 \times 84^1/_4$, and AMAT and KLAC are making new highs. Gauging by Level 2, I see MSCO is holding pretty firm at $94^1/_4$. In fact, he is selling right into the buyers. Stochastics is near the 100 band, so this is actually the tail end of the pop. Let me wait it out here to see where it goes; the high of the day was yesterday's close at $94^3/_4$.

2:45 p.m.   MSCO holds the $84^1/_4$ ask, and NVLS is selling off again. MSCO is on the inside ask. He is the ax, and he is very firm. Watching time of sales here for some block activity to signal that he is covering his shares. I am sure there are lots of buyers on the fence waiting for the large seller to cover. Stochastics is selling off; NVLS 3-minute moving averages charts are stabilizing here; looks like a consolidation with 15-period support at $83^1/2$. The buyers and sellers are slowing down. Spoos are turning back down.

3:00 p.m.   Bond market is closed. AMAT and KLAC are making new highs. They are very strong today, only wiggling on the futures pullbacks. NVLS is upticking, and MSCO is inside ask. NVLS at $83^7/8 \times 94$, and MSCO is inside ask at 84. Momentum tick buyers are coming in. I have my buy screen up for 500 shares at 94 if it breaks or if I see blocks. Just my luck, 50,000-share block at $93^3/4$ and MSCO upticks. He's covering! NVLS upticking fast now. MSCO at $84^1/4$. I SOES in at $94^1/4$ for 500 shares. I am in! Wow, INCA size bidder at $83^1/8$ 5000 shares! More buyers on the momentum tick. I'm am going to swing this one a bit here while AMAT and KLAC are still strong. NVLS 3-minute moving averages chart is looking to break out from the consolidation. Buyers coming after MSCO, and spoos are rising. Let's go, NVLS! Whee—another 25,000 block at 84, more short covering!

3:15 p.m.   NVLS at the high of the day here at $84^3/4$ ask. MSCO on the inside and bidders tightening the spread. The spoos and NDX futures are slowing down above the 80 band. AMAT and KLAC already pulling back off highs, but the NVLS buyers are still strong. The tier synergy laggard effect is pouring on here. The buyers on the fence smell blood as another 25,000-share block goes off at $84^1/2$. MSCO upticks. Here comes the 85 resistance. MSCO is out of there as his ask is not 96.

3:30 p.m.   Spoos buy program coming in, driving up the Dow. AMAT and KLAC breaking highs again. This time

WARR is holding the 84^1/$_4$ ask. NVLS moves with the futures when everything is in sync and there is no divergence. I figure at this point NVLS has some serious catching up to do. AMAT at the high of the day at +7, and KLAC just under the high of the day at +6^5/$_8$. Tier synergy and 3-minute charts holding me in NVLS for the swing and end-of-day buyers.

3:45 p.m. NVLS breaks the high of the day 86^1/$_2$, and it looks like WARR is a seller, but not supertight. I'm not planning on holding this one overnight, so I will try to sell the momentum tick even though NVLS still has some catch-up to do. I'll take a 50 percent gain versus the Tier 1 AMAT and NVLS gains. NVLS is holding 96^1/$_2$ pretty firm; no biggie. This one wiggles a lot, but the stochastics is toppy and reversing at the 90 band. I SOES out for the 500 shares at 96^1/$_4$ as the spoos are also reversing and AMAT and NVLS are a full point under their highs of the day.

500 × +2　·　Total gains: +$1,000

3:55 p.m. RWAV at the high of the day and breaking. Possible Linux mover here too. I'm in at 10 taking a change on 1000 shares. 10 is ticking—and ticking strong. Oh boy, should have looked at the stochastics. The damn thing is at 100! Come on, momentum! Let's go break that 10 momentum tick. Damn, NITE is holding that ask firm at 10. I am already seeing ISLD bids coming in at 10^1/$_{16}$. This one's looking like the momentum is dying. I try to place a sell for the 1000 at 10 on ISLD to try to get out even on this one. Too late—already 3000 shares to sell at 10. Momentum getting its legs chopped from underneath already. The bids are drying up fast from 9^{15}/$_{16}$ to 9^3/$_4$. Bad move. There's panic, yuck. I place my sell trigger at 9^1/$_2$ on ISLD in an attempt to sweep this one. RWAV moves on fast spreads and always favors the momentum trend of the moment. When I got in at 10, there were five market makers and 12,000 size ISLD boys bid at $9^{15}/_{16}$. That dried up before you could say panic. Biting the bullet and getting out before this one drops. Ooh, only get filled 300 out at $9^1/_2$. Now ISLD is at $9^1/_4$. This stinks. That was a bad impulse trade. Drop my ISLD sell order to 9 to try to sweep this one all the way down. This last-minute momentum is either up or down, and 10 held firm as superglue. Oh well, I'm filled 300 at $9^1/_4$ and 400 at 9. Ouch. So much for playing that one on the fly!

$300 \times -^1/_2$
$300 \times -^3/_4$
400×-1　　　Total losses: −$775.00

4:00 p.m.　RWAV bounces off $8^3/_4$ to close at $9^1/_2$ for the day. Oh well, not sweating it. I goofed on that one and jumped in prematurely. I thought the 10 would tick, but not having seen the Level 2 until seconds before the trade, there was no way I would have known NITE was the ax. Now I know. Another lesson learned on RWAV and the agony of defeat in impulse trading. I went too heavy, but my gains were nice today. Still, I got a little greedy and overconfident. Overall, I am happy for a nice day. Let's tally up my net profit-loss statement here:

Total gains:	+$4,037.50
Total losses:	−$1,599.99
Total commissions ($20 per trade × 21 trades):	−$ 420.00
Total net profit-loss:	+$2,017.51

Well, I managed to get 2 times my daily profit target of $1000. I am satisfied. My losing trades were caused mainly by making bad entries—according to the reversing toppy stochastics—and by miscalculating the momentum. Impulse trading without analyzing the charts first was my error. However, it could have been worse. At least I was familiar with the rhythms since I have played each stock before. That premarket trade on WALK was sweet and kicked my day off nicely. I don't usually play pre-market, but on mania momentum with nicely rising ISLD boy bids, I will take my chances for a quick pop. The trading site moderator had some nice calls today, and I got good fills. Since the markets were in a trading channel, I didn't play my basket stocks much because there was more momentum on the cheaper plays— although NVLS was a nice laggard play off my basket Tier 1 stock AMAT. A very nice trading day today!

TUESDAY

8:00 a.m. We turn on CNBC and see that the S&P are gapping 2 over fair value. I boot up Cybertrader (or Mbtrading, depending on your online broker). I log into the trading site to check for news, guidance, and potential plays. Say hi to the gang.

8:30 a.m. We go to www.briefing.com to check for morning upgrades, and we check for news on our basket stocks on www.yahoo.com. The moderator at the trading site logs and starts commentary and news. We go to www.isld.com and turn on two Java ISLD books as well as keep a window open with the Island top 20 volume movers premarket.

8:45 a.m. Let's see here. Some check junkers are gaining momentum premarket this morning according to the ISLD top 20. ASTM gapping 100 percent from 1 on some phase 2 cancer trials news. I've played this one before. I'm going to stay out of it. Keep looking for more gappers. I hate gap days. CSCO and AMAT are both gapping this morning. Usually, I expect gaps and then profit taking, at which time the stocks stay in a trading range long enough for a consolidation before breaking out to new highs. Takes patience and can get boring. It takes focus, which is why most traders end up getting hurt playing too much momentum on the fly.

9:23 a.m.   The trading site moderator gives the morning radar
            list and mentions that the semi makers look strong this
            morning with gaps across the board on NVLS,
            AMAT, and KLAC. CSCO has a nice gap this morn-
            ing. NEON has an alliance with MSFT. NEON has
            been on a tear lately, and stochastics on the daily chart
            is near the 90 band, so I will watch with caution. IZAP
            and AMZN in e-commerce pact. Big deal, I'm getting
            tired of these bogus little alliance press releases. They
            have been played out. Hmmm, WBVN looks very
            strong this morning. It's a recent IPO, and its gapping
            up +3 and no give. I will keep it on the radar.

9:31 a.m.   We are off! Ding ding! Watching my basket stocks
            AMAT and CSCO—both have buying on the open.
            Usually, I will wait for postopen to analyze the range.
            They rarely gap and so straight up, but today could be
            the day. WBVN selling from the 30 resistance here;
            closed yesterday at 27. WBVN just peaked at 30; met
            resistance and panic set in to $29\frac{1}{4}$. Market makers are
            holding the $29\frac{1}{4}$ tick. There's the gap—$29\frac{1}{4} \times 29\frac{3}{4}$;
            no more selling.

9:32am   WBVN trying to fill the gap, $29\frac{3}{8} \times \frac{3}{4}$, $29\frac{1}{2} \times \frac{3}{4}$. I see
            buyers. I see 4000 shares offered on ISLD at 30, the
            first resistance and peak. Looking for a gap fill, I'm
            going in for 1000 shares at 30 above the ask. I see
            chippies panicking to get in. I'm filled instantly.
            WBVN now $29\frac{7}{8} \times 30$. There's my gap fill!

9:36 a.m.   WBVN ticks through the $30\frac{1}{2}$ momentum tick; nice
            buying here. GSCO keeps trying to sell the momen-
            tum ticks, but he's getting overwhelmed with buying,
            and when he upticks, the stock moves to wherever he
            goes. WBVN has lots of heavy bids at $30\frac{7}{16}$ versus one
            lone market maker, GSCO, at $30\frac{1}{2}$. Let's go sqeeeze,
            baby. Watching the teenies and have my sell order lined
            up for $30\frac{1}{2}$ on the ask for ISLD for 1000 shares if I
            see the teenies build up at $\frac{9}{16}$ to sell.

9:38 a.m.   GSCO upticks under the hard buying pressure to 31. Tom Costello, reporter on CNBC, mentions WBVN's strength on CNBC—just what I needed, more buying pressure. Usually a mention on CNBC results in short-lived momentum pops. Locking in my profits at the 31 momentum tick while the buyers are hot and plenty. Pull my trigger to sell 1000 WBVN at the ask at 31 into the buyers. I'm out! Nicey-nice way to start the morning.

1 × 1000   Total gains: +$1,000

9:40 a.m.   Well, the spoos and NDX 100 futures are slipping here already. The Dow has gone negative. I'm going to sit back and wait here for a futures bottom. Looks like the semi makers are strong and CSCO is looking pretty good, but they are selling off, I'm going to measure their strength on this sell-off to see just how resilient they are. We are choppy already. WBVN holding support short-term here at $30^1/_4$. I'm glad I got out. Stochastics was topped out at 31 right at the 95 band. YHOO, AOL, and EBAY negative on the day—the Internet sector gapped and trapped.

9:46 a.m.   The site moderator mentions the gap fill on ASDS, a B2B Internet commerce play. I pull up the information quick and see nice buying here. Naturally stochastics is toppy, and this is only a momentum quick-in-and-out play. I'll bite. The trading site moderator calls the alert to buy ASDS at 30. Another 10 resistance momentum tick gap filler like WBVN. ASDS at $29^3/_4$ × 30. I know this stock from playing it last week, and it can be a heck of a choppy stock if you are caught on the wrong end of the momentum. I will go 500 shares. No way I'm getting filled at 30; too many buyers trying for that. I see ISLD at $30^3/_8$ for 1200 shares. I'm game for 500 shares; routed to ISLD directly and filled $30^3/_8$ for 500 shares. VOLP holding the 30 momentum tick firm, but he's feeling the squeeze. He upticks to 31, wow!

9:48 a.m.   The floodgates are open as ASDS clears through 31 with strength. Mostly the market makers are stepping up their quotes. I have my sell lined up for the 31½ momentum tick for 500 shares on ISLD, ready for me to pull the trigger. There's the 31½ momentum tick. No greed here. I am out into the buyers at 31½ for 500 shares on ISLD. In fact, I am out too fast, as I see market markers step off to 32.

$$1 \times 500 \qquad \text{Total gains: } +\$500$$

9:50 a.m.   ASDS cuts through 32 like a knife through hot butter, wowee! This momentum is overextended now. Stochastics 1-minute chart showing me a 97-band reading. Too toppy for my blood or for reentry for that matter. Happy to have profits this morning.

10:00 a.m. The trading site moderator asks how we are trading so far this morning. I reply, "I'm up 1.5 × DG, thnx!" *DG* stands for "daily goal," and mine is $1000. I've nailed it on two nice round-trips. I'm taking it easy from here. Market is just choppy as heck this morning. It's now going into postopen and I will look for consolidations and watch my basket stocks. A few rounds on NFL2K is not a bad idea either to keep me from overtrading.

10:35 a.m. CSCO is off just over 1 point from its intraday high of 95½. It's currently trading at 94¼ × 5/16, and it opened at 93⅞ on a gap. This is one of my basket stocks. I see a nice setup here. The CSCO 3-minute chart is in a consolidation with a ½-point trading channel. Stochastics reversing from the 10 band, and the futures are reversing up from the 20 band. This looks good. We need a nice ½ momentum tick break. I SOES in 1000 shares for 94 5/16, just looking for a scalp on the stochastics bounce.

10:37 a.m. Futures are rising stronger here through the 35 band. CSCO upticks, and stochastics is following through. There's the ½ tick, and momentum is coming in. Market makers stepping off. Looks like a buy program just hit. $spx.x is in buy-program territory, and I see the jerk on the NDX futures tick chart. CSCO ticking strong through the $1/2$ momentum tick; market makers always sell the teenies on this one. Now CSCO is at $94^1/2 \times 9/16$. Upticking.

10:40 a.m.   CSCO eats through to the $95^{11}/16 \times 95^3/4$ momentum tick. Stochastics approaching the 85 band. OK, I'm taking my scalp here since the $3/4$ momentum tick is stalling and stochastics is getting a tad toppy. I SOES out CSCO 1000 shares at $95^{11}/16$.

$7/16 \times 1000$ Total gains: +$487.50

11:00 a.m.   Man, markets are already slowing down for dead zone; am taking a break. Not going to overtrade.

1:00 p.m.   Markets are still in a consolidation on low volume. This is the middle of dead zone. I see nothing but light-volume movers up strong and head fakes.

2:00 p.m.   The trading site moderator has been watching VONE as it has been breaking new highs on a strong 3-minute uptrend. I am watching. This one is choppy and seems to retrace a full $1/2$ point once the momentum pop tops, but I see NITE holding supports at the tail end of the wiggle. The 3-minute chart is really a beauty. VONE has been stuck in the $4–$5 range for ages. Now it's trading $9^3/4 \times 7/8$ and looks to test 10. Stochastics toppy here at the 90 band, but there is some real momentum. I'm in at 10 for 500 shares on ISLD to test the momentum.

2:05 p.m.   The trading site moderator calls a buy alert at 10— nice break. 10 is deep and breaking here. Market makers are stepping off the teenies, letting the momentum tick move. $10 \times 10^1/4$ now. Here goes the $1/2$ tick whee! I have my sell cued up for 500 shares starting with the $10^1/2$ momentum tick, but not taking a shot yet.

2:08 p.m. $10^3/4$ momentum tick. Not pulling the trigger to sell yet. Buyers still coming in. Watching to see if I can get the 11 momentum tick, but watching the teenies here.

$^{13}/_{16}$, $^7/_8$ ask. Sizes everywhere. Oh, shoot! I see ISLD boys size 18,300 shares to sell at $^7/_8$. Great! The momentum is reversing fast here. Wow, market makers and ISLD bidders stepped right off the ask! I'm stuck; got too greedy. Downticking fast. I'm in at 10 so I won't panic, but that doesn't mean the world will cooperate here.

2:10 p.m.   VONE stochastics topped at 100, shoot! Looks like panic still going on here, and now VONE is at $10^1/_8 \times 10^3/_{16}$. ISLD boys still selling the teenies with size. The 3-minute chart is still in an uptrend, so I'm not going to panic too much on this one since I am up 2× DG already. I will risk a paring down from the $9^1/_2$ tick since momentum stocks tend to wiggle up to 1 point—need to give it some wiggle room.

2:15 p.m.   Well, VONE broke under 10 and finally saw some support at $9^3/_4$. I see ISLD boys loading the bid here with size. INCA coming in with size. Going to retest 10. Ah shoot, NITE selling the $9^{15}/_{16}$ teeny with size and no refreshing! VONE is at $9^{15}/_{16} \times 10$. I'm out of here at $9^{15}/_{16}$ on ISLD. I'm not fighting with NITE on this one.

$^1/_{16} \times 500$ Total losses = −$31.25

3:00 p.m.   VONE has a nice consolidation at that $9^3/_4 \times 10$ range. This is setting up for something here, and NITE is now a firm buyer. The site moderator mentions that we may get a short squeeze on this one since it is up almost 5 points on the day and no sign of real weakness with a strong 3-minute consolidation. I am watching AMAT for a breakout through the high of the day at 103. AMAT currently trading $102^3/_4 \times 102^7/_8$. 103 has been a tough nut to crack, and AMAT moves with the futures.

3:05 p.m.   VONE breaks 10 again. NITE is the inside bid and is taking it higher. I'm going in here with the 3-minute break from a 45-minute consolidation. I take 300 shares at $10^1/_2$ on ISLD filled. I will use a stop loss at the 15-period support on VONE, which is at $9^7/8$ now and rising. A small-lot short-term swing into the close. If we can hold the high ranges here, I agree with the site moderator—a squeeze is in order.

3:10 p.m.   In AMAT 103 for the break for 500 shares. Spoos are topping here near the 95 band. Let's go, AMAT! My stop loss on AMAT will be the 15-period, 3-minute support at $102^1/2$ even though the support is closer to $3/4$. I will give it some wiggle room. Wow, VONE is catching some momentum here on the 11 momentum tick test! I am upticking my stop loss on this one. VONE just broke the high of the day. It is choppy, but the wiggles are getting smaller and smaller. More momentum on this. Volume bars are rising.

3:33 p.m.   AMAT hits my stop. I'm out at $112^1/2$. Actually AMAT pulled back to $112^1/4$ and got a small stochastics bounce where I sold into the buyers.

$$-1/2 \times 500 \qquad \text{Total losses} = -\$250.00$$

3:35 p.m.   VONE is catching some real momentum. Level 2 is blazing and ticking through 12. OK, I am looking to lock in soon. Usually when stocks hit their highs intraday in the last $1/2$ hour of the day, I expect to see more momentum from end-of-day gap buyers. The moderator at the site is calling this one a buy again at $12^1/2$. Wow, nice read! VONE upticking strong through 13. Market makers are stepping off bids.

3:40 p.m.   VONE at $13^1/2$, and the stochastics has been riding the 100 band now. I am out 300 shares into the buyers at $13^1/2$. Whee! Nice score here. Buyers are still strong on this one.

$$+3 \times 300 \qquad \text{Total gains} = +\$900.00$$

3:50 p.m.   VONE at $14^1/2$ momentum tick taken out. The trading site moderator cautions to lock in profits on this one up to the 15 resistance tick. Bang, there's 15 and cutting through like a hot knife through ice cream! I'm going in for a quickie. I spot ISLD at $15^{1}/_{4}$. I get filled immediately at $15^{1}/_{16}$ for 1000 shares. Not a good sign when I get filled that cheap when offering more. Uh oh.

3:52 p.m.   VONE is falling on panic selling. Bright idea going in at the top! VONE is at $14^{1}/_{2} \times 14^{3}/_{4}$. First things first—stop the bleeding and cut my losses fast. Market makers are stepping off the bids and thinning it out. I see ISLD bidders at $14^{7}/_{16}$. Too much selling pressure. Time to bite the bullet. I enter a sweep sell order on ISLD to sell 14 for 1000 shares. I get filled all 1000 at $14^{3}/_{8}$. I am out. Yuck! I know where I screwed up—stochastics was too toppy, and it was a momentum run that peaked at the 15 resistance, like the trading site moderator said. That was the time to get out, not in. An impulse trade gone bad!

$$-{}^{5}/_{8} \times 1000 \qquad \text{Total losses} = -\$625.00$$

4:00 p.m.   Well, VONE closes at $13^{1}/_{2}$, so it could have been worse. Overall, I had a nice day, and I still exceeded my daily targets. My biggest mistake was going too heavy on the impulse trade at the end of the day on VONE. Still, it could have been worse.

Total gains:	+$2,887.50
Total losses:	−$ 906.25
Total commissions ($20 per trade × 14 trades):	−$ 280.00
Total net profit-loss:	+$1,701.25

Overall, the day went well—I exceeded my daily targets by 1.7 times. My biggest mistake was going too heavy on VONE at the end of the day. I am not going to beat myself up on that trade. I am happy I took the fast stops out. Overall, I stuck to charts and stops very nicely and have no real complaints about today. All that really matters is what is on my profit-loss statement at the end of the day, and I am in the green.

CHAPTER 14

Money Management and Risk Management

As stressed earlier, the immediate goal of trading is to preserve your capital. There will be times when your stock will pull back beyond your mental stop. However, you will have a very sure conviction that the stock will turn around—perhaps the bid is swelling or the market is gaining strength. But you are also nervous about losing capital. What do you do? At a time like this, you will need to take action, and many times it is beneficial to average your costs with another lot—provided you notice a turnaround in the trend and can anticipate it, and you have actual *proof of a trend reversal.* For example, you went long 2000 shares of XYZ at 18 ($^{1}/_{8}$ above the intraday low; the intraday high is 21 and the S&P futures are negative). XYZ continues to fall quickly on weakness to $16^{15}/_{16}$ × 17. You start seeing the bid size swell up at $16^{15}/_{16}$ and more market makers jumping on the best bid. You see market makers getting taken out at 17 and many jumping to a higher ask. Time of sales shows several block buys at ask and a flurry of trades at ask. Even better, you see GSCO and MSCO jump on the bid and are nowhere to be found on the first three asks. Then you see INCA jump on best ask with a 100 size. The S&P futures are reversing into positive territory. Everything looks good for a reversal trend. So you decide to jump in at the 17 on another 2000 shares, thereby averaging your cost basis to $17^{1}/_{2}$—just in time before the stock upticks and INCA follows to the very best bid with the same size because there are no sellers. The market makers sense a strong buying interest and immediately jump to higher asks, and INCA keeps chasing. Before you know it, the bid pops to $17^3/8 \times 1/2$, then $17^1/2 \times 5/8$, then $17^5/8 \times 3/4$. Now you start to see some profit takers coming in. You see the size on the bid starting to dwindle, however, it's still strong enough for another possible uptick. The market makers on the bid still outnumber the ones on the best ask—five market makers to one market maker. You still see strength as the stock reaches a slowdown at $17^3/4 \times {}^{13}/16$. Time of sales still shows buyers coming in at ${}^{13}/16$. Now you need to make a decision. Technically, you are $1/4$ in the money. Do you take the money off the table? Or do you wait and see what happens? Keep in mind that traders are contemplating their options on every tick. Here are the possible scenarios:

1. You decide to hold your position through a short profit taking session, which results in a minimal pullback to $17^5/8 \times {}^{11}/16$, at which time the trend resumes to break through 18. You see a lot of market maker resistance sitting at $18^1/8$, and therefore you sell into the strength at the ask, getting out at $18^1/16$ for a ${}^9/16$ profit = $2125 profit!

2. You decide to hold your position because you want to get at least a $1/2$ point (face it, you're just plain greedy!). Unfortunately, other traders see some selling and decide they want to lock in their profits and sell into the strength. Still other traders see this, and they in turn decide to take profits. The market makers sense this, and they will jump to a lower bid, thereby causing more traders to get nervous—not about locking their profits, but about how just to break even without a loss. The sellers wear out the market makers on the bid, and the stock now drops to $17^1/4 \times 5/16$. The traders are now trying to get out of the stock at any cost to preserve capital, thereby sending the stock crashing below 17, hitting more stop losses and causing the stop to fall to $16^1/2$ resistance and a new intraday low. Realizing that you are losing money now, you panic and sell at $16^3/4$, resulting in a loss of $-3/4 = -\$3000$!

3. You sense that there is still some strength and thereby put in a sell order at the ask at $17^{13}/16$. The best ask size is 10, and your

40 size steps in front of it, making you the best ask. The buyers buy up all your shares, and the stock upticks to $^{13}/_{16} \times ^7/_8$ before the rest of the traders take profits, dropping the price back down to $17^1/_2 \times ^9/_{16}$. You not only caught the top for this round but made yourself a nice $^5/_{16}$ profit on what could have been a losing trade: $^5/_{16} \times 4000$ shares = $1250!

This seems pretty drastic, but it happens every day. The market makers are not necessarily innocent bystanders. When they sense panic, they will continue to feed it until the panic dies, and then they will try to create panic on the buy side. It is really a work of art. Of course, they will often buy during the panic selling and sell during the panic buying—quite simple and effective.

Preserving capital is absolutely essential to one's long-term survival in the markets. A money management system will force you to cut your losses fast and let your profits ride. Most big losses usually started off as small losses, and failure to implement a disciplined money management system propelled them to large losses. Therefore, we cannot stress enough the absolute importance of a money management system.

Most novice traders and investors usually take a position in the stock with only one question in mind: "What is my upside or expected gain?" They fail to ask themselves: "What is my downside or potential loss?"

When given a choice between avoiding a potential loss or partaking fully in a gain, one's first impulse is usually to go for the gain. However, quantitatively speaking, avoiding a loss is more important to your longer-term performance than making a potential gain. The rational is quite simple: It takes a greater percentage gain to recover for a given percentage loss. For example, if you take a 20 percent loss on a trade assuming $100,000 in capital, you are sitting at $80,000. In order to make back the loss, you would actually need greater than a 20 percent gain. In this case, 20 percent would only bring your capital to $96,000. You would need a 25 percent gain to make back your full losses. The reality is that it takes a 100 percent gain to make back a 50 percent loss!

So does this mean that you should not be risking your capital in trades? Psychologically speaking, it is quite counterproductive to think too much about losing money while entering a trade. That's how you attain cold feet. The answer instead is to implement a risk management system while trading. To decrease your risk when entering a position, you have some basic options:

1. Take a ½ size position and average down or up from entry (on breakouts).
2. Wait for the price to hit your set limit.
3. Use a tight stop loss (mental, of course).
4. Hedge with an opposite position (straddle the same stock or the opposite stock).
5. Diversify your positions (take more than one position).

The more you diversify, the less you risk per trade. Risk and money management take discipline to implement. In fact, managing risk goes against the grain of our natural impulses. Prospect theory demonstrates that people have a natural tendency to become risk seeking after a series of losses and to become risk averse to protect a gain. Our nature is to double our bets when we are losing and to take quick profits when we are winning. But doing so virtually guarantees that we will chase good capital after bad and end up underfunding winning trades. Successful and profitable trading comes from doing what does not come naturally. This explains why so few are ever successful traders.

Most novice traders go into a trade on impulse and only consider the best-case scenario as far as profits and price movements go. We might add, only to get panicked out of a position simply because they failed to realize the worst-case scenario or to consider what they would do should a trend turn against them. Therefore, it is imperative that you consider your downside risk as well as your upside potential when entering a position. Your biggest foe will be your emotions.

Panic usually sets in when the unexpected happens and forces you to naturally take the quickest steps to cover your rear. Therefore, you must not only consider downside risk but anticipate it and incorporate it into your play.

First, we will consider the unexpected in regard to capital and its application to money management. The most basic money management technique is the x percent and y percent rule. This technique is easy enough to incorporate. You must promise yourself to never risk x percent on any given trade and no more than y percent on all open trades total. For example, you might go with no more than 2 percent risk on any single trade and no more than 10 percent risk on your total account on all open trades at any given moment. This does not prevent you from using your complete capital; yet it does require you to use tight stops or incorporate hedges via options so that your maximum loss per trade cannot exceed 2 percent of your total capital. Therefore, you immediately have a mental stop loss before going into any given trade. It is also wise to consider a third x percent risk component in regard to total loss per month. For example, you might promise yourself to stop trading if your total capital decreases by 7 percent at any given time during the month. This third component is very beneficial in more ways than one. It ends any further bleeding of capital. Most importantly, it forces you to cool off emotionally and be an observer, allowing you to see the trees from the forest. As stated earlier, the human tendency is to throw good money after bad and become less risk averse when losing capital, and so taking time off will put an immediate end to the downward spiral. During this off time for the month, it would be wise to paper-trade and observe. It is absolutely amazing how rational one becomes when there is no downside capital risk involved. It is truly an eye-opening experience so long as you have the discipline to hold back from trading.

Let's assume you have decided on a 2/10/7 percent rule. You never risk more than 2 percent of your total capital on any one trade, never risk more than 10 percent of your total account on all open trades, and will immediately stop trading if you decrease your total capital by 7 percent at any time during the month. Let's further assume you blew your first three trades and lost 7 percent of your total equity during the first 3 days of the month. Now you are stuck with only being able to paper-trade or watch. You have no hope of making back your losses, and it eats you up inside. You are forced to carry over the loss to the next month. You might have a very strong opinion on a stock trend or are totally convinced of a surefire play. You convince yourself 1 week into this prison sentence that you have learned your lesson and have changed your whole outlook. All you really need to do to confirm this is to put in a trade. Naturally, you violate your money management rule and enter this trade perhaps just once. To your surprise (and horror), the trade goes sour and turns against you fast, making you stop out at another 7 percent loss. Now you are down 14 percent for the month, and you are hating yourself for violating your rule. At this point, you figure, "Oh, screw it! I've broken my rules. I may as well go for it one more time." You convince yourself that this time will be different (prospect theory). To your absolute shame, you get stopped out with another 7 percent loss, bringing your equity loss to 21 percent for the month in a grueling downward spiral.

If this situation sounds all too familiar, you must downsize your risk right off the bat to perhaps only risking 1 percent per trade. The key is to take on smaller risk in the form of smaller positions. If you are in a losing trend, take on the most simple, boring, conservative trade just to regain your confidence. You can't always go for home runs. A single or double is sufficient enough to get back in the game. Always remember that money can be regained. However, self-confidence is much harder to get back once you've lost it.

Going back to the self-imposed hiatus, the hardest aspect of not trading is the feeling of missing an opportunity to make back your losses. Not taking an action—not doing something—is the hardest part of taking a break. Therefore, it is much easier and more beneficial to plan ahead what you will be doing during your hiatus.

You will inevitably feel stress from the guilt and shame of your losses. As cognitive dissonance theory states that people tend to reduce stress by either taking an action or changing their belief, you might convince yourself that the losses were a fluke and shrug off your misfortune and move on. You might even try to think about past good trades in an effort to forget the last bad trades.

But ignoring your losing trades in this fashion is the worst mistake you can make. This is because you can learn more from your losing trades than from your winning trades. Your losing trades allow you to learn the weaknesses of your system and also to explore your own vulnerability and thresholds.

Right from the start, you need to reprogram your frame of reference. Understand that trading is like a business and that losses are to be considered an expense, the cost of doing business. You did everything right and took the loss. This is called trading. It does no good to continue to torture yourself over taking too big of a loss. You are a speculator, not a gambler, and you are proving it. The difference between a speculator and a gambler is that the speculator can stop after a series of losses; the gambler can't.

The first thing you need to do is study your successful trades and develop a model of the setup, conditions, and chart patterns. Compare your winning trades with your losing trades and note the differences and the divergences in conditions. Was it the market in general? Not enough liquidity? Head fake? Fake breakout? Noise? Try to develop new rules or modify your old system so that you will recognize the conditions and setup the next time an identical trade or position is taken. This is why a trading journal is an absolute necessity when trading. Your trading journal should document the conditions of every trade, the reasons why you took the position, as well as your mental stops. One look at your trading journal should allow you to relive the trade as if you had just completed it. Use this self-imposed downtime to regain your confidence and self-esteem. Always realize that losses are unavoidable when trading. As well, however, realize that not only would you be a fool not to examine your trades and learn from your mistakes, but you would also be a gambler.

Successful trading is not based on your win-loss record. It is based on your profit and loss record. Remember that. You can have a 2-point gain and a 3-point stop loss and still end up positive for the day. How? Let's say you were playing an uptrend stock and gained 2 points on 1000 shares ($2000 profit). As the stock continued to rise, you managed your risk and took only 300 shares and pared out as it reversed, losing 3 points on 300 shares ($900 loss). The math is simple, $2000 (profits) − $900 (losses) = +$1100 profits netted before commissions. This is what we mean by risk management. Inherently a stock gets riskier the higher it moves, especially on momentum. A simple rule of thumb is to use smaller lots as a stock rises in value to protect your downside risk.

THE HOME RUN SYNDROME

When a trader makes a big score or a series of big scores, it is very important not to fall into the mentality that every trade should be just as big. When a trader lets a big score trade get to his head, we call this the home run syndrome. This is a very devastating mentality to adopt. The exception suddenly becomes the norm in a trader's mind; it make him sloppy and overconfident. Rather than taking stops, the trader sits through complete pullbacks, violating all rules in the hope that this trade will make big profits eventually.

When BAMM ran from $5 to over $50 in 1 week, many traders made gigantic profits on the run-up. The traders who made the most profits jumped in and held the stock like an investment, not knowing any better, thinking BAMM was a $100 stock. When BAMM started to fall back, these traders either continued to hold the trade or double-downed on the pullbacks. When the smoke cleared, lots of traders that made big money on BAMM either lost all their profits or lost more money on the next few stocks they played. The home run mentality blinded traders into looking for the next BAMM, only to strike out.

The sad irony is that most new day traders will hit that home run in the beginning and start off with a very dangerous precedent of basing their trades on sheer hope, luck, and will. They will think trading is very easy and will assume every other trade to be just as easy. This is like walking into a minefield for the first time, closing your eyes, and walking straight. When you make it out alive, you tell yourself that this is how you will survive every minefield you encounter. We can all guess what inevitably will happen in the long run—boom! Anyone can get lucky on a single trade. Luck runs out very fast. In the long run, skill is the only thing that will keep you alive.

The key is to go into every trade looking for a base hit, not the home run. Base hits are gains of $1/4$ to 1 point. Take what the stock will give you. It only takes one decent trade to hit your daily target. The game is to react and not to predict.

A Different Style of Trading

by Russell Arthur Lockhart, Ph.D.

Trading, whether as profession or pastime, is influenced heavily by a trader's personality, character, and psychological condition. Not every trader is cut out to be a momentum-scalping trader, for whom the earlier chapters of this book have been written. This appendix may be thought of as a bridge to an entirely different style of trading. The need for a different style rests not so much on the failure of a trader to develop momentum-scalping skills, but on the reality that there are different types of traders. Many traders, particularly those who are young, aggressive, and temperamentally suited to quick action, instant gratification, and near "combat" conditions, will find momentum scalping very appealing. There is something compelling about momentum scalping. The rules, as this book has made clear, are precise, straightforward, definite. You're in; you're out; you move on to the next trade. At day's end, you take your money off the table. Tomorrow, you come back and do it again. With proper training and education, many will be able to achieve considerable success.

Without question, momentum scalping is difficult. It constantly exposes the trader to the risks of *not* acting in a timely manner. The "storm" of shifting momentum and price oscillation then becomes threatening, and the trader becomes susceptible to fear and panic. Good trading under these emotional conditions is impossible. The trader needs to learn whether failure at momentum scalping is due to factors that can be surmounted or whether this style of trading is just not possible. Swing trading (holding a trade for longer periods during the trading day) may become an attractive alternative.

But for the trader not able to trade in these ways—for whatever reason—the choice of how to trade becomes more complex, so complex in fact that the frustrated trader, or one with mounting losses, is tempted to abandon trading altogether. It is for this trader that this appendix is written. The author has spent many years studying and trading just about every conceivable system, method, and strategy that any trader is likely to encounter—from the well known to the esoteric, even secret. The distillation of this experience has not led to an easy "day trading for dummies." The complexity of financial markets cannot be made simplistic. What the experience has produced is a challenging combination of principles and techniques that yields precise, objective, and unambiguous "action" signals while trading any market at any time. Once learned, these hints and helps will enable any trader to trade better, more profitably, and with genuine understanding of what to do under any trading condition. What you will find here may well change the way you experience the markets and the way you trade them. Most of all, what you will find here will help you trade with greater understanding, with less stress, and with clearer vision—the three factors that will enable you to achieve long-term success in active trading.

WHY DAY TRADING?

"Because it's there!" What has come to be known as *day trading* is new, and many are lured by it. Of course, day trading is as old as the first market, but it has generally been the preserve of professionals. Now one finds traders of all degrees of experience at innumerable trading houses hunched over computers, buying and selling in seconds or minutes, hundreds of trades a day, Uncountable trading rooms in cyberspace connect thousands of traders all over the world, responding instantly to "calls" made by head traders to buy or sell. And in countless chatrooms, this or that stock is touted or rumored into buying or selling frenzies by traders acting on this information alone.

Four factors converging in the last few years of the twentieth century have made this possible: the computer, the Internet, discount brokerage fees, and an unprecedented bull market. These, combined with the ever-present lust for quick fortune, have produced a new market dynamic: a massive degree of public participation in short-term trading. Volatility in some markets is obviously a direct result of day trading activity. Whether this amounts to more than day traders buying and selling to one another is not yet clear.

What is clear is that trading is *not* investing. If trading is "take the money and run," investing is "plant the money and let it grow." Trading is always short term in its orientation, whether for 6 seconds, 6 hours, or 6 days. Investment is always intended to be long term. Trading aspires to the growth of capital; investment to growth in ownership. The wealth of a trader is measured in units of currency; that of an investor in units of equity. The trader always seeks cash in pocket; the investor certificates of ownership (shares). Investment is long term because it generally takes a long time to accumulate a sizable degree of ownership. Unless an investment goes sour (e.g., a company fails), there is often no incentive to divest—even when there are large "profits" in the value of an investor's position.

The trader, however, seeks something quite different. The trader seeks gains *now!* The trader in effect attempts to reduce the time element to near zero. While a 15 percent return in a year's time would be considered satisfying to the investor, the trader wants this in a day!

Consider the capital multiplying potential that the "new" day trading makes possible. Figure A.1 illustrates the price action in a volatile stock over the course of a day's trading. In this example, the closing price is the same as the open price, so the nightly news will report that XYZ was "unchanged." As is clear, however, the price of XYZ was *full of changes* during the day. Imagine there exists a method that would work as follows. The trader buys on the open at 23, sells at that first peak at 25 (+2), buys again at 23, sells at the peak at 27 (+4), buys again at 25, sells at 29 (+4), buys again at 21, and closes out at 23 (+2). Adding up these gains, the trader would have a total gain of 12 points in four trades. That's more than a 50 percent return in one day! Imagine further that, in addition to buying at the lows of each move, the trader sold short at the peaks. In this case, the trader's total gain would be more than 100 percent in one day!

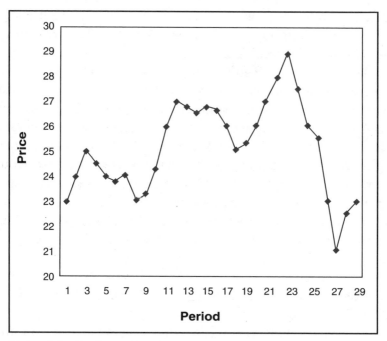

Figure A.1   13-minute price action during the trading day.

Thus, if it were possible to capitalize fully on the rise and fall of a stock's price during the day, a large percentage return of one's capital could be achieved in short order. In fact, there is no other mechanism of wealth-generating potential as potent as the multiplying effect of capital market price movements.

Perfect capture of price movement as illustrated in the above example, of course, is impossible. But impossible or not, it is some portion of that daily price potential that the day trader seeks to capture. And even if the trader captures only 10 percent of that total price movement on a daily basis, the annual income of that trader would be astronomical by most anyone's standards. *That* is the lure of day trading.

WHY DAY TRADERS LOSE MONEY

With the profit potential so high, why is it that so many day traders end up losing all or most of their money? Many reasons are obvious. Traders lack experience, education, and knowledge. They trade without method, discipline, or strategy. They fall prey to their emotions. This leads to compulsivity and behavior more akin to betting and gambling than to genuine understanding of either the markets or themselves. This is a prescription for disaster. Fortunate traders will discover early on that trading is not the easy way to riches it is often pictured to be, and will see that education is crucial. Most traders lose money because they do not have an understanding of the markets or themselves. Education through books such as this one and the many other fine books and training courses readily available to traders can help them to learn the necessity of method, the requirement of discipline, and the importance of money management. Even when armed with this understanding, traders will still have the daunting task of understanding themselves in relation to the market. This is the most difficult task of all. The psychological factors that lead traders into self-defeating behavior are very powerful and difficult to overcome.

Chief among the factors that lead to cycles of defeat is *stress*. In trading, one's money is always on the line, often on a tick-by-tick basis. One is always exposed to loss. The uncertainty of what will happen leads traders to "believe" certain things must happen, and these beliefs often interfere with correct observation about what is happening. In this state, traders will make substantial errors in judgment and action.

Most simply, traders lose money because they liquidate trades at a loss. Disciplined use of stop losses is one way to keep these losses to a minimum. If used properly, one's gains should always be more than one's losses. The first task of any trader is to minimize losses in order to preserve capital for more successful trades. Most traders never learn to do this well enough, and this is why perhaps as many as three-fourths of active traders ultimately fail.

Every trader, however, in looking over losing trades will discover an interesting fact. By far the majority of trades one enters into *do* become profitable—after the trader has exited the trade at a loss. This leads to all sorts of "if only" wishes and recriminations at oneself about "stupid" losses. Later in this appendix, I will describe a new strategy, which I have named the "basket" strategy. This approach does not use stops, but relies on the principle of alternation in conjunction with position size and price leveraging to reduce both losses and risk to an absolute minimum.

THE PRINCIPLE OF ACTION

Risk is uncertainty in relation to the future. In the financial markets, this uncertainty focuses on price and time. When faced with uncertainty, human beings—traders included—will make considerable effort to "predict" and "forecast" the future. When a trader *believes* that prices will rise—on whatever basis—the trader acts. Action follows belief.

What one believes will happen is very seductive. Most market analysis, whether simple-minded or sophisticated, fundamental or technical, emotional or mystical, is motivated by an invariable impulse to confirm and strengthen belief. Human belief processes seek only confirmation. Not only is evidence to the contrary *not* sought, but it is discounted, not seen, or distorted. Thus, built into the process of belief is a mechanism of denial. This denial engenders the emotional processes of greed and fear that serve to diminish the accuracy of perception, and, most critically, to inhibit action based on the reality and implication of contrary evidence. *This is fatal to the day trader.*

Success in day trading will be enhanced if one abandons all efforts at prediction and focuses instead on knowing what to do when and if certain prices occur in the market. No one can predict what the price will be in the next minute, the next hour, the next day, or the next year, because the underlying determinants of market behavior are *chaotic*.[1] For this reason the day trader must always be aware of the evidence that refutes the reasons for being in the trade, and when this evidence is confirmed, the trader must exit the trade without question, regardless of the strength of belief about what will or should happen. This principle of conjecture and refutation is counter to what happens in the natural phenomenology of belief and therefore is something the trader must learn.

Prediction is useless to the day trader. To profit consistently, the active trader will need to use techniques and methods that minimize risk, minimize dependence on prediction, and minimize the influence of belief. To accomplish this requires that the active trader must always know what to do when and if certain price behavior occurs in the market. This *principle of action* is designed to free the trader from those factors that undermine success. The secret to successful day trading is this: to know what to do when certain prices occur, to know with certainty that one will act on those prices when they do occur, and to let go of belief and prediction in order to focus more clearly on what actually is happening in the market.

METHODS, TECHNIQUES, AND THE PRINCIPLE OF ALTERNATION

One of the simplest observations of market behavior is that prices rise and fall. Without this ebb and flow of prices there would be no market. Two elements are always at work in this continual flux in prices. Of most importance is what might be likened to tidal action—the tide is in or out. This corresponds to what is called price *trend*. For certain periods of time, there is a general rise or fall in prices. Riding atop this trend is a shorter-term rise and fall in prices called price *oscillation*—analogous to ocean waves, whether the tide is coming in or going out. This general characteristic is *fractal*[2] in nature. This means that no matter what the time frame—1 minute, 1 day, or 1 year—price behavior *always* exhibits these two components: price trend and price oscillation. There are periods (again, in whatever time frame) when trend motion is strong—often strikingly so. This feature of price behavior is called *momentum*. When trend motion tends toward zero, a market is in *consolidation*.

Whatever a trader's time frame, it is obvious that underlying trends during momentum stages have the largest capital multiplying effect in the shortest period of time. Ideally, the active trader will seek to enter a trend as it develops momentum, will try to exit as the trend loses momentum, and will attempt to avoid periods of consolidation.

How does the trader actually do this? This is where the trader must call upon methods and techniques. Every trader has a method, whether it is just following the advice of a chatroom stock picker or acting on a signal from a neural network software program; whether it is following some gut feeling or getting an action signal from some telephone hot line. There is no end to the methods available to the active trader. Hundreds if not thousands of "methods" compete for the trader's attention.

It follows that the trader should seek out methods and techniques that have the capacity to identify trends early, to warn of trend exhaustion, and to identify likely periods of consolidation. While following most any method is better than none, many methods do *not* offer what the active trader most needs.

In my study of methods and markets, I have found eight factors that I believe are crucial in assessing the genuine effectiveness of any method. First, the methods must be of use in all markets and all time frames. Second, the methods must be totally objective and *not* subject to variable "interpretations." Third, the methods must use *actual* market prices, not averages, statistical manipulations, or other derivatives. Fourth, the methods must provide *actual* market prices on which to act in terms of entry, exit, and stop loss prices. Fifth, the methods must *objectively* identify trends, exhaustion points, and countertrends. Sixth, the methods must not rely on "predictions," but *always* on actual market behavior. Seventh, the methods must at all times, whether a trader is in a trade or not, provide actual market prices that tell the trader what to do. Eighth, the methods must sensitively and definitely incorporate the principle of alternation.

No method by itself will satisfy all these conditions. However, certain methods used in *combination* may approach these ideals. One such set of methods is described in the sections that follow.

THE THREE-PRICE BREAK METHOD
OF TREND DETERMINATION

Whatever the time frame of interest to the trader, it will be advantageous to know the trend state of the stock or market being traded. For this purpose the trader needs a method that will unambiguously identify the trend, its direction, precise entry and exit points, likely points of trend exhaustion, and market-based stop loss action points. This is a lot to ask of a single method. However, one method that satisfies these conditions is what I call the *three-price break method* (3PB). This method is an old Japanese trading method.[3] It works in all markets and in all time frames. This is important to the trader for three reasons: (1) Only one trend-determining method needs to be learned; (2) one can confidently trade shorter-term trends (e.g., 13-minute data) within the context of longer-term trends (daily); and (3) in combination with other methods (to be described shortly), the 3PB will provide extraordinarily effective guidance in terms of when to enter a trade, when to exit, when to reenter, or when to decline a trade altogether.

The best way to learn the 3PB method is to see it in action. Figure A.2 illustrates the price behavior of YHOO for 13-minute periods over the course of 3 days.[4] The chart is plotted using the Japanese candlestick method. The candlestick is composed of four "important" prices: the open, high, low, and close. Of these, the method considers the open and close to be the most important. The relationship between these two prices forms the "body" of the candlestick and produces a visual picture of the "outcome" of trading for the period by distinguishing between "up" and "down" candles. An up candle occurs when the close is higher than the open; a down candle when the close is lower than the open. In Figure A.2, up candles are gray, and down candles are black. The principle of alternation referred to earlier is clearly visible in a candlestick chart.

There are many types of candles as well as many relationships between candles that are important to the trader. Knowledge of candle types and candle patterns and their significance can be combined with the methods described here to increase a trader's effectiveness.

To use this chart to illustrate the 3PB method, the trader needs a starting point. The choice of starting point is quite arbitrary and is a matter of the trader's choice. Ordinarily, one would begin a 3PB chart at some obvious "low" point in a chart. In Figure

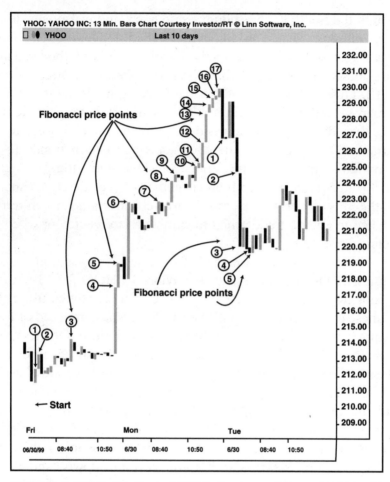

Figure A.2 Candlestick chart of YHOO showing each new price high and Fibonacci price points. (SOURCE: Chart by Investor/RT © 1996–2000 Linn Software, Inc., www.linnsoft.com. Reproduced with permission of Linn Software, Inc.)

A.2, notice the low price at 210 early Friday morning. This will be the arbitrary starting point in this example. For 3PB purposes, the *only* value we are interested in is the *closing* price in each 13-minute period. The close is the most important price because it reflects the net trading for the period. Note also that while this chart illustrates 13-minute periods, it could just as well be a 1-minute chart, a 30-minute chart, a daily chart, or a yearly chart. The principles of 3PB charting are exactly the same for any time period.

This first period of interest opened at 211.38, made a low at 210.00, went on to a high at 212.44, and closed at 212.38. This is an up candle, closing near the high of the period. So the first close is 212.38. Because a trend requires two data points, at this arbitrary starting point we choose the low price as the first data point and the close as the second data point. In this way, based on the information in a single period, we can determine the direction of the trend (up from 210.00 to 212.38). Moreover, we know as well what price would *reverse* the trend—that is, any price below 210.00.

In effect, the method says, that the trend is *long*, and will continue long until there is a close *below* 210.00. Notice, too, that the method is *not* predicting anything. We do not know whether the trend will continue up or whether the trend will reverse. But we do not need to predict in order to *act*. That is, if the trend is long, the trader buys YHOO at 212.38. The market itself has "issued" the buy signal. The market itself has also set a "reversal" price (less than 210.00). Using the 3PB method, the trader now *waits* until the close of the next period. All the ticks between closes are of no interest to the 3PB method.

The next period opens at 212.34 and promptly drops to 212.06. The trader who just bought at 212.38 now has a loss of 0.32. This may rattle the trader who hangs on every tick, but the method trader is looking for only two things: a closing price below 210.00 and a close higher than 212.38. Prices between these points are inconsequential. After hitting a low at 212.06, prices move ahead and close out the period near the high at 213.31. This is a new high. Again, the method does not predict; it yields only prices on which to act. The reversal or "break" price remains at 210.00.

At this point, the trader is feeling pleased. There is nearly a 1-point gain, the trend is long, and the trader is long. The trader knows that YHOO can move many points in a day and begins to want one of those 10- or 20-point moves *now*!

The next period opens at 213.31 and promptly drops like a rock to 211.31. The trader now has more than a 1-point loss, the gain has evaporated, and the trader asks if this is the beginning of one of YHOO's 10-point moves down or worse. All these thoughts and their attendant emotions of fear and greed will plague any trader, no matter how experienced. In this storm of emotion, the method provides a kind of beacon, guiding the trader to safe harbor. For what is most crucial to the trader is *not* the momentary gain or loss, but the *certainty* that *if* the next interval closes below 210.00, the long position will be sold and a short position will be initiated. This is the certainty of a trader's discipline, and it is the shortest road to genuine profits. The only certainty in the market is that prices will alternate. Therefore, the trader must seek certainty in *actions* based on prices. So the 3PB method trader does nothing as prices drop *unless* there is a close below 210.00. This is the trader's discipline. The period closed at 212.00. The trend is still long. The trader is still long. The trader has suffered through a natural period of alternation that did not break the trend. The trader's security is not that the trend will continue, but the certainty that *if* the trend breaks, the trader will act.

Now over the next eight periods, YHOO fails to make a new high. During this time, there was never a close below 210.00, so the trend remains intact. In the next period, YHOO spurts to a new high and closes at 214.19. This is the third new high. The break price remains at 210.00.

After hitting three new highs, there are twelve periods where prices trade in a narrow range without a new high and still no break. The trend remains intact but lackluster. In the next period, YHOO wakes up and moves dramatically higher to close at 217.50. This is the fourth new high.

With the fourth new high, the trend break price will change. This is illustrated in Figure A.3. This 3PB chart consists only of new prices and break points. Notice that this chart eliminates all the "inconsequential" prices (as well as time) and simply reveals the trend as it builds.

The break price is always determined by the third price back—hence the name, *three-price* break. When there are fewer than three prices in a new trend, the break price will be the starting price. Each new high is pictured in the chart by a stair-step box that has a beginning price (the prior close) and an end price

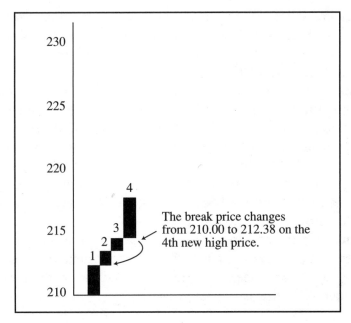

Figure A.3   Three-price break chart for YHOO showing the changing break price after the fourth new high price.

(the current new closing high). With each new box, the break price is found by starting at the *lower right corner* of the new box, counting this as 1, and then counting backward to 3. That will be the break price. So with the fourth new high, the new break price rises from 210.00 to 212.38. Notice that by the fourth new high, the break price becomes the entry price.

The next period brings the fifth new high at 218.94 and the closing for the day at 218.75. The short-term trader must always make a decision as the market closes about whether to liquidate the position and take the gain (6.38 points) or to carry the trade over. There is nothing in the 3PB data to suggest exiting the trade yet. At five new highs, the new break price is 213.31. Clearly, the 3PB method will stay long *until* there is a trend reversal. There is no way to predict when such a trend reversal will occur. The 3PB trader can simply follow the 3PB method, or the trader's resources can be "managed" with the addition of other methods. Such management will require acting on gain-taking signals and then following reentry signals. Examples of such methods will be described shortly.

Figure A.4 plots the trend data for YHOO over the next 2 days. Notice that YHOO reached 17 new highs at a price of 230.00. At this high, the break price was 229.00. This uptrend was broken in the following period on a close below 229.00 at 226.75.[5] If the trader had remained long during this period, there would be an "automatic" gain of 14.37 points, and the trader would now be short from 226.75 with a new break price of 230.00. Notice that the break price on the first reversal low is the price of the last high. Notice also that the method unambiguously indicates the trend and action prices for entry and reversal.

Just because the trend breaks at 226.75, the method is *not* predicting the price will go down. The very next interval could bring a new high price above 230.00. What the method *does* tell the trader—and this is crucial information—is what the market is

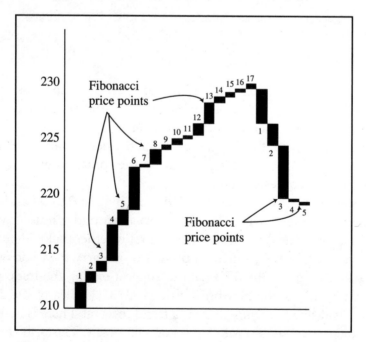

Figure A.4 Three-price break chart for YHOO showing the complete trend, three-price break downtrend, and Fibonacci price points.

actually doing. And what the market says in this respect, in the long run, is the trader's best friend. The trader will do best to listen to the market to see what it is doing. The 3PB method helps the trader do this.

YHOO promptly makes five new lows at 219.56 with a break price of 224.75, and for the rest of the day it makes no further lows and does not break. YHOO closed at 221.63, and the short position is worth 5.12 points. Again, the trader must decide whether to take this gain or to hold with the method.

By far, the majority of trades using the 3PB method will yield positive results with an active and volatile stock. There *will* be losses, but they will be more than offset by gains. The method is adaptable in a variety of ways. For example, one might choose to trade *only* the long signals in 13-minute data when the daily 3PB trend is long (or take short signals only when the daily trend is short). Or one might trade a high-priced stock like YHOO with *options,* instead of the stock itself, for greater leverage. In this case, one would buy calls on long signals and puts on short signals.

And to emphasize again: The 3PB method can be used in any market and in any time frame. The rules are the same. The trader can illustrate this by printing out a chart of prices without any price scale or time scale and doing the 3PB chart. The trend and action (reversal) points will be the same regardless of the time frame of the price chart. In this sense, the 3PB method is a *universal* trend-determining method and thus is the foundation on which additional methods can be built.

EAST MEETS WEST

Most any price chart in any time frame reveals periods of momentum (up or down), points at which change takes place (from one trend to another), and periods of relative stagnation. Prices rise to certain points, fall back and consolidate, rise again, reverse, drop to certain points, and so on. This ebb and flow is a constant feature of any price behavior in any time frame. The 3PB method simplifies trend determination by filtering out inconsequential price fluctuations. What 3PB does *not* do, however, is guide the trader during often lengthy periods of consolidation where the trader's money is at risk and inefficiently used.[6]

There is an old Japanese trading maxim that may be summarized as "sell half at 8 new prices, half again at 10 new prices, and the rest at 12 new prices." This clearly expresses the awareness that at some point every trend reverses, and that as a trend matures, one should begin to take profits and lessen risk. This is sound advice. In the YHOO trade above, if the trader had started with 100 shares of YHOO at 212.38, 50 shares would have been sold at 8 new highs (224.13 for a gain of $587.50), 25 shares at 10 new highs (225.13 for a gain of $318.75), and the remaining 25 shares at 12 new highs (226.63 for a gain of $356.25). This represents a total gain of $1262.50, or 5.9 percent, over the course of 2 days. This compares with the gain of $1437 if the trader had stayed fully invested until the trend broke. These values are to be compared with the "theoretical" maximum (i.e., if one had sold at the absolute high) of $1778.00.

As sound as this advice is, the method is not altogether satisfying. The initial gain-taking rule does not come into effect until after 8 new highs and therefore can be of no use to a trader in dealing with shorter-term trends. And since the position is liquidated completely at 12 new highs, there is no way of dealing with trends of longer duration. These are severe limitations and lead to the question of whether there may not be a more *general* approach that would enable the trader to deal with the shorter-term trend as well as the longer-term trend. Fortunately, there is a method that is ideal for this purpose.

The principle of alternation can also be thought of as a principle of growth and decay. It is meaningful to think of prices "growing" from a low to a high and then "decaying" by falling from a high to a low. Some periods produce small growth, others large growth, analogous to the different sizes and rates of growth of most anything that grows. When these growth characteristics are studied, it is found that a surprisingly large percentage of growth patterns are described by a surprisingly small number of definite patterns. These patterns are mathematical in nature. Even complex growth patterns are found to be expressions of relatively simple mathematical patterns. These patterns are generated by so-called number series.

A number series is simply a series of numbers generated according to well-defined rules. A simple number system is our ordinal number system: 0, 1, 2, 3, 4, 5, and so on to infinity. This number series has two rules: The first rule is that it has a beginning point (0), and the second rule is that 1 is added to each number in turn. So the series is generated by $0+1 = 1, 1+1 = 2, 2+1 = 3$, and so on. This is a simple summation series. Many things "grow" in this way: the years on a calendar, the rings on a tree, one's age, the sequence of trading periods.

Of course, many things do not grow this way. One's height or weight, for example. There are an infinite number of number series, and there are branches of mathematics devoted to their study. Fortunately relatively few such number series are of any interest or importance to the trader. One in particular, however, the so-called *Fibonacci* number series, turns out to have major relevance for the trader. In fact, this number series may underlie the growth characteristics of market prices, as it seems to underlie the growth characteristics of so many natural phenomena (from the growth of snail shells to the growth of galaxies!).

Here is the Fibonacci number series: 0, 1, 1, 2, 3, 5, 8, 13, 21, 34, 55, 89, 144, 233, … How is this generated? It begins as a simple ordinal series. In this case the growth rule is different: To get each new term add the *sum* of the preceding two terms. Thus: $0+1 = 1, 1+1 = 2, 1+2 = 3, 2+3 = 5, 3+5 = 8, 5+8 = 13$, and so on. Notice how the terms in this series get proportionally larger with each summation. In the next section, these proportions will be examined for their remarkable mathematical characteristics and their relevance to the trader.

For now, consider the relationship between these Fibonacci values and the 3PB method. Assume that Fibonacci numbers are important *price points* in a 3PB trend. The first price (1) is clearly the first "new" price following any start price or the first new price following a three-price break. The second price (2) is important because it *confirms* the trend. At this point, the trader is either in the trend on the first new price (1) or on the confirmation of the trend (2).[7]

Now consider that, once in a trade, all subsequent Fibonacci price points (3, 5, 8, 13, 21, 34, ...) are action points in terms of trade exit. It is obvious at once that this procedure solves the problems of both the short-term trend and the long-term trend. Underlying this idea is the assertion that the Fibonacci price points are points of price potential exhaustion.

Of course, once the trader exits a trade at a Fibonacci price point, there must be an objective rule to follow to reenter the trend in order to participate in the continuation of the trend. There are a number of such trend reentry rules. The simplest is that *following* a Fibonacci price-point exit (e.g., at three new highs), the trader will reenter only when price exceeds the previous high (the actual high, not the close) or when a new 3PB high occurs.

In the YHOO trade, then, the combined 3PB and Fibonacci price-point method would enter at 212.38 and exit on the third new high at 214.19 (see Figure A.2). The method has instructed the trader to *take gains* at three new highs. The instruction is clear and unambiguous. Once the gains are in pocket, the method further instructs the trader to reenter *only* if the price in a succeeding period hits a *higher* price than the high in the period in which the gains were taken. The high in that period was 214.38. After hitting the third high, YHOO went into a relatively long period of consolidation (12 periods). There is no predicting how long these price exhaustion periods may last. To watch the slow price erosion during the consolidation period on a tick-by-tick basis is very hard on the trader. The emotional stress during such a time tends to encourage wrong action.

However, with gains in pocket, the trader can *comfortably* watch for the action prices: either a break (below 210.00) or a reentry if and when prices hit 214.41 (a tick higher than 214.38, the previous high). Meanwhile, the funds are not at risk and could be employed elsewhere until YHOO gives a signal.

The reentry signal (214.41) was hit in the thirteenth period following the third new high. In this period, the uptrend accelerates, and YHOO makes a fourth new high at 217.50. As prices accelerate, the scalping trader may take a point or two. However, the disciplined 3PB trader is waiting for the next action point. This will be to take gains at five new highs. The trader does *not* know that there will be five new highs. As this fourth new high occurs, the break price rises from 210.00 to 212.38 (the original entry price). In the next period, YHOO continues its climb and closes at 218.94. This is a gain-taking price point. This yields 4.50 additional points. No further highs occurred by the close of trading. The 3PB trader ends the day with 6.31 points in pocket, and with definite instructions for the following day's trading: either to reenter on any price greater than 219.19 (the high price in the fifth new high period) or to go short on any 13-minute close below 213.31 (the new break price on the fifth new high). Notice that the method always has specific market prices to act on in terms of entry, exit, and reentry.

The next day, YHOO opens at 219.50. This is above the reentry price (219.19), and so the 3PB trader reenters. The break price is 213.31. The trader may ask what the stop is. From the perspective of the 3PB method, the stop is always the break price. This means that the market action itself sets the stops. For a trader used to setting close stops, this may seem to create considerable risk. Setting point stops or dollar-based stops, however, bears no relation to actual market behavior. Over time, the 3PB trader will observe that using the method's approach to stops (actually, reversals) is more profitable. To reenter at 219.19 with a break at 213.31 creates a "risk" of at least 5.88 points. However, this must be considered in the context of gains in pocket, 6.31 points. In effect, there is little risk because the trader has pocketed more than the risk being assumed. So, in general, as the 3PB trader takes gains at Fibonacci price points (3, 5, 8, 13, 21, ...), each succeeding reentry becomes essentially riskless.

The next gain-taking price point is at eight new highs (224.13) for an additional gain of 4.63 points. Reentry is at 224.25, with a break price of 218.94. The next gain-taking price point is 13 new highs (228.34) for an additional gain of 4.09 points. The reentry point is 228.75, with a break price of 225.13. With each new high, the break price rises. At 17 new highs, the break price is at 229.00. At this point, YHOO breaks *down* on a 13-minute close at 226.75. And at this point, the trader exits the long position and reverses to the short side. The last trade produced a loss of 2.00 points. The total gain on this long-side trade was 13.03 points.

The short-side trade is covered at 3 new lows (220.00), which nets 6.75 points. Reentry is at 219.63, and the trader exits on the fifth new low at 219.56. This nets the trader only 0.06 point. The 3PB trader reenters at 219.25 and remains short, with a break price at 224.75.

This example illustrates well the use of the 3PB method coupled with Fibonacci price points. The combined method yields precise market-based instructions on when to enter a trade, when to take gains, when to reenter and when to reverse. Used consistently and with discipline, this approach will be of particular value to the trader seeking major gains in relatively short periods of time.

The Fibonacci price points are obviously a useful addition to the general 3PB method. However, the price points themselves (3, 5, 8, 13, ...) do not tell the trader anything about the *extent* of the trend in terms of price at those price points. The YHOO example illustrates that as a trend *unfolds*, the price at the critical Fibonacci price points increases proportionally. The move from 1 to 3 was 1.87 points; to 5 was 6.56; to 8 was 11.75, and to 13 was 14.37. Quite obviously the trend grows. Can the Fibonacci number series help describe this growth in such a way that it would provide useful information for the trader?

FIBONACCI PRICE POTENTIAL TARGETS

Once a number series is generated, it is then possible to apply definite rules to the numbers generated. Table A.1 illustrates the application of simple rules to the Fibonacci number series which reveals the extraordinary properties of this series. The table shows the ordinal position of each Fibonacci number, the Fibonacci number itself, the result of dividing each Fibonacci number by the preceding one, the result of dividing each number by the subsequent one, the difference between these operations, the result of

Table A.1   Application of simple rules to the Fibonacci number series.

Ordinal Number	Fibonacci Value	Divide Number by Previous Number	Divide Number by Subsequent Number	Difference between Divisions	1.000–Difference	Ordinal Fibonacci
1	0					
2	1					
3	1	1.000	0.500	0.500	0.500	First
4	2	2.000	0.667	1.333	0.333	
5	3	1.500	0.600	0.900	0.400	Second
6	5	1.667	0.625	1.042	0.375	
7	8	1.600	0.615	0.985	0.385	
8	13	1.625	0.619	1.006	0.382	Third
9	21	1.615	0.618	0.997	0.382	
10	34	1.619	0.618	1.001	0.382	
11	55	1.618	0.618	1.000	0.382	
12	89	1.618	0.618	1.000	0.382	
13	144	1.618	0.618	1.000	0.382	
14	233	1.618	0.618	1.000	0.382	
15	377	1.618	0.681	1.000	0.382	
16	610	1.618	0.618	1.000	0.382	
17	987	1.618	0.618	1.000	0.382	
18	1597	1.618	0.618	1.000	0.382	
19	2584	1.618	0.618	1.000	0.382	
20	4181	1.618	0.618	1.000	0.382	
21	6765	1.618	0.618	1.000	0.382	Fifth

subtracting this difference from 1, and the ordinal positions in the series, which are themselves Fibonacci numbers.

Dividing each Fibonacci number by the preceding number soon produces an intriguing phenomenon: The result becomes the constant value 1.618. As well, dividing each number by the subsequent number yields the constant value 0.618. Subtracting the latter from the former soon leads to the constant value of 1. And subtracting the prior value from 1 soon produces the constant value 0.382.

Keeping in mind that the Fibonacci series is a series that mathematically describes the growth of many animals, plants, and other things, the table reveals that no matter how large something grows, it will grow by certain *constant* ratios that are independent of what is being described. What this means is that the growth of a snail's shell, the leafing of a plant, the growth of a galaxy—and the growth in stock prices—may all be described by the same mathematical structure, that is, the Fibonacci number series and its characteristics.

The constant 1.618 may be considered a *growth constant*. To relate this to the YHOO example, if we start at the price of 210 (the low on Figure A.2), multiplying 210 by 1.618 would yield a price of 339.78. We can consider this the growth potential of YHOO from 210. YHOO may indeed reach that price at some future time, but that potential is not likely to happen in the time frame of interest to the day trader. Since a constant remains a constant when operated on by a constant, the simplest way to bring a price potential move of interest to the day trader would be to divide this value 1.618 by a factor of 10. In this case, then, multiplying 210 by 0.1618 yields a value of 33.98 points. That is, the "reduced" Fibonacci growth factor yields a growth potential of 210 + 33.98 = 243.98.

We may regard this *potential* move of YHOO from 210 to 243.98 as one complete growth unit. The emphasis is on "potential" since no one has any idea what YHOO will do when it is at that 210 point. However, in using the 3PB method, the trader has taken a long position at 212.38, with a break price at less than 210.00. The trader needs some "reference" price points, and application of the Fibonacci growth constant gives the trader a price target. The growth price of 243.98 is *not* a prediction but an action point. Should prices rise to that level, it would be a *sell* point.

The complete wave from 210 to 243.98 can be considered a "whole" unit of growth. Table A.1 treats any whole unit as the constant 1. Additionally, *any* whole unit of growth may be divided according to the important Fibonacci ratios of 0.38 and 0.62. Put another way, as YHOO "grows" to 243.98, it must first hit the 0.38 growth point, then the 0.62 growth point, then the 1.00 growth point, and finally the 1.618 growth point that "completes" that growth wave. Just as the Fibonacci ordinal price points (3, 5, 8, 13, 21, …) are points at which gains are to be taken, the Fibonacci price potential points of 0.38, 0.62, 1.0, and 1.62 are also points of price potential exhaustion and thus gain-taking points.

The trader knows that prices rarely move in straight lines (from 210 to 243.98). If the trend "grows" from 210 to 243.98, the trader can expect there to be an ebb and flow of prices as the underlying trend grows. Each of the important Fibonacci points (0.382 and 0.618) of that trend may themselves be considered a unit and further subdivided into 0.382 and 0.618 price points. That is, once prices grow to the 0.382 point, the trader would anticipate that a retreat ("correction," consolidation," etc.) would occur and that the point to which prices retreat may be related to the Fibonacci division of that interval. Knowledge of these dynamic price points during the unfolding of a trend will be extremely useful to the trader.

Figure A.5 once again illustrates the YHOO example. Multiplying 210 (the starting price) by 0.0382 yields an initial price potential of 8.02 points. Added to 210, this yields a price potential target 1 at 218.02. Notice that this target price is reached in the same period that the 3PB is making five new highs. At this point, the trader has two reasons to sell: Prices have hit a Fibonacci price point (5) and a Fibonacci price potential point (218.02). The trader can use this *convergence* of methods to take gains. Yes, prices may go higher; they may also go lower. But that is prediction. What the trader *knows* at this point is that prices have hit an action price and discipline *requires* selling. Again, the knowledge that is most crucial to the successful trader is that an action signal will be acted on. Once the gains are in pocket, the trader can then deal with the question of reentry as previously described.

Figure A.5 also illustrates the 0.0618 price potential point at 222.98 (210+12.98). Notice how YHOO hits that price area and immediately retreats for several periods. This is the kind of consolidation and possible reversal behavior expected at price exhaustion targets. This is the reason for *selling* into target price momentum. However, this occurs during new high number 6. The 3PB price point for selling is not until new high number 8. Are these methods in conflict? No! At this point the trader does not know that prices will continue to rise to 8 new highs, but does know for *certain* that a price potential target has been hit. This

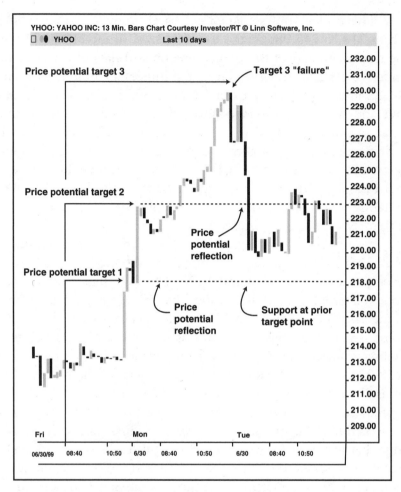

Figure A.5 YHOO showing price potential targets and their forward reflection. (SOURCE: Chart by Investor/RT © 1996–2000 Linn Software, Inc., www.linnsoft.com. Reproduced with permission of Linn Software, Inc.)

knowledge requires the trader to sell. The trader needs to remember that neither 3PB price points (3, 5, 6, 13, …) nor target projections are predictions. They are *action* points. So the trading rule is that action must be taken on whichever occurs *first:* a Fibonacci price point or a Fibonacci price potential target. Once action is taken and gains are in pocket, then the trader can consider the question of reentry.

As noted earlier, there are numerous methods of reentry. In this example, we will assume the same reentry methods as before, that is, requiring a *higher* price than the candle in which the action signal was taken, or on a new 3PB high, as long as that new 3PB high is *not* a Fibonacci price point. In this illustration, YHOO makes a seventh new high at 222.88, and so that is an entry point. Notice, again, that the action signals are very clear and precise. Now the next target is target 3 at 231.00. But the next price point action signal is at eight new highs. Once again, the disciplined trader will prepare to sell on eight new highs or target 3, whichever occurs first. In the example, the eighth new high occurs first. Reentry is in the next period when the high price of the previous interval is exceeded. Now the trader continues to have two price points in mind: the target 3 at 231.00 and thirteen new highs. At 9 new highs, the break price is less than 222.75.

The thirteenth new high is achieved before target 3. Again, discipline requires selling at this point. Reentry occurs in the following period on the "new high" rule. Now the next price point target is 21 new highs. The next price potential target is 231.00. Notice that YHOO makes a seventeenth new high at 230.16 and in the next period suffers a substantial downmove of more than 3 points. As noted earlier, this is a break in the trend and a reversal point. As is evident, the price action at or near a target price can be very rapid, and reversals can occur within very brief time periods. Generally speaking, the further along in the trend, the more rapid these reversals can be. For this reason, trends beyond 13 periods often require an examination of the *risk-reward* potential of the trade. That is, the trader knows that if trade entry is at a price greater than 228.63 (the reentry price), the sell point is at 231.00. So the gain on this trade would be 2.37 points if YHOO hit the price potential target 3. The potential loss is a minimum of 3.38 (the break price after 13 new highs). For this reason, the trader may simply *decline* the trade because of its risk parameters, since the potential loss is greater than the potential gain.

Clearly, as one approaches a target price point, the risk increases. This does not mean that one should not enter following the thirteenth new high, but it does raise the question of whether there are additional methods that could provide the trader with additional guidance in maximizing the potential gain while minimizing the potential loss in a risky trade.

While the 3PB data provide a picture of what the market is doing at any point in time, the price potential projections remain fixedly related to a single price point in time, that is, the starting price at 210.00. Is there a general method for "updating" price potential projections as prices unfold?

THE CONCEPT OF MARKET STRUCTURE

The low at 210 has a particular characteristic. That is, there are higher prices on either side of it. This pattern of low, lower, higher low, in three *consecutive* periods, is termed a *market structure low*.[8] The significance of a market structure low is that it is a *reversal* formation. That is, prices were moving lower and in the third period a new low was not achieved. Similarly, a market structure high would have the form of a high price, followed by a higher high, followed in turn by a lower high in three consecutive periods. This is also a reversal formation in that the third period does not yield a new high.

Market structure points are always *important* price points because of this reversal characteristic. Moreover, market structure points become points from which new estimates of target potentials may be calculated. Of most interest to the trader will be estimating the price potential from the market structure low point that occurs after the price hits the price potential targets. For example, after price potential target 2, prices retreat, form a market structure low (marked *a*), and then a lower market structure low (marked *b*), as shown in Figure A.6. Prices then make a new high (number 7), followed by a higher market structure low (marked *c*). This *sequence* of market structure points, which themselves form a market structure low pattern, often is seen just *before* a new momentum move. Since a new high has occurred (number 7), the price at the lowest market structure low becomes an important price, and one the trader can use to project a new price potential. Multiplying that low at 220.63 by 0.0382 yields a value of 229.06. That is, that price point has a target 1 price potential of

229.06 before price exhaustion would be expected. Now this gives the trader a *price exhaustion zone* formed by the target 3 price potential at 231 and this new target 1 price potential at 229.06 from a major market structure point. Thus, the trader will be looking to sell as prices enter that zone. This information may further dissuade the trader from reentry following 13 new highs since the reentry is just fractionally below the start of the selling zone. This

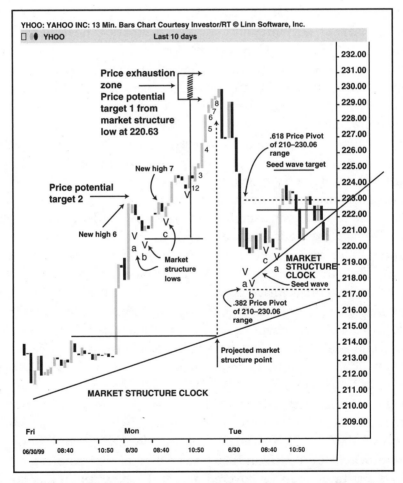

Figure A.6 YHOO illustrating market structure low formations, market structure clock projections, price exhaustion zones, pivot points of range, and seed wave formation and confirmation. (SOURCE: Chart by Investor/RT © 1996–2000 Linn Software, Inc., www.linnsoft.com. Reproduced with permission of Linn Software, Inc.)

kind of "zone filtering" of riskier trades will eliminate a significant proportion of otherwise losing trades.

Another way market structure can assist the trader is the observation that during *momentum* moves, prices tend to make new highs *without* forming market structure points. The further a move continues without making a market structure point, the more *vulnerable* the move becomes to reversal. Here, too, the Fibonacci numbers can be very helpful to the trader. Notice the last market structure low in YHOO before the reversal and break in the trend. That market structure low is at 223.63. Following that point, there is a momentum surge that makes 8 new highs. If a trader went long following 13 new highs, the Fibonacci number of 8 new momentum highs at 230.16 would be a signal to sell. Prices may surely go higher, but the risk increases beyond 8 new highs without a market structure "rest." This knowledge of market structure momentum characteristics would have enabled the trader to sell at the exact high. Obviously, this will not always be the case—but it is always the case that paying attention to this market structure characteristic will serve the trader well. The 3PB price points, the use of price potential targets, and attention to market structure characteristics combine to offer the trader a set of highly objective methods that can serve as extraordinarily effective guides to action in relation to market prices.

When the trend breaks, the trader enters on the short side at 226.75. The break price is less than 230.00, the previous 3PB high. The minimum risk is 3.25 points (230.00 − 226.75). Once the 3PB trend has changed to the short side, the Fibonacci price projection calculator can be used to project downside price point targets. The first target from the high at 230.16 is 221.37 (230.16 × 0.0382). The target is 5.38 points below the entry price and is larger than the risk estimate. This risk-reward ratio suggests the trade is viable. In Figure A.6, this target price is hit in the same interval that the 3PB makes the third new low. Once again, the congruence of the 3PB and the price potential target indicates that the short trade is to be covered at 221.37. Now the trader must decide on reentry. Once again, the risk-reward potential is an initial guide. After three new lows, the break price is greater than

229.50 and target 2 is at 215.94. The risk is 13.56 points, and the reward potential is the reentry price (219.72) less the target price (215.94), or 3.78 points. The discerning trader would decline this trade. With each successive low, a new risk-reward ratio can be calculated easily. In this example, with each new low, the risk-reward continues to favor risk, and so a further short position would be declined.

FIBONACCI PIVOT POINTS

The risk-reward filter will allow the trader to decline many trades that often end up being losing trades. There are other features illustrated in this example which can also help the trader to decide whether to take a trade or decline it. In any complete trend cycle, in this case the rise to 17 new 3PB highs, the *range* of that cycle, from the lowest market structure low to the highest market structure high, may be considered a complete growth unit for which the Fibonacci divisions at .0618 and 0.382 are likely to become meaningful price points. These divisions of a "whole" are referred to as Fibonacci price *pivots*. The term *pivot* indicates a meaningful price point at which a *reversal* may be considered a distinct possibility. At the break following the high at 230.06, the range is from 210.00 to 230.06, or 20.06 points. Dividing this into Fibonacci points tells the trader to be mindful of price action at 222.98 (the 0.618 price pivot) and 217.66 (the 0.38 pivot). The midpoint between these pivots is also an important price point (the 0.50 pivot at 220.03).

How prices behave at target and pivot price points can also give the trader an additional clue about market dynamics. When a trend is strong, it will hit price point targets before retreating. When retreating, if the trend is strong, prices will retreat generally only to the 0.618 pivot before turning upward again. Notice in the YHOO example that prices hit the target 1 and target 2 points and the retreats were minor and substantially above the 0.618 pivot points. Even though YHOO came close to hitting T3, the target 3 point, it did not do so. When a target is not hit, the trend weakens, and in this example, the failure to hit the target was followed immediately by a 3PB down. Moreover, the resulting rapid retreat was not supported at the 0.618 pivot, falling to 218.00, very near to the 0.382 pivot point at 217.66.

TARGET AND PIVOT POINT REFLECTION IN FUTURE PRICES

Once a target price or pivot price point is known, these price levels are important to keep in mind for a period of time, as they often become meaningful price points in future price action. For example, the price potential target 1 value of 218.02, which was a gain-taking target in the initial rise, can be seen to be the exact point to which prices fell in the downturn. This illustrates as well the principle of alternation, that is, a price that was initially an exhaustion point for an upmove subsequently becomes an exhaustion point for the downmove. In addition, the convergence of the prior price potential 1 target at 218.02 and the 0.38 pivot point at 217.66 alerts the trader to potential uptrend reversal in this price zone.

THE CONCEPT OF SEED WAVE

Prices move in spurts or waves as they grow. It is obviously quite easy to identify a growth trend once prices have moved substantially. Is it possible to identify such trends in their more "incipient" or "seed" form early in a trend? Certainly the 3PB method alerts the trader to trend reversal. When there is a 3PB break, the trend has reversed. Frequently, as in the case of the YHOO example, the break price for establishing a new trend is often "far away." No one knows what will happen to YHOO after it hits that 218 price level. If this is the initial stage of a strong trend to the downside, then that 218 price area will not hold. At some point, on a new 3PB low, the risk-reward will favor going short and the trader will take up a short position. However, if this retreat is only a correction of the move to the 230 area, then the trader must be alert to the possibility of an upmove. What are some of the early signs that an upmove may unfold following the retreat to 218? Since *all* upmoves begin from a *low*, what should the trader look for to find the seed of any new upmove?

Earlier, it was noted that a market structure low point that consisted of three distinct market structure low formations often signaled an incipient momentum move. So one thing the trader can look for at potential reversal points (e.g., the 0.38 price pivot) is this specific market structure formation. In the case of YHOO, this formation occurs with a market structure low at 218.38, followed by the market structure low at 218.00, followed by a higher market structure low at 220. This formation sets the stage for a potential rally.

A second element to look for is a higher market structure low between 8 and 13 time periods from the low point. The first higher market structure low occurs after 5 time periods and does not qualify. But the higher market structure low at 219.25 occurs at 8 time periods following the low price at 218. This formally defines a *seed wave* and is often the beginning of a strong move.

A seed wave is important because it is frequently the *earliest* indication of a coming trend reversal. Notice the price movement in the period following the higher market structure low point at 219.25. That is the kind of momentum action one expects from a seed wave formation. There are two subsequent "tests" of a seed wave if it is to succeed in giving rise to a new larger uptrend. The first test is, does it "grow?" This may be objectified in the following manner. From the low price at 218.00, the highest price between that low and the seed defining higher market structure low (at 219.25) is determined. That price is 222.25. This is 4.25 points above the low at 218.00, and is the amplitude of the seed wave. This amplitude is then multiplied by the Fibonacci growth factor of 1.618. This yields a value of 6.88. Adding this to the low price of 218.00 yields a price of 224.88. Thus, if YHOO hits 224.88, a "confirmed" seed wave will be in place. Notice that the high price within a short period was 225.25, thus confirming a seed wave formation.

The second test for a seed wave is that *following* confirmation, the subsequent low must *not* break the higher market structure low at 219.25. Notice on Figure A.6 that following the confirmation high, the next low point was at 220.00. This seed wave passes both tests. This is *not* a prediction that prices will go higher. But it does give the trader a basis for early entry on the long side before the trend breaks on a 3PB basis. And once the 3PB trend breaks up, it gives additional support for taking the trade.

FURTHER USES OF MARKET STRUCTURE PRICE POINTS

While the 3PB chart uses the *closing* price in each time period to determine the 3PB trend, a 3PB chart can be constructed from market structure points as well. The market structure chart can be constructed from market structure high points, market structure low points, or a combination of both. In the case of a market structure high chart, a new entry is made for each successive new market structure high. For the trend to change, a market structure high has to occur below the break price. The same rules for taking gains at Fibonacci price points (3, 5, 8, 13, 21, ...) and price potential targets apply to market structure charts as well as 3PB charts. Used together, the 3PB and market structure charts provide the trader with complementary information on price dynamics.

Market structure points can be utilized also to generate *time* estimations for future market structure points. For example, consider the rising line between the market structure low at 210 and the market structure low at 211.88 (see Figure A.6). If you draw a straight line from the market structure high *between* these points, that line will intersect the rising line at a particular point. This point will quite frequently correspond to a *subsequent* and meaningful market structure point. Notice that this time point corresponds almost exactly to the high at 230.06. A similar market structure clock is drawn in for the seed wave described earlier. This projects a market structure high at a point in the future that is not on the chart. The clock projects market structure, not price level, so there is no guarantee that prices will be higher—only that an important market structure point will likely occur at that projected time point. This information can be exceedingly useful to the trader when prices are approaching a target point and a time point. This congruence must not be ignored by the trader, as the conjunction of price point exhaustion and time point exhaustion is often the exact conditions for remarkably swift reversal action, as is the case in the YHOO example.

THE NATURAL TRADING UNIT

The Fibonacci natural growth constant of 1.618 gives rise to the concept of a unit of growth. As was shown earlier, any complete unit of growth can be divided meaningfully into the Fibonacci pivot ratios of 0.618 and 0.382. Each of these divisions can also be treated as complete units and further subdivided. Because of the fractal nature of the Fibonacci number series, no matter how large or small these units are, their significance remains the same. A unit of growth meaningfully related to the Fibonacci number series may be useful to the trader interested in nonscalping methods of trading. There are many ways to approach this concept. To provide a flavor of this approach, recall that the growth constant (1.618) was divided by 10 to provide a meaningful day trading *range*. This gave a value of 33.98 points as a meaningful range of interest to the day trader. Now consider a further division of this range by another factor of 10. This would yield a value of 3.40 points as a Fibonacci-based unit of trading. What is meant by this? Given the starting point at 210, it means that nothing happens until YHOO reaches 213.40 or falls to 206.60. In the YHOO example, once prices hit 213.40, the trader would buy. The trend is 1 natural trading unit (NTU) up. To "break" this trend, prices must fall to 206.60. The trader now remains long until YHOO hits 216.80 or falls below 206.60. Notice that the stop is always 2 × NTU.

Figure A.7 illustrates the NTU price action for the data in Figure A.2. When combined with Fibonacci price points, the trader would take gains at 3 NTU up and again at 5 NTU up, for a total of 13.6 points. This compares favorably with the 3PB methods described earlier. There are many useful combinations of NTU trading with the other methods described earlier. Because the natural trading unit is based on the Fibonacci growth factor, it will always be related to the underlying price dynamics of the market of interest to the trader. And because the NTU method filters all inconsequential prices, it is a relatively stress-free method of trading.

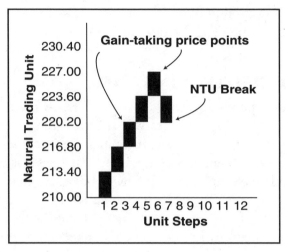

Figure A.7   YHOO trading using the natural trading unit (NTU) based on the scaled Fibonacci growth constant (1.618/100) from the starting price at 210.00.

CONCLUSION

This appendix has offered only a brief glimpse into a combination of methods available to the trader who wishes to explore non-scalping methods of trading. The methods described always provide a market-based price for entry, exit, and reentry. The methods in combination are relatively simple to use and enable the trader to trade with considerably less stress than is characteristic of scalp trading. The methods build in automatic points of gain-taking actions, enabling the trader to put in pocket a large percentage of trend-generated gains. The methods are applicable in any market and in any time frame and so are of general use and value to the day trader.

NOTES

[1]*Chaotic* as used here does not mean "disorderly," but rather "not predictable." Modern chaos theory has shown that in spite of unpredictability, patterns of order do exist in chaotic systems. These patterns of order can be revealed through the use

of fractal methods, nonlinear analysis, and application of concepts such as strange attractors. The methods described in this chapter are simple examples of these concepts. For an introduction to these concepts, see Edgar E. Peters, *Chaos and Order in the Capital Markets: A New View of Cycles, Prices, and Market Volatility* (New York: John Wiley & Sons, 1991).

[2] *Fractal* is used here in its most general sense, that is, a pattern that is "self-similar" regardless of the *range* of observation. Thus, a chart of daily prices over the course of a year will have the same general characteristics as a chart of 1-minute prices over the course of a trading day. Another way to think of this is that if all scale identifiers were removed, one could not tell which chart was which.

[3] The best readily available source for all Japanese trading methods is Steve Nison's *Japanese Candlestick Charting Techniques: A Contemporary Guide to the Ancient Investment Techniques of the Far East* (New York: New York Institute of Finance, 1991) and *Beyond Candlesticks: New Japanese Charting Techniques Revealed* (New York: John Wiley & Sons, 1994). The latter volume contains an excellent section on the 3PB method (Chapter 6) which Nison calls "three-line break charts."

[4] I will illustrate all methods using the price behavior in this figure. This particular selection is in no way special. The methods would be equally applicable over any 3-day period.

[5] Notice that while the break price is 229.00 (and for a break to occur the price must be below this price), the actual price at the close of the break period was substantially below this, at 226.75. This is typical of "pronounced" reversals and is one of the reasons for attending to this possibility by instituting specific "gain protection" stops following extensive 3PB trends (i.e., greater than 13 new prices), by declining trades when the risk-reward ratio does not favor the trader, and by using more technical approaches to anticipate trend reversal.

[6] Consolidation periods always follow trend exhaustion. In this sense, these periods are periods of indecision. The trend may continue, or it may reverse. During these periods the range of price fluctuation is minimal and trading is difficult. Ideally, the trader should not have exposure during consolidation periods. Resources are not being efficiently utilized in such periods. A better approach would be to reenter upon the first indications that the trend is continuing or on indications that the trend is reversing. The methods illustrated here make this possible.

[7] Occasionally, a first break will *not* be confirmed and the prior trend will continue. For this reason, more conservative traders may wait for confirmation, while more aggressive traders generally act on first break.

[8] The concept of market structure was initially observed by Larry Williams in volume 1 of *The Definitive Guide to Futures Trading* (Beverly Hills, Calif.: Windsor Books, 1988).

APPENDIX B

Hardware Setup and Brokers

In order to day-trade successfully, there are minimal requirements that you need in the way of tools. Failure to obtain these tools makes day trading nothing more than a shot in the dark. We will describe everything that you need in order to mount a worthy offense as a day trader. Please do not be cheap on your system setup. We often hear how beginner traders state that they will "work up" their systems and brokers as they get "better." This is like telling someone you will work up to buying a helmet and pads once you get better at riding a motorcycle. You do not need unforced technical errors in this game, especially as they may materialize down the road in the form of bad fills, computer crashes in the middle of a trade, and dropped Internet connections. So let's break down the tools into three separate categories: computers, connections, and brokers.

COMPUTERS

Computers are the hardware portion of your arsenal. The more powerful your computer, the better. Your computer(s) should have a fast processor and plenty of RAM (random access memory). In fact, RAM is the most important facet of your hardware system that you will need. A minimum of 128 megabytes of RAM is needed. Remember that the higher your RAM, the less often you will face having your computer lock up on you when it is downloading tons of data and crunching out charts. If you really want cream-of-the-crop processing, we suggest getting a Windows NT box with Pentium III 500-megahertz dual processors.

Monitors

The bigger your monitor is, the better off you will be. The more monitors you have, the better. In fact, we highly recommend starting with two separate 19-inch monitors that are connected to a box. Two monitors allow for more screen capacity, and allow your mouse to glide smoothly from one monitor to another.

CONNECTION

The faster your connection to the Internet, the quicker your executions and the shorter the delay of information. A *minimum* of 56 kilobits per second is required for your Internet connection. We say minimum in italic letters because 56 kbits/s is subpar. We highly recommend ADSL (asymmetric digital subscriber line—not available in all areas but growing fast) if you have the capacity in your area. ADSL also requires you (as of this writing) to be within 16,000 feet of your local telephone company. Speed is a major issue. Mere seconds can mean the difference between a fill and a rejection. When major money is on the line with every trade, your connection costs are the least of your worries. The faster connection is worth the money hands down. As the Internet continues its massive growth, with more and more people clicking onto the Internet everyday, as well as more and more day traders taking up more and more bandwidth, you must be prepared for backbone outages and Internet network problems—problems that are turning into an everyday, common theme. This underscores the necessity of having at least two backup ISPs (Internet service providers) in case your main ISP goes down. And you should expect your Internet connection to go down during the week sometime, because the Internet gets more and more crowded everyday and bandwidth is a major issue. The heaviest connection problems will happen in the mornings on the open. Whenever you find yourself experiencing lags or quote problems, turn off some of your charts to see if that frees up some bandwidth. In addition, should you ever get stuck, always use the ISLD book in the sweep manner to exit your trade. Never rely on SelectNet or SOES. Most importantly, if you are experiencing connection problems, do not trade.

BROKERS

Here is your greatest tool in day trading—the right broker. We do not advise any of the popular browser-based brokers, as they are too slow and still fill through market makers. Forget those $5 or $10 commission advertisements. You get what you pay for, and that is slow, pathetic market maker fills. They are fine for investment or swing hold accounts but completely inadequate for day trading purposes. You do not work your way up to a professional day trading broker. You start there with all the right tools. When selecting a day trading broker, you need to make sure you have ECN access. We recommend CyBerTrader (www.cybercorp.com) and MB Trading (www.mbtrading.com). Both offer superfast point-and-click order routing, which is exactly as it implies. Point your mouse to the market maker or ECN, click, and own the stock seconds later. CyBerTrader has its patented Smartroute execution system (as mentioned previously in the order-routing section) which has the benefit of SOES. MB Trading uses the RealTick™ platform which gives access to ARCA. These are the only day trading brokers that we recommend for anyone who is serious about day trading. Both brokers offer free Nasdaq Level 2 and free charts with a certain amount of trades per month. The futures feeds require an extra monthly fee and a special contract with the CBOE (Chicago Board Options Exchange). Do not try to piecemeal your system with a browser-based broker and different chart services. Get the complete package integrated and all inclusive with the above brokers.

Here is a basic system setup:

One Pentium III 500-megahertz computer with 256 megabytes of RAM

One 19-inch monitor

One 56-kbits/s modem

Three ISPs (different backbones—Sprint, UUNET, MCI)

CyBerTrader or MB Trading broker

Here is a very nice system setup:

Two Pentium III 500-megahertz computers, with 512 megabytes of RAM each

Four 19-inch monitors (two monitors for each box)

One ADSL modem/56-kps backup

One ADSL connection with two ISPs as backup (one for each computer)

CyBerTrader or MB Trading broker

Backup broker for swing holds

Backup quote provider from www.atfi.com

Somewhere in between the two systems is where you should start off. As you get better, you can continue to upgrade your existing system by adding more computers and more monitors. Bandwidth is a major issue, and we highly recommend ADSL, as there are packages that will supply up to 7.1 megabytes downstream of data for under $250 a month.

Index

ABOUT THE AUTHOR

Jea Yu is the managing partner and cofounder and the lead instructor of www.undergroundtrader.com, an Internet online day trading chatroom and instructional Web site. Mr. Yu actively day-traded the U.S. equities markets while writing the infamous *Underground Level 2 Daytraders Handbook.* He graduated from the University of Maryland with a major in business management and speech communications and was a business management consultant prior to his successful career as a day trader.

★★★

If you wish to continue your journey with like minded hard-core day traders, Jea Yu happily invites you to visit www.undergroundtrader.com and take a free trial at the Trading Pit where they practice everything outlined in this book daily from the trenches.